The Britannica Guide to
Matter

PHYSICS EXPLAINED

The Britannica Guide to
Matter

EDITED BY ERIK GREGERSEN, ASSOCIATE EDITOR,
SCIENCE AND TECHNOLOGY

Britannica
Educational Publishing

IN ASSOCIATION WITH

ROSEN
EDUCATIONAL SERVICES

Published in 2011 by Britannica Educational Publishing
(a trademark of Encyclopædia Britannica, Inc.)
in association with Rosen Educational Services, LLC
29 East 21st Street, New York, NY 10010.

For a listing of additional Britannica Educational Publishing titles, call toll free (800) 237-9932.

First Edition

Britannica Educational Publishing
Michael I. Levy: Executive Editor
J.E. Luebering: Senior Manager
Marilyn L. Barton: Senior Coordinator, Production Control
Steven Bosco: Director, Editorial Technologies
Lisa S. Braucher: Senior Producer and Data Editor
Yvette Charboneau: Senior Copy Editor
Kathy Nakamura: Manager, Media Acquisition
Erik Gregersen: Associate Editor, Science and Technology

Rosen Educational Services
Jeanne Nagle: Senior Editor
Nelson Sá: Art Director
Cindy Reiman: Photography Manager
Matthew Cauli: Designer, Cover Design
Introduction by Erik Gregersen

Library of Congress Cataloging-in-Publication Data

The Britannica guide to matter / edited by Erik Gregersen.
    p. cm.—(Physics explained)
"In association with Britannica Educational Publishing, Rosen Educational Services."
Includes bibliographical references and index.
ISBN 978-1-61530-323-6 (library binding)
1. Matter—Popular works. I. Gregersen, Erik. II. Title: Guide to matter. III. Title: Matter.
QC171.2.B67 2011
530.4—dc22

                                                                        2010024080

Manufactured in the United States of America

On page x: Aurora borealis as seen from Yellowknife, Northwest Territories, Canada.
Auroras are a beautiful phenomenon caused by plasma in Earth's space environment. *David
Brosha Photography/Flickr/Getty Images*

On page xviii: Bathers enjoy the hot springs in Slovakia's Low Tatras National Park. Water
is visible in three forms of matter: liquid (pooled water), gaseous (steam), and solid (ice and
snow). *isifa/Getty Images*

On pages 1, 9, 39, 56, 73, 115, 164, 197, 228, 256, 258, 267: Water in all its forms, represented by the famous Blue Lagoon in Iceland. *Shutterstock.com*

CONTENTS

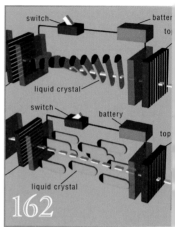

236

241

INTRODUCTION

Matter is one of the most basic subjects of physics. One could say that everything else depends on it. Matter is everything from raindrops that fall from the sky to the wind that rustles grassy fields, to the stars that shine in the most distant galaxies. This book goes beyond these and other manifestations of manner to examine its primary components, its behaviours, and the scientific discoveries that have made the study of matter possible.

The ordinary experience of matter encompasses three different types or phases: solid, liquid, and gas. These phases follow how a substance holds itself together. Solids remain, for lack of a better word, solid. Liquids do not hold themselves together. They need to be contained, as anyone who has dropped a glass of water on the ground has discovered. Once contained, liquids pool and settle to the lowest part of the container. Gases also need to be contained. However, they neither pool nor settle. They fill a container.

Gases are made of atoms or molecules. Aside from collisions, there is no relation between one atom or molecule and another atom or molecule. Since collisions are the most important process in a gas, knowing physical parameters such as the distance between molecules, the average speed at which a molecule travels, how far a molecule travels before it collides with another molecule, and how often molecules collide can reveal much about how gases work. The molecules travel at a speed determined by the temperature. Temperature can be considered as a measurement of the kinetic energy in a gas.

The chief way to describe a gas is the ideal gas equation of state, which says that the pressure of a gas times its volume is equal to a constant times the temperature. Equations of state are formulas that relate pressure, volume, and temperature, and are extremely useful for describing a material's behavior. For example if the volume of a gas is increased and the temperature is held constant, this would mean that the gas's pressure would have to decrease. (This last is Boyle's law, which has been known since 1662.)

The limiting conditions of matter also can be discerned using the concept of the phase diagram. The three phases are not immutable categories. By changing the temperature of a substance, it is possible to go from one phase to another. The transmutability of water is the most recognizable example of this. When the temperature drops below 0 °C (32 °F), liquid water freezes into ice. When the temperature rises above 100 °C (212 °F), liquid water evaporates into steam.

It is also possible to go from one phase to another by changing the pressure. For example, by increasing the pressure, water vapour can be condensed into liquid. Because both pressure and temperature are important in determining the phase of a substance, the phase diagram, which graphs temperature on the horizontal axis and pressure on the vertical axis, is quite important. The temperatures and pressures where, for example, water vapour condenses form a curved line in the phase diagram. These curved lines can intersect at interesting points on the phase diagram called the triple point and the critical point. At the triple point the curves demarcating sublimation (solid to gas), fusion (solid to liquid), and vaporization (gas to liquid) intersect. At this point, gas, liquid, and solid are in equilibrium with each other. At the critical point, the line of vaporization ends and the line between gas and liquid is blurred so the substance is a single fluid.

Solids are classified on the basis of the order of their internal structure, with the most ordered of all being the crystalline solids. Crystals have what is called long-range order, wherein the place of any atom in the crystal can be pinpointed once one knows the basis of its structure. The basis of any crystalline structure is the unit cell, which is repeated over and over throughout the crystal. The main unit cells (hexagonal close packed, face-centred cubic, and body-centred cubic) occur in many materials with extremely different compositions. These crystal structures were deduced as far back as 1912 by German physicist Max von Laue, who aimed a beam of X rays at a crystal to produce a diffraction pattern, which is a regular series of spots. By examining the spacing of the spots, one can deduce how far apart are the atoms in a crystal. Von Laue won the Nobel Prize in Physics for this discovery.

As mentioned, the "solidity" of solids arises from the fact that the atoms are bound together. There are four main types of bonds. In ionic bonds, such as in table salt (a.k.a. sodium chloride), atoms exchange electrons so as to fill their outermost electron shells. In covalent bonds, atoms share electrons. In metallic bonds, electrons can travel throughout the crystal unbound from their atoms. (These conduction electrons allow metals to be excellent conductors of electricity.) In molecular bonding, also referred to as the van der Waals force, interactions between the dipole moments—the measure of how charge is distributed within a molecule—of neighbouring molecules that arise on a quantum mechanical level bind the two molecules together. The van der Waals force is unlike other forces such as the gravitational force between two masses or the Coulomb force between two charges, in which the strength of the force decreases as the square of the distance. If the distance between two masses is doubled, the gravitational force falls to one-quarter of its original value. The van der Waals force decreases as the seventh power of the distance. If the distance between two molecular dipole moments is increased, the force falls to 1/128th of its original value. Therefore the van der Waals force has quite a short range.

Aside from the three forms of gas, liquid, and solid are intermediate forms that partake of the properties of two different phases. One of these forms is the liquid crystal, which has some of the properties of a liquid and some of a crystalline solid. For example, in the nematic liquid crystal form, the molecules do not have translational symmetry but they do have rotational symmetry. This form of matter is pervasive in today's computerized society in the LCD, or liquid crystal display.

The amorphous solid is held together by the same chemical bonds that bind the crystalline solids. However, it lacks the pattern that rigidly describes the crystal. Amorphous solids do not have unit cells, some of which can have very unusual structures. Plastics have molecular structures that consist of long chains of up to 100,000 atoms, with these long chains randomly tangled together like shoelaces in a bag.

Glass is an amorphous solid and not a crystal, as one would suppose. It is a long-standing urban legend that glass is actually a liquid that flows very, very slowly. Thus, the pieces of stained-glass windows in Gothic cathedrals are supposedly thicker at the bottom than at the top, having had centuries to flow. (Presumably in millennia, these medieval masterpieces would be puddles on the ancient stones beneath them.) However, glass is indeed solid. As for the stained-glass "mystery," it appears that the pieces of glass were originally made thicker at the bottom.

Another intermediate form is that of the quasicrystals, so called because they have some of the regular pattern behaviour of crystals but also the irregularity of the amorphous solids. Quasicrystals are one of the most recent types of matter to be discovered, in 1984. Quasicrystals display the interesting mathematical property of quasiperiodicity, meaning that the pattern of the crystal can be mathematically described but the pattern never repeats itself. More than 100 quasicrystals are known. Such an unusual substance has one very down-to-earth application as a nonstick coating for pots and pans.

Beyond solid, liquid, and gas there is plasma, which has been called the fourth state of matter. Plasmas are gas in which the atoms are ionized such that there are as many atoms that are negatively charged as positively charged. This state of matter is of great interest to astronomers, since nearly the entire universe is occupied by plasma. The interiors of stars are in a plasma state. The vast spaces between the stars, the interstellar medium, is not empty space, but is filled with a tenuous plasma of hydrogen. In the solar system, the spaces between the planets — the interplanetary medium — is filled with the plasma of the solar wind, charged particles blown outwards by the Sun. Earth's magnetic field stretches out into space in the magnetosphere, and the solar wind plasma within it gives rise to the beautiful aurorae.

On Earth's surface, plasma is also a subject of great interest. There are plasma TVs, in which a small plasma is created in cells behind the screen. This plasma gives rise to ultraviolet light that excites the phosphors on the screen that emit in visible light. Since plasma TVs do not need the electron beam apparatus required in regular televisions, they are much thinner. Aside from bringing to many the latest reality television shows, plasmas are also of great interest in the energy field. Some scientists hope to make controlled nuclear fusion a reality and thus power everything by the same process that makes the Sun shine. To do this requires confining an extremely hot plasma in a small space.

Clusters are another form of matter, made up of groups of atoms and molecules that form in solids and liquids. These groups have unusual properties in that they occupy the space between individual atoms and "bulk matter," that is, objects closer to the sizes of everyday experience. For example, in something like a block of wood, nearly all of the atoms are on the inside. In a cluster of tens of atoms, most of the atoms are on the surface. This means that the atoms in the bulk are surrounded by other atoms, while those in the cluster have the freedom to leave. Also since the cluster is smaller than the block of wood, the effects of quantum mechanics are much more prominent. A block of wood can be in any one of billions of quantum states. The cluster of 10 atoms can only be in a few states.

The most famous cluster is buckminsterfullerene, a spherical molecule of 60 carbon atoms (C_{60}), named after Buckminster Fuller, the maverick architect whose geodesic domes prefigure this cluster's structure. The discovery of C_{60} led to an entire family of fullerenes, including a cylindrical tube of carbon, or nanotube, which may someday become the material for extremely strong cables.

The subject of matter contains nearly everything in everyday experience and much that is beyond it. Despite the seemingly reductive classification of every substance into three phases (four, if plasma is included), the material presented in this volume shows that initial classification to be merely the beginning steps in the understanding of matter.

CHAPTER 1

MATTER AND
ITS PHASES

M atter is the material substance that constitutes the observable universe and, together with energy, forms the basis of all objective phenomena. At its most fundamental level, matter is composed of elementary particles, known as quarks and leptons (the class of elementary particles that includes electrons). Quarks combine into protons and neutrons and, along with electrons, form atoms of the elements of the periodic table, such as hydrogen, oxygen, and iron. Atoms may combine further into molecules such as the water molecule, H_2O. Large groups of atoms or molecules in turn form the bulk matter of everyday life.

However, all matter of any type shares the fundamental property of inertia, which—as formulated within Isaac Newton's three laws of motion—prevents a material body from responding instantaneously to attempts to change its state of rest or motion. The mass of a body is a measure of this resistance to change. For example, it is enormously harder to set in motion a massive ocean liner than it is to push a bicycle. Another universal property is gravitational mass, whereby every physical entity in the universe acts so as to attract every other one, as first stated by Newton and later refined into a new conceptual form by Albert Einstein.

Depending on temperature and other conditions, matter may appear in any of several states. At ordinary temperatures, for instance, gold is a solid, water is a liquid, and nitrogen is a gas, as defined by certain characteristics: solids hold their shape, liquids take on the shape of the container that holds them, and gases fill an entire container. These states can be further categorized into subgroups. Solids, for example, may be divided into those with crystalline or amorphous structures or into metallic, ionic, covalent, or molecular solids, on the basis of the kinds of bonds that hold together the constituent atoms. Less clearly defined states of matter include plasmas, which are ionized gases at very high temperatures; foams, which combine aspects of liquids and solids; and clusters, which are assemblies of small numbers of atoms or molecules that display both atomic-level and bulklike properties.

These states of matter are called phases. The three fundamental phases of matter are solid, liquid, and gas (vapour), but others are considered to exist, including crystalline, colloid, glassy, amorphous, and plasma phases. When a phase in one form is altered to another form, a phase change is said to have occurred.

GENERAL CONSIDERATIONS

A system is a portion of the universe that has been chosen for studying the changes that take place within it in response to varying conditions. A system may be complex, such as a planet, or relatively simple, as the liquid within a glass. Those portions of a system that are physically distinct and mechanically separable from other portions of the system are called phases.

Phases within a system exist in a gaseous, liquid, or solid state. Solids are characterized by strong atomic bonding and high viscosity, resulting in a rigid shape. Most solids are crystalline, inasmuch as they have a three-dimensional periodic atomic arrangement. Some solids (such as glass) lack this periodic arrangement and are noncrystalline, or amorphous. Gases, which consist of weakly bonded atoms with no long-range periodicity, expand to fill any available space. Liquids have properties intermediate between those of solids and gases. The molecules of a liquid are condensed like those of a solid. Liquids have a definite volume, but their low viscosity enables them to change shape as a function of time. The matter within a system may consist of more than one solid or liquid phase, but a system can contain only a single gas phase, which must be of homogeneous composition because the molecules of gases mix completely in all proportions.

SYSTEM VARIABLES

Systems respond to changes in pressure, temperature, and chemical composition, and, as this happens, phases may be created, eliminated, or altered in composition. For example, an increase in pressure may cause a low-density liquid to convert to a denser solid, while an increase in temperature may cause a solid to melt. A change of composition might result in the compositional modification of a preexisting phase or in the gain or loss of a phase.

THE PHASE RULE

The classification and limitations of phase changes are described by the phase rule, as proposed by the American chemist J. Willard Gibbs in 1876 and based on a rigorous thermodynamic relationship. The phase rule is commonly given in the form $P + F = C + 2$. The term P refers to the number of phases that are present within the system, and C is the minimum number of independent chemical components that are necessary to describe the composition of all phases within the system. The term F, called the variance, or degrees of freedom, describes the minimum

Theoretical chemist J. Willard Gibbs, whose work changed the face of physical chemistry. Hulton Archive/Getty Images

number of variables that must be fixed in order to define a particular condition of the system.

PHASE DIAGRAMS

Phase relations are commonly described graphically in terms of phase diagrams. Each point within the diagram indicates a particular combination of pressure and temperature, as well as the phase or phases that exist stably at this pressure and temperature.

UNARY SYSTEMS

For example, in the diagram for silicon dioxide, SiO_2, all phases have the same composition. The diagram in that case is a representation of a one-component (unary) system, in contrast to a two-component (binary), three-component (ternary), or four-component (quaternary) system. The phases coesite, low quartz, high quartz, tridymite, and cristobalite are solid phases composed of silicon dioxide; each has its own atomic arrangement and distinctive set of physical and chemical properties. The most common form of quartz (found in beach sands and granites) is low quartz. The region labeled anhydrous melt consists of silicon dioxide liquid.

Different portions of the silicon dioxide system may be examined in terms of the phase rule. Consider a point A where a single solid phase exists—low quartz. Substituting the appropriate values into the phase rule $P + F = C + 2$ yields $1 + F = 1 + 2$, so $F = 2$. For point A (or any point in which only a single phase is stable) the system is divariant—i.e., two degrees of freedom exist. Thus, the two variables (pressure and temperature) can be changed independently, and the same phase assemblage continues to exist.

For a point B located on the boundary curve between the stability fields of low quartz and high quartz, these two phases coexist at all points along this curve. Substituting values in the phase rule ($2 + F = 1 + 2$) will cause a variance of 1 to be obtained. This indicates that one independent variable can be changed such that the same pair of phases will be retained. A second variable must be changed to conform to the first in order for the phase assemblage to remain on the boundary between low and high quartz. The same result holds for the other boundary curves in this system.

For a point C located at a triple point, a condition in which three stability fields intersect, the phase rule ($3 + F = 1 + 2$) indicates that the variance is 0. Point C is therefore an invariant point; a change in either pressure or temperature results in the loss of one or more phases. The phase rule also reveals that no more than three phases can stably coexist in a one-component system because additional phases would lead to negative variance.

BINARY SYSTEMS

Consider the binary system that describes the freezing and melting of the minerals titanite ($CaSiTiO_5$) and anorthite feldspar ($CaAl_2Si_2O_8$). The melt can range in composition from pure $CaSiTiO_5$ to pure $CaAl_2Si_2O_8$, but the solids show no compositional substitution. All phases therefore have the composition of $CaSiTiO_5$, $CaAl_2Si_2O_8$, or a liquid mixture of the two. The system in the figure has been examined at atmospheric pressure; because the pressure variable is fixed, the phase rule is expressed as $P + F = C + 1$. In this form it is called the condensed phase rule, for any gas phase is either condensed to a liquid or is present in negligible amounts. The phase diagram shows a vertical temperature coordinate and a horizontal compositional coordinate (ranging from pure $CaSiTiO_5$ at the left to pure $CaAl_2Si_2O_8$ at the right).

The phase fields contain either one or two phases. Any point in a one-phase field corresponds to a single phase whose composition is indicated directly below on the horizontal axis. For example, point A would present a liquid whose composition is 70 percent $CaAl_2Si_2O_8$ and 30 percent $CaSiTiO_5$. The compositions of phases in a two-phase field are determined by construction of a horizontal (constant-temperature) line from the point of interest to the extremities of the two-phase field. Thus, a sample with composition B would consist of liquid C (43 percent $CaSiTiO_5$ and 57 percent $CaAl_2Si_2O_8$) and solid anorthite D. A sample at point E at a lower temperature would consist of the solids titanite (F) and anorthite (G).

Liquid $CaAl_2Si_2O_8$ cools to produce solid anorthite at 1,550 °C, whereas liquid $CaSiTiO_5$ cools to produce solid titanite at 1,390 °C. If the batch were a mixture of the two components, the freezing temperature of each of these minerals would be depressed. In a melt consisting of a single component, such as $CaSiTiO_5$, all atoms could add to titanite nuclei to form crystals of titanite. If, however, the melt contained 30 percent $CaAl_2Si_2O_8$, the rate of formation of titanite nuclei would be decreased, as 30 percent of the melt could not contribute to their formation. In order to increase the rate of formation of titanite nuclei and promote crystallization, the temperature of the melt must be decreased below the freezing point of pure $CaSiTiO_5$. When cooled, liquid A does not begin crystallization until temperature H is reached. Pure anorthite crystals precipitate from the melt. Depletion of $CaAl_2Si_2O_8$ from the melt causes the melt composition to become relatively enriched in $CaSiTiO_5$, with consequent additional depression of the anorthite freezing point.

As freezing continues, the liquid composition changes until the minimum point is reached at I. This point is called the eutectic. It is the lowest temperature at which a liquid can exist in this system. At the eutectic, both anorthite and titanite crystallize together at a fixed temperature and in a fixed ratio until the remaining liquid is consumed. All intermediate liquid compositions migrate during crystallization to the eutectic. The melting sequence of titanite-anorthite mixtures is exactly the opposite of the freezing sequence (i.e., melting of any anorthite-titanite mixture begins at the eutectic).

Depression of the freezing point of a compound by the addition of a second component is common in both binary and more complex systems. This usually occurs when the solid phases either have a fixed composition or show limited solid solution. Common examples are the mixing of ice and salt (NaCl) or the use of ethylene glycol (antifreeze) to depress the freezing point of water.

CHAPTER 2

PROPERTIES
OF GASES

The remarkable feature of gases is that they appear to have no structure at all. They have neither a definite size nor shape, whereas ordinary solids have both a definite size and a definite shape, and liquids have a definite size, or volume, even though they adapt their shape to that of the container in which they are placed. Gases will completely fill any closed container; their properties depend on the volume of a container but not on its shape.

KINETIC-MOLECULAR PICTURE

Gases nevertheless do have a structure of sorts on a molecular scale. They consist of a vast number of molecules moving chaotically in all directions and colliding with one another and with the walls of their container. Beyond this, there is no structure—the molecules are distributed essentially randomly in space, traveling in arbitrary directions at speeds that are distributed randomly about an average determined by the gas temperature. The pressure exerted by a gas is the result of the innumerable impacts of the molecules on the container walls and appears steady to human senses because so many collisions occur each second on all sections of the walls. More subtle properties such as heat conductivity, viscosity (resistance to flow), and diffusion are attributed to the molecules themselves carrying the mechanical quantities of energy, momentum, and mass, respectively. These are called transport properties, and the rate of transport is dominated by the collisions between molecules, which force their trajectories into tortuous shapes. The molecular collisions are in turn controlled by the forces between the molecules and are described by the laws of mechanics.

Thus, gases are treated as a large collection of tiny particles subject to the laws of physics. Their properties are attributed primarily to the motion of the molecules and can be explained by the kinetic theory of gases. It is not obvious that this should be the case, and for many years a static picture of gases was instead espoused, in which the pressure, for instance, was attributed to repulsive forces between essentially stationary particles pushing on the container walls.

Any theory of gas behaviour based on this kinetic model must also be a statistical one because of the enormous numbers of particles involved. The kinetic theory of gases is now a classical part of statistical physics and is indeed a sort of miniature display case for many of the fundamental concepts and methods of science. Such important modern concepts as distribution functions, cross-sections, microscopic reversibility, and time-reversal invariance have their historical roots in kinetic theory, as does the entire atomistic view of matter.

NUMERICAL MAGNITUDES

When considering various physical phenomena, it is helpful for one to have some idea of the numerical magnitudes involved. In particular, there are several characteristics whose values should be known, at least within an order of magnitude (a factor of 10), in order for one to obtain a clear idea of the nature of gaseous molecules. These features include the size, average speed, and intermolecular separation at ordinary temperatures and pressures. In addition, other important considerations are how many collisions a typical molecule makes in one second under these conditions and how far such a typical molecule travels before colliding with another molecule. It has been established that molecules have sizes on the order of a few angstrom units (1 Å $= 10^{-8}$ cm) and that there are about 6×10^{23} molecules in one mole, which is defined as the amount of a substance whose mass in grams is equal to its molecular weight (e.g., 1 mole of water, H_2O, is 18.0152 grams [0.6355 ounce]). With this knowledge, one could calculate at least some of the gas values. It is interesting to see how the answers could be estimated from simple observations and then to compare the results to the accepted values that are based on more precise measurements and theories.

INTERMOLECULAR SEPARATION AND AVERAGE SPEED

One of the easiest properties to work out is the average distance between molecules compared to their diameter; water will be used here for this purpose. Consider 1 gram (0.04 ounce) of H_2O at 100 °C (212 °F) and atmospheric pressure, which are the normal boiling point conditions. The liquid occupies a volume of 1.04 cubic cm (0.06 cubic inch); once converted to steam it occupies a volume of 1.67×10^3 cubic cm. Thus, the average volume occupied by one molecule in the gas is larger than the corresponding volume occupied in the liquid by a factor of $1.67 \times 10^3/1.04$, or about 1,600. Since volume varies as the cube of distance, the ratio of the mean separation distance in the gas to that in the liquid is roughly equal to the cube root of 1,600, or about 12. If the molecules in the liquid are considered to be touching each other, the ratio of the intermolecular separation to the molecular diameter in ordinary gases is on the order of 10 under ordinary conditions. It should be noted that the actual separation and diameter cannot be determined in this way; only their ratio can be calculated.

It is also relatively simple to estimate the average speed of gas molecules. Consider a sound wave in a gas, which is just the propagation of a small pressure disturbance. If pressure is attributed to molecular impacts on a test surface, then surely a pressure disturbance cannot travel faster than the molecules themselves. In other words, the average molecular speed in a gas should be somewhat greater than the speed of sound in the gas. The speed of sound in air at ordinary temperatures is about 330 metres (1,100 feet) per second, so the molecular speed will be estimated here to be somewhat greater, say, about 500 metres (1,600 feet) per second. This value depends on the particular gas and the temperature, but it will be sufficient for the kind of estimates sought here.

MEAN FREE PATH AND COLLISION RATE

The average molecular speed, along with an observed rate of the diffusion of gases, can be used to estimate the length and tortuosity of the path traveled by a typical molecule. If a bottle of ammonia is opened in a closed room, at least a few minutes pass before the ammonia can be detected at a distance of just one metre. (Ammonia, NH_3, is a gas; the familiar bottle of "ammonia" typically seen is actually a solution of the gas in water.) Yet, if the ammonia molecules traveled directly to an observer at a speed somewhat faster than that of sound, the odour should be detectable in only a few milliseconds. The explanation for the discrepancy is that the ammonia molecules collide with many air molecules, and their paths are greatly distorted as a result.

For a quantitative estimate of the diffusion time, a more controlled system must be considered, because even gentle stray air currents in a closed room greatly speed up the spreading of the ammonia. To eliminate the effect of such air currents, a closed tube—say, a glass tube 1 cm (0.4 inch) in diameter and 1 metre (39 inches) in length—can be used. A small amount of ammonia gas is released at one end, and both ends are then closed. In order to measure how long it takes for the ammonia to travel to the other end, a piece of moist red litmus paper might be used as a detector; it will turn blue when the ammonia reaches it. This process takes quite a long time—about several hours—because diffusion occurs at such a slow rate. In this case, the time will be taken to be approximately 3 hours, or roughly 10^4 seconds (s). During this time interval, a typical ammonia molecule actually travels a distance of $(5 \times 10^4 \text{ cm/s})(10^4 \text{ s}) = 5 \times 10^8$ cm = 5,000 km (3,000 miles), roughly the distance across the United States. In other words, such a molecule travels a total distance of five million metres in order to progress a net distance of only one metre.

The solution to a basic statistical problem can be used to estimate the number of collisions such a typical diffusing molecule experienced (N) and the average distance traveled between collisions (l), called the mean free path. The product of N and l must equal the total distance traveled— i.e., $Nl = 5 \times 10^8$ cm. This distance can be thought of as a chain 5,000 km long, made up of N links, each of length l. The statistical question then is as follows: If such a chain is randomly jumbled, how far apart will its ends be on the average? This end-to-end distance corresponds to the length of the diffusion tube (one metre). This is a venerable statistical problem that recurs in many applications. One of the more vivid ways of illustrating the concept is known as the "drunkard's walk." In this scenario a drunkard takes steps of length l but, because of inebriation, takes them in random directions. After N steps, how far will he be from his starting point?

The answer is that his progress is proportional not to N but to $N^{1/2}$. For example, if the drunkard takes four steps, each of length l, he will end up at a distance of $2l$ from his starting point. Gas molecules move in three dimensions, whereas the drunkard moves in two dimensions; however, the result is the same. Thus, the square root of N multiplied by the length of the mean free path equals the length of the diffusion tube: $N^{1/2}l$ = 10^2 cm = 1 metre. From the equations for Nl and $N^{1/2}l$, it can readily be calculated that N = 2.5 × 10^{13} collisions and l = 2.0 × 10^{-5} cm. The mean time between collisions, τ, is found by dividing the time of the diffusion experiment by the number of collisions during that time: τ = $(10^4)/(2.5 \times 10^{13})$ = 4 × 10^{-10} seconds between collisions, corresponding to a collision frequency of 2.5 × 10^9 collisions per second. It is thus understandable that gases appear to be continuous fluids on ordinary scales of time and distance.

MOLECULAR SIZES

Molecular sizes can be estimated from the foregoing information on the intermolecular separation, speed, mean free path, and collision rate of gas molecules. It would seem logical that large molecules should have a better chance of colliding than do small molecules. The collision frequency and mean free path must therefore be related to molecular size.

To find this relationship, consider a single molecule in motion. During a time interval t it will sweep out a certain volume, hitting any other molecules present in this so-called collision volume. If molecules are located by their centres and each molecule has a diameter d, then the collision volume will be a long cylinder of cross-sectional area πd^2. The cylinder must be sufficiently long to include enough molecules so that good statistics on the number of collisions are obtained, but otherwise the length does not matter. If the molecule is observed for a time t, then the length of the collision cylinder will be $\bar{v}t$, where $\bar{v}$ is the average speed of the molecule, and the volume of the cylinder will be $(\pi d^2)(\bar{v}t)$, the product of its cross-sectional area and its length. Every molecule in the cylinder will be struck within time t, so the number of molecules in the collision cylinder will equal the number of collisions that occur in time t. Each collision will put a kink in the cylinder, but this will not affect the results as long as the number of collisions is not too large.

If the gas is uniform, the number of molecules per volume will be consistent throughout the entire gas. Suppose that there are N molecules in volume V; then there will be $(N/V)(\pi d^2)(\bar{v}t)$ molecules in the collision volume; this is the number of collisions in time t. The mean free path is equal to the total length of the collision cylinder divided by the number of collisions that occur in it:

$$l = \frac{(\bar{v}t)}{(N/V)(\pi d^2)(\bar{v}t)} = \frac{1}{(N/V)(\pi d^2)}.$$

Since l has been shown to be roughly 2.0×10^{-5} cm, d could be calculated if N/V was known.

It is relatively easy to find $(N/V)d^3$, from which both d and N/V can be determined. Recall that the volume of one gram of steam is about 1,600 times larger than the volume of one gram of liquid water. In other words, there are roughly 1,600 N molecules in a volume V of liquid, and, if the molecules are just touching (i.e., the separation distance between their centres is one molecular diameter), the volume V of the liquid is 1,600 Nd^3. When this equation for volume is combined with the above expression for l, the following values are obtained: $d = \pi(2.0 \times 10^{-5})/1,600 = 3.9 \times 10^{-8}$ cm = 3.9 Å, and $N/V = 1/\pi d^2 l = 1.0 \times 10^{19}$ molecules per cubic cm. Thus, a typical molecule is exceedingly small, and there is an impressively large number of them in 1 cubic cm of gas.

Between collisions, a gas molecule travels a distance of about $l/d = (2.0 \times 10^{-5})/(3.9 \times 10^{-8}) = 500$ times its diameter.

Since it was calculated above that the average separation between molecules is about 10 times the molecular diameter, the mean free path is approximately 50 times greater than the mean molecular separation. Accordingly, a typical molecule passes roughly 50 other molecules before it hits one.

Summary of Numerical Magnitudes

The following is a summary of the above estimates of molecular quantities in a gas, with a little spread in the numbers to allow for molecules both smaller and larger than the typical ones used here—which are H_2O, NH_3, and the nitrogen (N_2) plus oxygen (O_2) mixture that is air—and to allow for the fact that some of these quantities depend on temperature and pressure. It is important to note that these estimates and calculations are rather simplified, although fundamentally correct, and that there may well be missing factors such as $3\pi/8$ or $\sqrt{2}$. The numerical estimates for gases at ordinary pressure and temperature are:

molecular diameter	10^{-8} to 10^{-7} cm
molecular number density	10^{19} molecules/cm^3
average molecular speed	10^4 to 10^5 cm/s
average distance between molecules	10^{-7} to 10^{-6} cm
collision rate per molecule	10^9 to 10^{10} collisions/s
average time between collisions	10^{-10} to 10^{-9} s
average distance traveled between collisions (mean free path)	10^{-5} to 10^{-4} cm

The general impression of gas molecules given by these numbers is that they are exceedingly small, that there are enormous numbers of them in even 1 cubic cm, that they are moving very fast, and that they collide many times in one second. Two other facts are especially important. The first is that the lengths involved, especially the mean free path, are minute compared with ordinary lengths, even with the diameter of a capillary tube. This means that gas behaviour and properties are dominated by collisions between molecules and that collisions with walls play only a secondary (though important) role. The second is that the mean free path is much larger than the molecular diameter. Thus, collisions between pairs of molecules are of paramount importance in determining ordinary gas behaviour, while collisions that involve three or more molecules at the same time can basically be ignored.

A cautious reader might feel a bit uneasy about the glibness of the preceding estimates, so a simple check will be made here by calculating the number of molecules in one mole of gas, a quantity known as Avogadro's number. The number density of a gas was approximated to be about 1.0×10^{19} molecules per cubic cm, and from experiment it is known that 1 mole of gas occupies a volume of about 25 litres (2.5×10^4 cubic centimetres) under ordinary conditions. Using these values, an estimate of Avogadro's number is $(1.0 \times 10^{19})(2.5 \times 10^4) = 2.5 \times 10^{23}$ molecules per mole. This deviates somewhat from the accepted value of 6.022×10^{23} molecules per mole, but the order of magnitude is certainly correct.

In point of historical fact, a value for Avogadro's number as good as this estimate was not obtained until 1865, when Josef Loschmidt in Vienna made a calculation similar to the one here but based on gas viscosity rather than on gas diffusion. In the older German scientific literature, Avogadro's number is often referred to as Loschmidt's number for this reason. In current English-language scientific literature, Loschmidt's number is usually taken to mean the number of gas molecules in one cubic centimetre at 0 °C (32 °F) and one atmosphere pressure (2.687 × 10^{19} molecules per cubic centimetre).

There are other ways by which molecular sizes and Avogadro's number could have been estimated, such as from the spreading of a surface oil film on water or from the surface tension and the energy of evaporation of a liquid, but they will not be discussed here.

The foregoing picture of a gas as a collection of molecules dominated by binary molecular collisions is in reality only a limited view. Two limitations of the model are briefly discussed below.

FREE-MOLECULE GAS

The mean free path in a gas may easily be increased by decreasing the pressure. If the pressure is halved, the mean free path doubles in length. Thus, at low enough pressures the mean free path can become sufficiently large that collisions of the gas molecules with surfaces become more important than collisions with other gas molecules. In such a case, the molecules can be envisioned as moving freely through space until they encounter some solid surface; hence, they are termed free-molecule gases. Such gases are sometimes called Knudsen gases, after the Danish physicist Martin Knudsen, who studied them experimentally.

Many of their properties are strikingly different from those of ordinary gases (also known as continuum gases). A radiometer is a four-vaned mill that depends essentially on free-molecule effects. A temperature difference in the free-molecule gas causes a thermomolecular pressure difference that drives the vanes. The radiometer will stop spinning if enough air leaks into its glass envelope. (It will also stop spinning if all the air is removed from the envelope.) The flight of objects at high altitudes, where the mean free path is very long, is also subject to free-molecule effects. Such effects can even occur at ordinary pressures if a significant physical dimension becomes small enough. Important examples are found in many chemical process industries, where reactions are forced by catalysts to proceed at reasonable speeds. Many of these catalysts are porous materials whose pore sizes are smaller than molecular mean free paths. The speed of the desired chemical reaction may be controlled by how fast the reactant gases diffuse into the porous catalyst and by how fast the product gases can diffuse out so more reactants can enter the pores.

There is a large transition region between free-molecule behaviour and continuum behaviour, where both molecule-molecule and molecule-surface collisions are significant. This region is rather difficult to describe theoretically and remains an active field of research.

CONTINUITY OF GASEOUS AND LIQUID STATES

It may be somewhat surprising to learn that there is no fundamental distinction between a gas and a liquid. It was noted above that a gas occupies a volume about 1,600 times greater than that of an equal weight of liquid. The question arises as to the behaviour of a gas that has been compressed to 1/1,600 of its volume by application of sufficiently high pressure. If this compression is carried out above a specific temperature called the critical temperature, which is different for each gas, no phase change occurs, and the resulting substance is a gas that is just as dense as a liquid. If the compression is carried out at a fixed temperature below the critical temperature, an astonishing phenomenon occurs—at a particular pressure liquid suddenly forms. Attempts to compress the gas further simply increase the amount of liquid present and decrease the amount of gas, with the pressure remaining constant until all the gas has been converted to liquid. The applied pressure must subsequently rise a great deal to reduce the volume further, since liquids are much less compressible than gases.

The abrupt condensation of a gas to a liquid usually does not seem astonishing because it is so commonplace — nearly everyone has boiled water, for example, which is the reverse process. From the standpoint of the kinetic-molecular theory of gases, however, it is something of a mystery. Why does it occur so abruptly and only at temperatures below a critical temperature? Equations have been written down that describe condensation, but an explanation is still lacking in the sense that no one has been able to show that it must occur, given only the forces between the molecules and the fact that their motion is described by ordinary mechanics. Condensation, which is an example of a first-order phase transition, remains one of the outstanding unsolved problems of statistical physics.

The critical temperature marks the separation between an abrupt change and a continuous change. Other peculiar phenomena occur near the critical temperature. The densities of the coexisting liquid and gas (which is usually called a vapour in this case) become closer as the critical temperature is approached from below, and at the critical temperature they are identical. There is a unique point for every fluid, called the critical point. It is described by a critical temperature, a critical volume, and a critical pressure, at which liquid and vapour become identical. Above that temperature there is no distinction between gas and liquid; there is only a single fluid. Moreover, it is possible to pass continuously from an apparently definite gas or vapour to an apparently definite liquid with no abrupt condensation occurring. This can be accomplished by heating the vapour above the critical temperature while keeping the volume constant, then compressing it to a high density characteristic of a liquid, and finally cooling it at constant volume to its original temperature, where it is now clearly a liquid.

In short, gases and liquids are just the extreme stages of a fluid, with no fundamental distinction between the two. For this reason, an arbitrary decision has been made for the present discussion to define what is meant by the gaseous state. The definition will be based on the number density (i.e., molecules per unit volume): the number density of the fluid must be low enough that only collisions between two molecules at a time need to be considered. More specifically, the mean free path must be much larger than the molecular diameter. Such a fluid shall be termed a dilute gas.

A few brief historical remarks are in order before leaving the subject of the continuity of the gaseous and liquid states. The first extensive experimental study that clearly demonstrated the phenomena involved was performed on carbon dioxide, CO_2. (Carbon dioxide, whose solid form is called dry ice, has a critical temperature of 31 °C [88 °F].) The experiment was conducted by Thomas Andrews at what is now the Queen's University of Belfast in Northern Ireland, and its results were summarized in 1869 in a Bakerian lecture to the Royal Society of London entitled "On the Continuity of the Gaseous and Liquid States of Matter." In 1873 a Dutch thesis was presented to the University of Leiden by Johannes D. van der Waals with virtually the same title (but in Dutch) as Andrews's lecture. In his study van der Waals used some ingenious approximations to obtain a simple equation relating the pressure, temperature, and molar volume of a fluid, based on a model that considered molecules as hard spheres with weak long-range attractive forces between them. This equation can be used to locate the critical point of a system, and it is also consistent with the occurrence of condensation when supplemented with a thermodynamic condition. This is possibly one of the most-quoted but little-read theses in science.

Nevertheless, van der Waals started a scientific trend that continues to the present. His pressure-volume-temperature relation, called an equation of state, is the standard equation of state for real gases in physical chemistry, and at least one new equation of state is proposed every year in an attempt to improve on its quantitative accuracy (which is not very good). It furnished the impetus for the development of theories of liquids and of solutions. The equation is compatible with a unifying idea called the principle of corresponding states. This principle states that, if the pressure (p), volume (V), and temperature (T) of a gas are replaced, respectively, with the corresponding reduced variables—i.e., the pressure divided by the critical pressure (p/p_c), the volume divided by the critical volume (V/V_c), and the temperature divided by the critical temperature (T/T_c)—all gases will behave in essentially the same manner.

The critical point has itself proved to be a rich and deep subject. The gas-liquid critical point turns out to be only one of many types of critical points, including those of a magnetic variety, with the common feature that long-range correlations develop regardless of the molecular details of the system. That is, any small part of a system near its critical point seems to "know" what quite distant parts are doing. The mathematical description of the behaviour of a system near its critical point also becomes rather unusual.

BEHAVIOUR AND PROPERTIES

The enormous number of molecules in even a small volume of a dilute gas produces not complication, as might be expected, but rather simplification. The reason is that ordinarily only statistical averages are observed in the study of the behaviour and properties of gases, and statistical methods are quite accurate when large numbers are involved. Compared to the numbers of molecules involved, there are only a few properties of gases that warrant attention here, namely, pressure, density, temperature, internal energy, viscosity, heat conductivity, and diffusivity. (More subtle properties can be brought into view by the application of electric and magnetic fields, but they are of minor interest.)

It is a remarkable fact that these properties are not independent. If two are known, the rest can be determined from them. That is to say, for a given gas, the specification of only two properties—usually chosen to be temperature and density or temperature and pressure—fixes all the others. Thus, if the temperature and density of carbon dioxide are specified, the gas can have only one possible pressure, one internal energy, one viscosity, and so on. In order to determine the values of these other properties, they must either be measured or calculated from the known properties of the molecules themselves. Such calculations are the ultimate goal of statistical mechanics and kinetic theory, and dilute gases constitute the case for which the most progress toward that goal has been made.

EQUILIBRIUM PROPERTIES

In discussing the behaviour of gases, it is useful to separate the equilibrium properties and the nonequilibrium transport properties. By definition, a system in equilibrium can undergo no net change unless some external action is performed on it (e.g., pushing in a piston or adding heat). Its behaviour is steady with time, and no changes appear to be occurring, even though the molecules are in ceaseless motion. In contrast, the nonequilibrium properties describe how a system responds to some external action, such as the imposition of a temperature or pressure difference. Equilibrium behaviour is much easier to analyze, because any change that occurs on the molecular level must be compensated by some other change or changes on the molecular level in order for the system to remain in equilibrium.

IDEAL GAS EQUATION OF STATE

Among the most obvious properties of a dilute gas, other than its low density compared with liquids and solids, are its great elasticity or compressibility and its large volume expansion on heating. These properties are nearly the same for all dilute gases, and virtually all such gases can be described quite accurately by the following universal equation of state:

$$pv = RT. \tag{15}$$

This expression is called the ideal, or perfect, gas equation of state, since all real gases show small deviations from it, although these deviations become less significant as the density is decreased. Here p is the pressure, v is the volume per mole, or molar volume, R is the universal gas constant, and T is the absolute thermodynamic temperature. To a rough degree, the expression is accurate within a few percent if the volume is more than 10 times the critical volume; the accuracy improves as the volume increases. The expression eventually fails at both high and low temperatures, owing to ionization at high temperatures and to condensation to a liquid or solid at low temperatures.

The ideal gas equation of state is an amalgamation of three ideal gas laws that were formulated independently. The first is Boyle's law, which refers to the elastic properties of the gas; it was described by the Anglo-Irish scientist Robert Boyle in 1662 in his famous " . . . Experiments . . .

Touching the Spring of the Air . . . ." It states that the volume of a gas at constant temperature is inversely proportional to the pressure; i.e., if the pressure on a gas is doubled, for example, its volume decreases by one-half. The second, usually called Charles's law, is concerned with the thermal expansion of the gas. It is named in honour of the French experimental physicist Jacques-Alexandre-César Charles for the work he carried out in about 1787. The law states that the volume of a gas at constant pressure is directly proportional to the absolute temperature; i.e., an increase of temperature of 1 °C (1.8 °F) at room temperature causes the volume to increase by about 1 part in 300, or 0.3 percent.

The third law embodied in equation (15) is based on the 1811 hypothesis of the Italian scientist Amedeo Avogadro—namely, that equal volumes of gases at the same temperature and pressure contain equal numbers of particles. The number of particles (or molecules) is proportional to the number of moles n, the constant of proportionality being Avogadro's number, N_o. Thus, at constant temperature and pressure the volume of a gas is proportional to the number of moles. If the total volume V contains n moles of gas, then only $v = V/n$ appears in the equation of state. By measuring the quantity of gas in moles rather than grams, the constant R is made universal; if mass were measured in grams (and hence v in volume per gram), then R would have a different value for each gas.

The ideal gas law is easily extended to mixtures by letting n represent the total number of moles of all species present in volume V. That is, if there are n_1 moles of species 1, n_2 moles of species 2, etc., in the mixture, then $n = n_1 + n_2 + \cdots$ and $v = V/n$ as before. This result can also be rewritten and reinterpreted in terms of the partial pressures of the different species, such that $p_1 = n_1 RT/V$ is the

Robert Boyle. Hulton Archive/Getty Images

partial pressure of species 1 and so on. The total pressure is then given as $p = p_1 + p_2 + \cdots$. This rule is known as Dalton's law of partial pressures in honour of the British chemist and physicist John Dalton, who formulated it about 1801.

A brief aside on units and temperature scales is in order. The (metric) unit of pressure in the scientific international system of units (known as the SI system) is newton per square metre (N/m^2), where one newton (N) is the force that gives a mass of 1 kg an acceleration of 1 m/s^2. The unit N/m^2 is given the name pascal (Pa), where one standard atmosphere is exactly 101,325 Pa (approximately 14.7 pounds per square inch). The unit of volume in the SI system is the cubic metre (1 cubic metre = 10^6 cubic cm), and the unit of temperature is the kelvin (K). The Kelvin thermodynamic temperature scale is defined through the laws of thermodynamics so as to be absolute or universal, in the sense that its definition does not depend on the specific properties of any particular kind of matter. Its numerical values, however, are assigned by defining the triple point of water—i.e., the unique temperature at which ice, liquid water, and water vapour are all in equilibrium—to be exactly 273.16 K. The freezing point of water under one atmosphere of air then turns out to be (by measurement) 273.1500 K. The freezing point is 0° on the Celsius scale (or 32° on the Fahrenheit scale), by definition. The precise thermodynamic definition of the Kelvin scale and the rather peculiar number chosen to define its numerical values (i.e., 273.16) are historical choices made so that the ideal gas equation of state will have the simple mathematical form given by the right-hand side of equation (15).

The gas constant R is determined by measurement. The best value so far obtained is that of the U.S. National

Institute of Standards and Technology—namely, 8.314472 J/mol · K. Here the unit J is one of work or energy, one joule (J) being equal to one newton-metre.

INTERNAL ENERGY

Once the equation of state is known for an ideal gas, only its internal energy, E, needs to be determined in order for all other equilibrium properties to be deducible from the laws of thermodynamics. That is to say, if the equation of state and the internal energy of a fluid are known, then all the other thermodynamic properties (e.g., enthalpy, entropy, and free energy) are fixed by the condition that it must be impossible to construct perpetual motion machines from the fluid. Proofs of such statements are usually rather subtle and involved and constitute a large part of the subject of thermodynamics, but conclusions based on thermodynamic principles are among the most reliable results of science.

A thermodynamic result of relevance here is that the ideal gas equation of state requires that the internal energy depend on temperature alone, not on pressure or density. The actual relationship between E and T must be measured or calculated from known molecular properties by means of statistical mechanics. The internal energy is not directly measurable, but its behaviour can be determined from measurements of the molar heat capacity (i.e., the specific heat) of the gas. The molar heat capacity is the amount of energy required to raise the temperature of one mole of a substance by one degree. Its units in the SI system are J/mol · K. A system with many kinds of motion on a molecular scale absorbs more energy than one with only a few kinds of motion. The interpretation of the temperature dependence of E is particularly simple for dilute gases, as shown in the discussion of the kinetic theory of gases in Chapter 3. The following highlights only the major aspects.

Every gas molecule moves in three-dimensional space, and this translational motion contributes $(3/2)RT$ (per mole) to the internal energy E. For monatomic gases, such as helium, neon, argon, krypton, and xenon, this is the sole energy contribution. Gases that contain two or more atoms per molecule also contribute additional terms because of their internal motions:

$$E\,(\text{per mole}) = \frac{3}{2}RT + E_{int},\qquad (16)$$

where E_{int} may include contributions from molecular rotations and internal vibrations and occasionally from internal electronic excitations. Some of these internal motions may not contribute at ordinary temperatures because of special conditions imposed by quantum mechanics, however, so that the temperature dependence of E_{int} can be rather complex.

The extension to gas mixtures is straightforward—the total internal energy E (per mole) is the weighted sum of the internal energies of each of the species: $nE = n_1E_1 + n_2E_2 + \cdots$, where $n = n_1 + n_2 + \cdots$.

It is the task of the kinetic theory of gases to account for these results concerning the equation of state and the internal energy of dilute gases.

TRANSPORT PROPERTIES

The following is a summary of the three main transport properties: viscosity, heat conductivity, and diffusivity. These properties correspond to the transfer of momentum, energy, and matter, respectively.

VISCOSITY

All ordinary fluids exhibit viscosity, which is a type of internal friction. A continuous application of force is needed to keep a fluid flowing, just as a continuous force is needed to keep a solid body moving in the presence of friction. Consider the case of a fluid slowly flowing through a long capillary tube. A pressure difference of Δp must be maintained across the ends to keep the fluid flowing, and the resulting flow rate is proportional to Δp. The rate is inversely proportional to the viscosity (η) since the friction that opposes the flow increases as η increases. It also depends on the geometry of the tube, but this effect will not be considered here. The SI units of η are $N \cdot s/m^2$ or $Pa \cdot s$. An older unit of the centimetre-gram-second version of the metric system that is still often used is the poise ($1 \, Pa \cdot s = 10$ poise). At 20 °C (68 °F) the viscosity of water is $1.0 \times 10^{-3} \, Pa \cdot s$ and that of air is $1.8 \times 10^{-5} \, Pa \cdot s$. To a rough approximation, liquids are about 100 times more viscous than gases.

There are three important properties of the viscosity of dilute gases that seem to defy common sense. All can be explained, however, by the kinetic theory. The first property is the lack of a dependence on pressure or density. Intuition suggests that gas viscosity should increase with increasing density, inasmuch as liquids are much more viscous than gases, but gas viscosity is actually independent of density. This result can be illustrated by a pendulum swinging on a solid support. It eventually slows down owing to the viscous friction of the air. If a bell jar is placed over the pendulum and half the air is pumped out, the air remaining in the jar damps the pendulum just as fast as a full jar of air would have done. Robert Boyle noted this peculiar phenomenon in 1660, but his results were largely either ignored or forgotten. The Scottish chemist Thomas

James Clerk Maxwell. Hulton Archive/Getty Images

Graham studied the flow of gases through long capillaries, which he called transpiration, in 1846 and 1849, but it was not until 1877 that the German physicist O.E. Meyer pointed out that Graham's measurements had shown the independence of viscosity on density. Prior to Meyer's investigations, the kinetic theory had suggested the result, so he was looking for experimental proof to support the prediction. When James Clerk Maxwell discovered (in 1865) that his kinetic theory suggested this result, he found it difficult to believe and attempted to check it experimentally. He designed an oscillating disk apparatus (which is still much copied) to verify the prediction.

The second unusual property of viscosity is its relationship with temperature. One might expect the viscosity of a fluid to increase as the temperature is lowered, as suggested by the phrase "as slow as molasses in January." The viscosity of a dilute gas behaves in exactly the opposite way: the viscosity increases as the temperature is raised. The rate of increase varies approximately as T^s, where s is between ½ and 1, and depends on the particular gas. This behaviour was clearly established in 1849 by Graham.

The third property pertains to the viscosity of mixtures. A viscous syrup, for example, can be made less so by the addition of a liquid with a lower viscosity, such as water. By analogy, one would expect that a mixture of carbon dioxide, which is fairly viscous, with a gas like hydrogen, which is much less viscous, would have a viscosity intermediate to that of carbon dioxide and hydrogen. Surprisingly, the viscosity of the mixture is even greater than that of carbon dioxide. This phenomenon was also observed by Graham in 1849.

Finally, there is no obvious correlation of gas viscosity with molecular weight. Heavy gases are often more viscous than light gases, but there are many exceptions, and no simple pattern is apparent.

HEAT CONDUCTION

If a temperature difference is maintained across a fluid, a flow of energy through the fluid will result. The energy flow is proportional to the temperature difference according to Fourier's law, where the constant of proportionality (aside from the geometric factors of the apparatus) is called the heat conductivity or thermal conductivity of the fluid, λ. Mechanisms other than conduction can transport energy, in particular convection and radiation; here it is assumed that these can be eliminated or adjusted for. The SI units for λ are J/m $\cdot$ s $\cdot$ K or watt per metre degree (W/m $\cdot$ K), but sometimes calories are used for the energy term instead of joules (one calorie = 4.184 J). At 20 °C (68 °F) the thermal conductivity of water is 0.60 W/m $\cdot$ K, and that of many organic liquids is roughly only one-third as large. The thermal conductivity of air at 20 °C is only about 2.5 $\times 10^{-2}$ W/m $\cdot$ K. To a rough approximation, liquids conduct heat about 10 times better than do gases.

The properties of the thermal conductivity of dilute gases parallel those of viscosity in some respects. The most striking is the lack of dependence on pressure or density. Based on this fact, there seems to be no advantage to pumping out the inner chambers of thermos bottles. As far as conduction is concerned, it does not provide any benefits until practically all the air has been removed and free-molecule conduction is occurring. Convection, however, does depend on density, so some degree of insulation is provided by pumping out only some of the air.

The thermal conductivity of a dilute gas increases with increasing temperature, much like its viscosity. In this case, such behaviour does not seem particularly odd, probably because most people do not have a preconceived idea of how thermal conductivity should behave, unlike the situation with viscosity.

There are some differences in the behaviour of thermal conductivity and viscosity; one of the most notable has to do with mixtures. At first glance the thermal conductivity of a gaseous mixture seems to be as expected, since it falls between the conductivities of its components, but a closer look reveals an odd regularity. The conductivity of the mixture is always less than an average based on the number of moles (or molecules) of each component in the mixture. This appears to be related to the different effect that molecular weight has on thermal conductivity and viscosity. Light gases are usually better conductors than are heavy gases, whereas heavy gases are often (but not always) more viscous than are light gases. There also seems to be some correlation between molar heat capacity and thermal conductivity. The foregoing properties of thermal conductivity pose more puzzles that the kinetic theory of gases must address.

DIFFUSION

Diffusion in dilute gases is in some ways more complex, or at least more subtle, than either viscosity or thermal conductivity. First, a mixture is necessarily involved, inasmuch as a gas diffusing through itself makes no sense physically unless the molecules are in some way distinguishable from one another. Second, diffusion measurements are rather sensitive to the details of the experimental conditions. This sensitivity can be illustrated by the following considerations.

Light molecules have higher average speeds than do heavy molecules at the same temperature. This result follows from kinetic theory, as explained in the next chapter, but it can also be seen by noting that the speed of sound is greater in a light gas than in a heavy gas. This is the basis of the well-known demonstration that breathing helium causes one to speak with a high-pitched voice. If a light and a heavy gas are interdiffusing, the light molecules should move into the heavy-gas region faster than the heavy molecules move into the light-gas region, thereby causing the pressure to rise in the heavy-gas region. If the diffusion takes place in a closed vessel, the pressure difference drives the heavy gas into the light-gas region at a faster rate than it would otherwise diffuse, and a steady state is quickly reached in which the number of heavy molecules traveling in one direction equals, on the average, the number of light molecules traveling in the opposite direction. This method, called equimolar countercurrent diffusion, is the usual manner in which gaseous diffusion measurements are now carried out.

The steady-state pressure difference that develops is almost unmeasurably small unless the diffusion occurs through a fine capillary or a fine-grained porous material. Nevertheless, experimenters have been able to devise clever schemes either to measure it or to prevent its development. The first to do the latter was Graham in 1831; he kept the pressure uniform by allowing the gas mixture to flow. The results of this work now appear in elementary textbooks as Graham's law of diffusion. Most of these accounts are incorrect or incomplete or both, owing to the fact that the writers confuse the uniform-pressure experiment either with the equal countercurrent experiment or with the phenomenon of effusion (described in Chapter 3 on the kinetic theory of gases). Graham also performed equal countercurrent experiments in 1863, using a long closed-tube apparatus he devised. This sort of apparatus is now usually called a Loschmidt diffusion tube after Loschmidt, who used a modified version of the tube in 1870 to make a series of accurate diffusion measurements on a number of gas pairs.

A quantitative description of diffusion follows. A composition difference in a two-component gas mixture causes a relative flow of the components that tends to make the composition uniform. The flow of one component is proportional to its concentration difference, and in an equal countercurrent experiment this is balanced by an equal and opposite flow of the other component. The constant of proportionality is the same for both components and is called the diffusion coefficient, D_{12}, for that gas pair. This relationship between the flow rate and the concentration difference is called Fick's law of diffusion. The SI units for the diffusion coefficient are square metres per second (m^2/s). Diffusion, even in gases, is an extremely slow process, as was pointed out above in estimating molecular sizes and collision rates. Gaseous diffusion coefficients at one atmosphere pressure and ordinary temperatures lie largely in the range of 10^{-5} to 10^{-4} m^2/s, but diffusion coefficients for liquids and solutions lie in the range of only 10^{-10} to 10^{-9} m^2/s. To a rough approximation, gases diffuse about 100,000 times faster than do liquids.

Diffusion coefficients are inversely proportional to total pressure or total molar density and are therefore reported by convention at a standard pressure of one atmosphere. Doubling the pressure of a diffusing mixture halves the diffusion coefficient, but the actual rate of diffusion remains unchanged. This seemingly paradoxical result occurs because doubling the pressure also doubles the concentration, according to the ideal gas equation of state, and hence doubles the concentration difference, which is the driving force for diffusion. The two effects exactly compensate.

Diffusion coefficients increase with increasing temperature at a rate that depends on whether the pressure or the total molar density is held constant as the temperature is changed. If the rate increases as T^s at constant molar density (where s usually lies between ½ and 1), then it will increase as T^{1+s} at constant pressure, according to the ideal gas equation of state.

Perhaps the most surprising property of gaseous diffusion coefficients is that they are virtually independent of the mixture's composition, varying by at most a few percent over the whole composition range, even for very dissimilar gases. A trace of hydrogen, for example, diffuses through carbon dioxide at virtually the same rate that a trace of carbon dioxide diffuses through hydrogen. Liquid mixtures do not behave this way, and liquid diffusion coefficients may vary by as much as a factor of 10 from one end of the composition range to the other. The lack of composition dependence of gaseous diffusion coefficients is one of the odder properties to be explained by kinetic theory.

THERMAL DIFFUSION

If a temperature difference is applied to a uniform mixture of two gases, the mixture will partially separate into its components, with the heavier, larger molecules usually (but not invariably) concentrating at the lower temperature. This behaviour was predicted theoretically before it was observed experimentally, but a rather elaborate explanation was required because simple theory suggests no such phenomenon. It was predicted in 1911–12 by David Enskog in Sweden and independently in 1917 by Sydney Chapman in England, but the validity of their theoretical results was questioned until Chapman (who was an applied mathematician) enlisted the aid of the chemist F. W. Dootson to verify it experimentally.

Thermal diffusion can be used to separate isotopes. The amount of separation for any reasonable temperature difference is quite small for isotopes, but the effect can be amplified by combining it with slow thermal convection in a columnar arrangement devised in 1938 by Klaus Clusius and Gerhard Dickel in Germany. While the apparatus is quite simple, the theory of its operation is not: a long cylinder with a diameter of several centimetres is mounted vertically with an electrically heated hot wire along its central axis. The thermal diffusion occurs horizontally between the hot wire and the cold wall of the cylinder, and the convection takes place vertically to bring new gas regions into contact.

There is also an effect that is the inverse of thermal diffusion, called the diffusion thermoeffect, in which an imposed concentration difference causes a temperature difference to develop. That is, a diffusing gas mixture develops small temperature differences, on the order of 1 °C (0.6 °F), which die out as the composition approaches uniformity. The transport coefficient describing the diffusion thermoeffect must be equal to the coefficient describing thermal diffusion, according to the reciprocal relations central to the thermodynamics of irreversible processes.

CHAPTER 3
KINETIC THEORY
OF GASES

The aim of kinetic theory is to account for the properties of gases in terms of the forces between the molecules, assuming that their motions are described by the laws of mechanics (usually classical Newtonian mechanics, although quantum mechanics is needed in some cases). The present discussion focuses on dilute ideal gases, in which molecular collisions of at most two bodies are of primary importance. Only the simplest theories are treated here in order to avoid obscuring the fundamental physics with complex mathematics.

IDEAL GAS

The ideal gas equation of state can be deduced by calculating the pressure as caused by molecular impacts on a container wall. The internal energy and John Dalton's law of partial pressures also emerge from this calculation, along with some free-molecule phenomena. The calculation is significant because it is basically the same one used to explain all dilute-gas phenomena.

PRESSURE

Sir Isaac Newton's second law of motion can be stated in not-so-familiar form as impulse equals change in momentum, where impulse is force multiplied by the time during which it acts. A molecule experiences a change in momentum when it collides with a container wall. During the collision an impulse is imparted by the wall to the molecule that is equal and opposite to the impulse imparted by the molecule to the wall. This is required by Newton's third law. The sum of the impulses imparted by all the molecules to the wall is, in effect, the pressure.

Consider a system of molecules of mass m traveling with a velocity v in an enclosed container. In order to arrive at an expression for the pressure, a calculation will be made of the impulse imparted to one of the walls by a single impact, followed by a calculation of how many impacts occur on that wall during a time t. Although the molecules are moving in all directions, only those with a component of velocity toward the wall can collide with it; call this component v_z, where z represents the direction directly toward the wall. Not all molecules have the same v_z, of course; perhaps only N_z out of a total of N molecules do. To find the total pressure, the contributions from molecules with all different values of v_z must be summed. A molecule approaches the wall with an initial momentum mv_z, and after impact it moves away from the wall with an equal momentum in the opposite direction, $-mv_z$. Thus, the total change in momentum is $mv_z - (-mv_z) = 2mv_z$, which is equal to the total impulse imparted to the wall.

The number of impacts on a small area A of the wall in time t is equal to the number of molecules that reach the wall in time t. Since the molecules are traveling at speed v_z, only those within a distance $v_z t$ and moving toward the wall will reach it in that time. Thus, the molecules that are traveling toward the wall and are within a volume $Av_z t$ will strike the area A of the wall in time t. On the average, half of the molecules in this volume will be moving toward the wall. If N_z molecules with speed component v_z are present in the total volume V, then $(1/2)(N_z/V)(A)(v_z t)$ molecules in the collision volume will hit, and each one contributes an impulse of $2mv_z$. The total impulse in time t is therefore $(1/2)(N_z/V)(A)(v_z t)(2mv_z) = (N_z/V)(mv_z^2)(At)$, which is equal to Ft, where

F is the force on the wall due to the impacts. Equating these two expressions, the time factor t cancels out. Since pressure is defined as the force per unit area (F/A), it follows that the contribution to the pressure from the molecules with speed v_z is thus (Nz/V)mv_z^2. Because there are different values of v_z^2 for different molecules, the average value, denoted $\overline{v_z^2}$, is used to take into account the contributions from all the molecules. The pressure is thus given as $p = (N/V)m\overline{v_z^2}$.

Since the molecules are in random motion, this result is independent of the choice of axis. For any choice of (x, y, z) axes, the magnitude of the velocity is $v^2 = v_x^2 + v_y^2 + v_z^2$ (which is just the Pythagorean theorem in three dimensions), and taking the average gives $\overline{v^2} = \overline{v_x^2} + \overline{v_y^2} + \overline{v_z^2}$. The gas is in equilibrium, so it must appear the same in any direction, and the average velocities are therefore the same in all directions—i.e., $\overline{v_x^2} = \overline{v_y^2} = \overline{v_z^2}$; thus $\overline{v^2} = 3\overline{v_z^2}$. When the value $(1/3)\overline{v^2}$ is substituted for $\overline{v_z^2}$ in the expression for pressure, the following equation is obtained:

$$p = \frac{1}{3}\frac{N}{V}m\overline{v^2}, \quad \text{or} \quad pV = \frac{1}{3}Nm\overline{v^2}. \tag{17}$$

To rewrite this in molar units, N is set equal to nN_o—i.e., the product of the number of moles n and Avogadro's number N_o—to give

$$pv = \frac{1}{3}M\overline{v^2}, \tag{18}$$

where $M = N_o m$ is the molecular weight of the gas and v is the volume per mole (V/n). Since the ideal gas equation of state relates pressure, molar volume, and temperature as $pv = RT$, the temperature T must be related to the average kinetic energy of the molecules as

$$\frac{1}{2}M\overline{v^2} = \frac{3}{2}RT. \tag{19}$$

This expression is often written in molecular (rather than molar) terms as $(1/2)[mv^2] = (3/2)kT$, where $k = R/N_o$ is called Boltzmann's constant, named after Ludwig Boltzmann, a 19th-century Austrian physicist who substantially contributed to the foundation and development of statistical mechanics. If the gas is a mixture, the foregoing calculation shows that the impacts of the different species are simply added separately, and Dalton's law of partial pressures follows directly.

The energy law given as equation (16) also follows from equation (19): the kinetic energy of translational motion per mole is $(3/2)RT$. Any energy residing in the internal motions of the individual molecules is simply carried separately without contributing to the pressure.

Average molecular speeds can be calculated from the results of kinetic theory in terms of the so-called root-mean-square speed v_{rms}. The v_{rms} is the square root of the average of the squares of the speeds of the molecules: $(v^2)^{1/2}$. From equation (19) the v_{rms} is $(3RT/M)^{1/2}$. At 20 °C (68 °F) the value for air ($M = 29$) is 502 metres (1,647 feet) per second, a result very close to the rough estimate of 500 metres per second given above.

Molecule-molecule collisions were not considered in the calculation of the expression for pressure even though many such collisions occur. Such collisions could be ignored because they are elastic; i.e., linear momentum is conserved in the collision, provided that no external forces act. Two molecules therefore continue to carry the same momentum to the wall even if they collide with one another before striking it. The ideal gas equation of state remains valid as the density is decreased, even holding for a free-molecule gas. The equation eventually fails as the density is increased, however, because other molecules exert forces and change the rate of collisions with the walls.

It was not until the mid- to late 19th century that kinetic theory was successfully applied to such calculations as gas pressure. Such notable scientists as Newton and Dalton had believed that gas pressure was caused by repulsions between molecules that pushed them against the container walls. For many reasons, the kinetic theory had overshadowed such static theories (and others such as vortex theories) by about 1860. It was not until 1875, however, that James Clerk Maxwell actually proved that a static theory was in conflict with experiment.

EFFUSION

Consider the system described above in the calculation of gas pressure, but with the area A in the container wall replaced with a small hole. The number of molecules that escape through the hole in time t is equal to $(1/2)(N/V)v_z(At)$. In this case, collisions between molecules are significant, and the result holds only for tiny holes in very thin walls (as compared to the mean free path), so that a molecule that approaches near the hole will get through without colliding with another molecule and being deflected away. The relationship between v_z and the average speed $\bar{v}$ is rather straightforward: $v_z = (1/2)\bar{v}$.

If the rates for two different gases effusing through the same hole are compared, starting with the same gas density each time, it is found that much more light gas escapes than heavy gas and that more gas escapes at a high temperature than at a low temperature, other things being equal. In particular,

$$\frac{\text{effusion rate of gas 1}}{\text{effusion rate of gas 2}} = \frac{\overline{v}_1}{\overline{v}_2} = \left(\frac{m_2}{m_1}\right)^{1/2}\left(\frac{T_1}{T_2}\right)^{1/2}. \qquad (20)$$

The last step follows from the energy formula, $(1/2)mv^2 = (3/2)kT$, where $(v^2)^{1/2}$ is approximated to be v, even though v^2 and $(\bar{v})^2$ actually differ by a numerical factor near unity (namely, $3\pi/8$). This result was discovered experimentally in 1846 by Graham for the case of constant temperature and is known as Graham's law of effusion. It can be used to measure molecular weights, to measure the vapour pressure of a material with a low vapour pressure, or to calculate the rate of evaporation of molecules from a liquid or solid surface.

Thermal Transpiration

Suppose that two containers of the same gas but at different temperatures are connected by a tiny hole and that the gas is brought to a steady state. If the hole is small enough and the gas density is low enough that only effusion occurs, the equilibrium pressure will be greater on the high-temperature side. But, if the initial pressures on both sides are equal, gas will flow from the low-temperature side to the high-temperature side to cause the high-temperature pressure to increase. The latter situation is called thermal transpiration, and the steady-state result is called the thermomolecular pressure difference. These results follow simply from the effusion formula if the ideal gas law is used to replace N/V with p/T;

$$\frac{\text{effusion rate from container 1}}{\text{effusion rate from container 2}} = \frac{p_1}{p_2}\left(\frac{T_2}{T_1}\right)^{1/2}. \qquad (21)$$

When a steady state is reached, the effusion rates are equal, and thus

$$\frac{p_1}{p_2} = \left(\frac{T_1}{T_2}\right)^{1/2}. \qquad (22)$$

This phenomenon was first investigated experimentally by Osborne Reynolds in 1879 in Manchester, England. Errors can result if a gas pressure is measured in a vessel at very low or very high temperature by connecting it via a fine tube to a manometer at room temperature. A continuous circulation of gas can be produced by connecting the two containers with another tube whose diameter is large compared with the mean free path. The pressure difference drives gas through this tube by viscous flow. A heat engine based on this circulating flow unfortunately has a low efficiency.

VISCOSITY

The kinetic-theory explanation of viscosity can be simplified by examining it in qualitative terms. Viscosity is caused by the transfer of momentum between two planes sliding parallel to one another but at different rates, and this momentum is transferred by molecules moving between the planes. Molecules from the faster plane move to the slower plane and tend to speed it up, while molecules from the slower plane travel to the faster plane and tend to slow it down. This is the mechanism by which one plane experiences the drag of the other. A simple analogy is two mail trains passing each other, with workers throwing mailbags between the trains. Every time a mailbag from the fast-moving train lands on the slow one, it imparts its momentum to the slow train, speeding it up a little; likewise each mailbag from the slow train that lands on the fast one slows it down a bit.

If the trains are too far apart, the mailbags cannot be passed between them. Similarly, the planes of a gas must be only about a mean free path apart in order for molecules to pass between them without being deflected by collisions. If one uses this approach, a simple calculation can be carried out, much as in the case of the gas pressure, with the result that

$$\eta = a\frac{N}{V}\bar{v}lm, \tag{23}$$

where a is a numerical constant of order unity, the term $(N/V)\bar{v}l$ is a measure of the number of molecules contained in a small counting cylinder, and the mass m is a measure of the momentum carried between the sliding planes. The cross-sectional area of the counting cylinder and the relative speed of the sliding planes do not appear in the equation because they cancel one another when the drag force is divided by the area and speed of the planes in order to find η.

It can now be seen why η is independent of gas density or pressure. The term (N/V) in equation (23) is the number of carriers of momentum, but l measures the number of collisions that interfere with these carriers and is inversely proportional to (N/V). The two effects exactly cancel each other. Viscosity increases with temperature because the average velocity $\bar{v}$ does; that is, momentum is carried more quickly when the molecules move faster. Although $\bar{v}$ increases as $T^{1/2}$, η increases somewhat faster because the mean free path also increases with temperature, since it is harder to deflect a fast molecule than a slow one. This feature depends explicitly on the forces between the molecules and is difficult to calculate accurately, as is the value of the constant a, which turns out to be close to $1/2$.

The behaviour of the viscosity of a mixture can also be explained by the foregoing calculation. In a mixture of a light gas and a viscous heavy gas, both types of molecules have the same average energy. However, most of the momentum is carried by the heavy molecules, which are therefore the main contributors to the viscosity. The light molecules are rather ineffective in deflecting the heavy molecules, so that the latter continue to carry virtually as much momentum as they would in the absence of light molecules. The addition of a light gas to a heavy gas therefore does not reduce the viscosity substantially and may in fact increase it because of the small extra momentum carried by the light molecules. The viscosity will eventually decrease when there are only a few heavy molecules remaining in a large sea of light molecules.

The main dependence of η on the molecular mass is through the product $\bar{v}m$ in equation (23), which varies as $m^{1/2}$ since $\bar{v}$ varies as $1/m^{1/2}$. Owing to this effect, heavy gases tend to be more viscous than light gases, but this tendency is compensated for to some degree by the behaviour of l, which tends to be smaller for heavy molecules because they are usually larger than light molecules and therefore more likely to collide. The often confusing connection between viscosity and molecular weight can thus be accounted for by equation (23).

Finally, in a free-molecule gas there are no collisions with other molecules to impede the transport of momentum, and the viscosity thus increases linearly with pressure or density until the number of collisions becomes great enough so that the viscosity assumes the constant value given by equation (23). The nonideal behaviour of the gas that accompanies further increases in density eventually leads to an increase in viscosity, and the viscosity of an extremely dense gas becomes much like that of a liquid.

THERMAL CONDUCTIVITY

The kinetic-theory explanation of heat conduction is similar to that for viscosity, but in this case the molecules carry net energy from a region of higher energy (i.e., temperature) to one of lower energy (temperature). Internal molecular motions must be accounted for because, though they do not transport momentum, they do transport energy. Monatomic gases, which carry only their kinetic energy of translational motion, are the simplest case. The resulting expression for thermal conductivity is

$$\lambda = a' \frac{N}{V} \overline{v} l \left(\frac{3}{2} k \right), \tag{24}$$

which has the same basic form as equation (23) for viscosity, with ($3k/2$) replacing m. The ($3k/2$) is the heat capacity per molecule and is the conversion factor from an energy difference to a temperature difference.

It can be shown from equation (24) that the independence of density and the increase with temperature is the same for thermal conductivity as it is for viscosity. The dependence on molecular mass is different, however, with λ varying as $1/m^{1/2}$ owing to the factor $\overline{v}$. Thus, light gases tend to be better conductors of heat than are heavy gases, and this tendency is usually augmented by the behaviour of l.

The behaviour of the thermal conductivity of mixtures may be qualitatively explained. Adding heavy gas to light gas reduces the thermal conductivity because the heavy molecules carry less energy and also interfere with the energy transport of the light molecules.

The similar behaviour of λ and η suggests that their ratio might provide information about the constants a and a'. The ratio of a'/a is given as

$$\frac{\lambda}{\eta} \frac{m}{(3k/2)} = \frac{a'}{a}. \tag{25}$$

Although simple theory suggests that this ratio should be about one, both experiment and more refined theory give a value close to 5/2. This means that molecules do not "forget" their past history in every collision, but some persistence of their precollision velocities occurs. Molecules transport both energy and momentum from a somewhat greater distance than just one mean free path, but this distance is greater for energy than for momentum. This is plausible, for molecules with higher kinetic energies might be expected to have greater persistences.

Attempts to calculate the constants a and a' by tracing collision histories to find the "persistence of velocities" have not met with much success. The molecular "memory" fades slowly, too many previous collisions have to be traced, and the calculations become almost hopelessly complicated. A different theoretical approach is needed, which was supplied about 1916–17 independently by David Enskog and Sydney Chapman. Their theory also shows that the same value of l applies to both η and λ, a fact that is not obvious in the simple theory described here.

The thermal conductivity of polyatomic molecules is accounted for by simply adding on a contribution for the energy carried by the internal molecular motions:

$$\lambda = a'\left(\frac{N}{V}\right)\overline{v}\,l\left(\frac{3}{2}k\right) + a''\left(\frac{N}{V}\right)\overline{v}\,l\,c_{int}, \qquad (26)$$

where c_{int} is the contribution of the internal motions to the heat capacity (per molecule) and is easily found by subtracting $(3k/2)$ from the total measured heat capacity. As might be expected, the constant a'' is only about half as large as a'.

The pressure or density dependence of λ must be similar to that of η—an initial linear increase in the free-molecule region, followed by a constant value in the dilute-gas region and finally an increase in the dense-fluid region.

DIFFUSION AND THERMAL DIFFUSION

Both of these properties present difficulties for the simple mean free path version of kinetic theory. In the case of diffusion it must be argued that collisions of the molecules of species 1 with other species 1 molecules do not inhibit the interdiffusion of species 1 and 2, and similarly for 2–2 collisions. If this is not assumed, the calculated value of the diffusion coefficient for the 1–2 gas pair, D_{12}, depends strongly on the mixture composition instead of being virtually independent of it, as is shown by experiment. The neglect of 1–1 and 2–2 collisions can be rationalized by noting that the flow of momentum is not disturbed by such like-molecule collisions owing to the conservation of momentum, but it can be contended that the argument was simply invented to make the theory agree with experiment. A more charitable view is that the experimental results demonstrate that collisions between like molecules have little affect on D_{12}. It is one of the triumphs of the accurate kinetic theory of Enskog and Chapman that this result clearly emerges.

If 1–1 and 2–2 collisions are ignored, a simple calculation gives a result much like those for η and λ:

$$D_{12} = a_{12} \overline{v_{12}}\, l_{12}, \qquad (27)$$

where a_{12} is a numerical constant, v_{12} is an average relative speed for 1–2 collisions given by $v_{12}^2 = (1/2)(v_1^2 + v_2^2)$, and l_{12} is a mean free path for 1–2 collisions that is inversely proportional to the total molecular number density, $(N_1 + N_2)/V$. Thus, D_{12} is inversely proportional to gas density or pressure, unlike η and λ, but the concentration difference is proportional to pressure, with the two effects canceling one another, as pointed out previously. The actual transport of molecules is therefore independent of pressure. The numerical value of a_{12}, as obtained by refined calculations, is close to 3/5.

The pressure dependence of pD_{12} should be qualitatively similar to that of η and λ—an initial linear increase in the free-molecule region, a constant value in the dilute-gas region, and finally an increase in the dense-fluid region.

Thermal diffusion presents special difficulties for kinetic theory. The transport coefficients η, λ, and D_{12} are always positive regardless of the nature of the intermolecular forces that produce the collisions—the mere existence of collisions suffices to account for their important features. The transport coefficient that describes thermal diffusion, however, depends critically on the nature of the intermolecular forces and the collisions and can be positive, negative, or zero. Its dependence on composition is also rather complicated. There have been a number of attempts to explain thermal diffusion with a simple mean free path model, but none has been satisfactory. No simple physical explanation of thermal diffusion has been devised, and recourse to the accurate, but complicated, kinetic theory is necessary.

BOLTZMANN EQUATION

The simple mean free path description of gas transport coefficients accounts for the major observed phenomena, but it is quantitatively unsatisfactory with respect to two major points: the values of numerical constants such as a, a', a'', and a_{12}, and the description of the molecular collisions that define a mean free path. Indeed, collisions remain a somewhat vague concept except when they are considered to take place between molecules modeled as hard spheres. Improvement has required a different, somewhat indirect, and more mathematical approach through a quantity called the velocity distribution function. This function describes how molecular velocities are distributed on the average: a few very slow molecules, a few very fast ones, and most near some average value — namely, $v_{rms} = (v^2)^{1/2} = (3kT/2)^{1/2}$. If this function is known, all gas properties can be calculated by using it to obtain various averages. For example, the average momentum carried in a certain direction would give the viscosity.

The velocity distribution for a gas at equilibrium was suggested by Maxwell in 1859 and is represented by the familiar bell-shaped curve that describes the normal, or Gaussian, distribution of random variables in large populations. Attempts to support more definitively this result and to extend it to nonequilibrium gases led to the formulation of the Boltzmann equation, which describes how collisions and external forces cause the velocity distribution to change. This equation is difficult to solve in any general sense, but some progress can be made by assuming that the deviations from the equilibrium distribution are small and are proportional to the external influences that cause the deviations, such as temperature, pressure, and composition differences.

Even the resulting simpler equations remained unsolved for nearly 50 years until the work of Enskog and Chapman, with a single notable exception. The one case that was solvable dealt with molecules that interact with forces that fall off as the fifth power of their separation (i.e., as $1/r^5$), for which Maxwell found an exact solution. Unfortunately, thermal diffusion happens to be exactly zero for molecules subject to this force law, so that phenomenon was missed.

It was later discovered that it is possible to use the solutions for the $1/r^5$ Maxwell model as a starting point and then calculate successive corrections for more general interactions. Although the calculations quickly increase in complexity, the improvement in accuracy is rapid, unlike the persistence-of-velocities corrections applied in mean free path theory. This refined version of kinetic theory is now highly developed, but it is quite mathematical and is not described here.

DEVIATIONS FROM THE IDEAL MODEL

Deviations from ideal gas behaviour occur both at low densities, where molecule-surface collisions become important, and at high densities, where a description in terms of only two-body collisions becomes inadequate. The low-density case can be handled in principle by including both molecule-surface and molecule-molecule collisions in the Boltzmann equation. Since this branch of the subject is now quite advanced and mathematical in character, only the high-density case will be discussed here.

EQUATION OF STATE

To a first approximation, molecule-molecule collisions do not affect the ideal gas equation of state, $pv = RT$, but real gases at nonzero densities show deviations from this equation that are due to interactions among the molecules. Ever since the great advance made by van der Waals in 1873, an accurate universal formula relating p, v, and T has been sought. No completely satisfactory equation of state has been found, though important advances occurred in the 1970s and '80s. The only rigorous theoretical result available is an infinite-series expansion in powers of $1/v$, known as the virial equation of state:

$$\frac{pv}{RT} = 1 + \frac{B(T)}{v} + \frac{C(T)}{v^2} + \cdots, \qquad (28)$$

where $B(T)$, $C(T)$, ... are called the second, third, ... virial coefficients and depend only on the temperature and the particular gas. The virtue of this equation is that there is a rigorous connection between the virial coefficients and intermolecular forces, and experimental values of $B(T)$ were an early source (and still a useful one) of quantitative information on intermolecular forces. The drawback of the virial equation of state is that it is an infinite series and becomes essentially useless at high densities, which in practice are those greater than about the critical density. Also, the equation is wanting in that it does not predict condensation.

The most practical approaches to the equation of state for real fluids remain the versions of the principle of corresponding states first proposed by van der Waals.

TRANSPORT PROPERTIES

Despite many attempts, there is still no satisfactory theory of the transport properties of dense fluids. Even the extension of the Boltzmann equation to include collisions of more than two bodies is not entirely clear. An important advance was made in 1921 by Enskog, but it is restricted to hard spheres and has not been extended to real molecules except in an empirical way to fit experimental measurements.

Attempts to develop a virial type of expansion in $1/v$ for the transport coefficients have failed in a surprising way. A formal theory was formulated, but, when the virial coefficients were evaluated for the tractable case of hard spheres, an infinite result was obtained for the coefficient of the $1/v^2$ term. This is a signal that a virial expansion is not accurate in a mathematical sense, and subsequent research showed that the error arose from a neglected term of the form $(1/v^2)\ln(1/v)$. It remains unknown how many similar problematic mathematical terms exist in the theory. Transport coefficients of dense fluids are usually described by some empirical extension of the Enskog hard-sphere theory or more commonly by some version of a principle of corresponding states. Much work clearly remains to be done.

CHAPTER 4
PROPERTIES OF LIQUIDS

The most obvious physical properties of a liquid are its retention of volume and its conformation to the shape of its container. When a liquid substance is poured into a vessel, it takes the shape of the vessel, and, as long as the substance stays in the liquid state, it will remain inside the vessel. Furthermore, when a liquid is poured from one vessel to another, it retains its volume (as long as there is no vaporization or change in temperature) but not its shape. These properties serve as convenient criteria for distinguishing the liquid state from the solid and gaseous states. Gases, for example, expand to fill their container so that the volume they occupy is the same as that of the container. Solids retain both their shape and volume when moved from one container to another.

On Earth, water is the most abundant liquid, although much of the water with which organisms come into contact is not in pure form but is a mixture in which various substances are dissolved. Such mixtures include those fluids essential to life—blood, for example—beverages, and seawater. Seawater is a liquid mixture in which a variety of salts have been dissolved in water. Even though in pure form these salts are solids, in oceans they are part of the liquid phase. Thus, liquid mixtures contain substances that in their pure form may themselves be liquids, solids, or even gases.

The liquid state sometimes is described simply as the state that occurs between the solid and gaseous states, and for simple molecules this distinction is unambiguous. However, clear distinction between the liquid, gaseous, and solid states holds only for those substances whose molecules are composed of a small number of atoms. When the number exceeds about 20, the liquid may often be cooled below the true melting point to form a glass, which has many of the mechanical properties of a solid but lacks crystalline order. If the number of atoms in the molecule exceeds about 100–200, the classification into solid, liquid, and gas ceases to be useful. At low temperatures such substances are usually glasses or amorphous solids, and their rigidity falls with increasing temperature — i.e., they do not have fixed melting points; some may, however, form true liquids. With these large molecules, the gaseous state is not attainable, because they decompose chemically before the temperature is high enough for the liquid to evaporate. Synthetic and natural high polymers (e.g., nylon and rubber) behave in this way.

If the molecules are large, rigid, and either roughly planar or linear, as in cholesteryl acetate or p-azoxyanisole, the solid may melt to an anisotropic liquid (i.e., one that is not uniform in all directions) in which the molecules are free to move about but have great difficulty in rotating. Such a state is called a liquid crystal, and the anisotropy produces changes of the refractive index (a measure of the change in direction of light when it passes from one medium into another) with the direction of the incident light and hence leads to unusual optical effects. Liquid crystals have found widespread applications in temperature-sensing devices and in displays for watches and calculators. However, no inorganic compounds and only about 5 percent of the known organic compounds form liquid crystals. The theory of normal liquids is, therefore, predominantly the theory of the behaviour of substances consisting of simple molecules.

A liquid lacks both the strong spatial order of a solid, though it has the high density of solids, and the absence of order of a gas that results from the low density of gases—i.e., gas molecules are relatively free of each other's influence. The combination of high density and of partial order in liquids has led to difficulties in developing quantitatively acceptable theories of liquids. Understanding of the liquid state, as of all states of matter, came with the kinetic molecular theory, which stated that matter consisted of particles in constant motion and that this motion was the manifestation of thermal energy. The greater the thermal energy of the particle, the faster it moved.

TRANSITIONS BETWEEN STATES OF MATTER

In very general terms, the particles that constitute matter include molecules, atoms, ions, and electrons. In a gas these particles are far enough from one another and are moving fast enough to escape each other's influence, which may be of various kinds—such as attraction or repulsion due to electrical charges and specific forces of attraction that involve the electrons orbiting around atomic nuclei. The motion of particles is in a straight line, and the collisions that result occur with no loss of energy, although an exchange of energies may result between colliding particles. When a gas is cooled, its particles move more slowly, and those slow enough to linger in each other's vicinity will coalesce, because a force of attraction will overcome their lowered kinetic energy and, by definition, thermal energy.

Each particle, when it joins others in the liquid state, gives up a measure of heat called the latent heat of liquefaction, but each continues to move at the same speed within the liquid as long as the temperature remains at the condensation point. The distances that the particles can travel in a liquid without colliding are on the order of molecular diameters. As the liquid is cooled, the particles move more slowly still, until at the freezing temperature the attractive energy produces so high a density that the liquid freezes into the solid state. They continue to vibrate, however, at the same speed as long as the temperature remains at the freezing point, and their latent heat of fusion is released in the freezing process.

Heating a solid provides the particles with the heat of fusion necessary to allow them to escape one another's influence enough to move about in the liquid state. Further heating provides the liquid particles with their heat of evaporation, which enables them to escape one another completely and enter the vapour, or gaseous, state.

This starkly simplified view of the states of matter ignores many complicating factors, the most important being the fact that no two particles need be moving at the same speed in a gas, liquid, or solid and the related fact that even in a solid some particles may have acquired the energy necessary to exist as gas particles, while even in a gas some particles may be practically motionless for a brief time. It is the average kinetic energy of the particles that must be considered, together with the fact that the motion is random. At the interface between liquid and gas and between liquid and solid, an exchange of particles is always taking place; slow gas molecules condensing at the liquid surface and fast liquid molecules escaping into the gas. An equilibrium state is reached in any closed system, so that the number of exchanges in either direction is the same. Because the kinetic energy of particles in the liquid state can be defined only in statistical terms (i.e., every possible value can be found), discussion of the liquid (as well as the gaseous) state at the molecular level involves formulations in terms of probability functions.

BEHAVIOUR OF PURE LIQUIDS

Liquids may be divided into two general categories: pure liquids and liquid mixtures. Liquid mixtures can contain substances in the gas and solid phase and thus have somewhat different behaviour than the pure liquids discussed below.

PHASE DIAGRAM OF A PURE SUBSTANCE

When the temperature and pressure of a pure substance are fixed, the equilibrium state of the substance is also fixed. Consider the phase diagram for pure argon. In this diagram a single phase is shown as an area, two as a line, and three as the intersection of the lines at the triple point, T. Along a line TC, called the vapour-pressure curve, liquid and vapour exist in equilibrium. The liquid region exists to the left and above this line while the gas, or vapour, region exists below it. At the upper extreme, this curve ends at the critical point, C. If line TC is crossed by moving directly from point P to S, there is a distinct phase change accompanied by abrupt changes in the physical properties of the substance (e.g., density, heat capacity, viscosity, and dielectric constant) because the vapour and liquid phases have distinctly different properties. At the critical point, however, the vapour and liquid phases become identical, and above the critical point, the two phases are no longer distinct. Thus, if the substance moves from point P to S by the path $PQRS$ so that no phase-change lines are crossed, the change in properties will be smooth and continuous, and the specific moment when the substance converts from a liquid to a gas is not clearly defined.

In fact, the path $PQRS$ demonstrates the essential continuity of state between liquid and gas, which differ

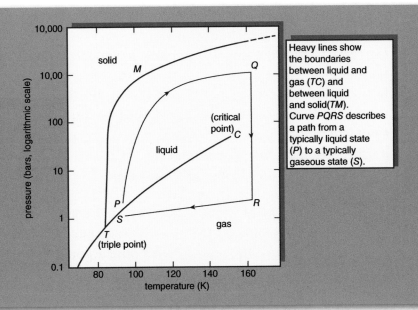

Phase diagram of argon. Copyright Encyclopædia Britannica; rendering for this edition by Rosen Educational Services

in degree but which together constitute the single fluid state. Strictly speaking, the term *liquid* should be applied only to the denser of the two phases on the line *TC*, but it is generally extended to any dense fluid state at low temperatures—i.e., to the area lying within the angle *CTM*.

The extension of line *TC* below the triple point is called the sublimation curve. It represents the equilibrium between solid and gas, and when the sublimation curve is crossed, the substance changes directly from solid to gas. This conversion occurs when dry ice (solid carbon dioxide) vaporizes at atmospheric pressure to form gaseous carbon dioxide because the triple-point pressure for carbon dioxide is greater than atmospheric pressure. Line *TM* is the melting curve and represents an equilibrium between solid and liquid. When this curve is crossed from left to right, solid changes to liquid with the associated abrupt change in properties.

The melting curve is initially much steeper than the vapour-pressure curve; hence, as the pressure is changed, the temperature does not change much, and the melting temperature is little affected by pressure. No substance has been found to have a critical point on this line, and there are theoretical reasons for supposing that it continues indefinitely to high temperatures and pressures, until the substance is so compressed that the molecules break up into atoms, ions, and electrons. At pressures above 10^6 bars (one bar is equal to 0.987 atmosphere, where one atmosphere is the pressure exerted by the air at sea level), it is believed that most substances pass into a metallic state.

It is possible to cool a gas at constant pressure to a temperature lower than that of the vapour-pressure line without producing immediate condensation, since the liquid phase forms readily only in the presence of suitable nuclei (e.g., dust particles or ions) about which the drops can grow. Unless the gas is scrupulously cleaned, such nuclei remain; a subcooled vapour is unstable and will ultimately condense. It is similarly possible to superheat a liquid to a temperature where, though still a liquid, the gas is the stable phase. Again, this occurs most readily with clean liquids heated in smooth vessels, because bubble formation occurs around foreign particles or sharp points. When the superheated liquid changes to gas, it does so with almost explosive violence. A liquid also may be subcooled to below its freezing temperature.

Representative Values of Phase-Diagram Parameters

To a certain extent the behaviour of all substances is similar in that the parameters that vary from substance to substance are the particular values of the triple-point and critical-point temperature and pressure, the size of the various regions, and the slopes of the lines. Triple-point temperatures range from 14 K (-259 °C [-434 °F]) for hydrogen to temperatures too high for accurate measurement. Triple-point pressures are generally low, that of carbon dioxide at 5.2 bars being one of the highest. Most are around 10^{-3} bar, and those of some hydrocarbons are as low as 10^{-7} bar. The normal melting point of a substance is defined as the melting temperature at a pressure of one atmosphere (equivalent to 1.01325 bars); it differs little from the triple-point temperature, because of the steepness of melting lines. Critical temperatures (the maximum temperature at which a gas can be liquefied by pressure) range from 5.2 K (-268 °C [-450.3 °F]), for helium, to temperatures too high to measure. Critical pressures (the vapour pressure at the critical temperature) are generally about 40–100 bars. The normal boiling point is the temperature at which the vapour pressure reaches one atmosphere. The normal liquid range is defined as the temperature interval between the normal melting point and the normal boiling point, but such a restriction is artificial, the true liquid range being from triple point to critical point. Substances whose triple-point pressures are above atmospheric (e.g., carbon dioxide) have no normal liquid range but sublime at atmospheric pressure.

Each of the three two-phase lines in a phase diagram canbe described by the Clapeyron equation:

$$\frac{dp}{dT} = \frac{\Delta H}{T \Delta V}. \tag{1}$$

In this equation, dp/dT is the slope of the curve under consideration—i.e., either the melting, sublimation, or vapour-pressure curve. ΔH is the latent heat required for the phase change, and ΔV is the change in volume associated with the phase change. Thus, for the sublimation and vapour-pressure curves, since ΔH and ΔV are both positive (i.e., heat is required for vaporization, and the volume increases on vaporization), the slope is always positive. The slope of the sublimation curve immediately below the triple point is greater than the slope of the vapour-pressure curve immediately above it, so that the vapour-pressure curve is not continuous through the triple point. This is consistent with equation (1) because the heat of sublimation for a substance is somewhat larger than its heat of vaporization.

The slope of the melting line is usually positive, but there are a few substances, such as water and bismuth, for which the melting-line slope is negative. The negative melting-line slope is consistent with equation (1) because, for these two substances, the density of the solid is less than the density of the liquid. This is the reason ice floats. For water, this negative volume change (i.e., shrinking) persists to 2.1 kilobars and -22 °C (-8 °F), at which point the normal form of ice changes to a denser form, and thereafter the change in volume on melting is positive.

BEHAVIOUR OF SUBSTANCES NEAR CRITICAL AND TRIPLE POINTS

At the critical point the liquid is identical to the vapour phase, and near the critical point the liquid behaviour is somewhat similar to vapour-phase behaviour. While the particular values of the critical temperature and pressure vary from substance to substance, the nature of the behaviour in the vicinity of the critical point is similar for all compounds. This fact has led to a method that is commonly referred to as the law of corresponding states. Roughly speaking, this approach presumes that, if the phase diagram is plotted using reduced variables, the behaviour of all substances will be more or less the same. Reduced variables are defined by dividing the actual variable by its associated critical constant; the reduced temperature, T_r, equals T/T_c, and the reduced pressure, p_r, equals p/p_c. Then, for all substances, the critical point occurs at a value of T_r and p_r equal to unity.

This approach has been used successfully to develop equations to correlate and predict a number of liquid-phase properties including vapour pressures, saturated and compressed liquid densities, heat capacities, and latent heats of vaporization. The corresponding states approach works remarkably well at temperatures between the normal boiling point and the critical point for many compounds but tends to break down near and below the triple-point temperature. At these temperatures the liquid is influenced more by the behaviour of the solid, which has not been successfully correlated by corresponding states methods.

Many of the properties of a liquid near its triple point are closer to those of the solid than to those of the gas. It has a high density (typically 0.5–1.5 grams per cubic cm [0.02–0.05 pound per cubic inch]), a high refractive index (which varies from 1.3 to 1.8 for liquids), a high heat capacity at constant pressure (2–4 joules per gram per kelvin, 1 joule being equal to 0.239 calorie), and a low compressibility (0.5–1 × 10⁻⁴ per bar). The compressibility falls to values characteristic of a solid (0.1 × 10⁻⁴ per bar or less) as the pressure increases. A simple and widely used equation describes the change of specific volume with pressure. If $V(p)$ is the volume at pressure p, $V(o)$ is volume at zero pressure, and A and B are positive parameters (constants whose values may be arbitrarily assigned), then the difference in volume resulting from a change in pressure equals the product of A, the pressure, and the volume at zero pressure, divided by the sum of B and the pressure. This is written:

$$V(0) - V(p) = \frac{A p V(0)}{(B + p)}. \qquad (2)$$

The pressure parameter B is close to the pressure at which the compressibility has fallen to half its initial value and is generally about 500 bars for liquids near their triple points. It falls rapidly with increasing temperature.

As a liquid is heated along its vapour-pressure curve, TC, its density falls and its compressibility rises. Conversely, the density of the saturated vapour in equilibrium with the liquid rises; i.e., the number of gas molecules in a fixed space above the liquid increases. Liquid and gas states approach each other with increasing rapidity as the temperature approaches C, until at this point they become identical and have a density about one-third that of the liquid at point T. The change of saturated-gas density (ρ_g) and liquid density (ρ_l) with temperature T can be expressed by a simple equation when the temperature is close to critical. If ρ_c is the density at the critical temperature T_c, then the difference between densities equals the difference between temperatures raised to a factor called beta, β:

$$(\rho_l - \rho_c) = (\rho_c - \rho_g) = (T_c - T)^{\beta}, \qquad (3)$$

where β is about 0.34. The compressibility and the heat capacity of the gas at constant pressure (C_p) become infinite as T approaches T_c from above along the path of constant density. The infinite compressibility implies that the pressure no longer restrains local fluctuations of density. The fluctuations grow to such an extent that their size is comparable with the wavelength of light, which is therefore strongly scattered. Hence, at the critical point, a normally transparent liquid is almost opaque and usually dark brown in colour. The classical description of the critical point and the results of modern measurement do not agree in detail, but recent considerations of thermodynamic stability show that there are certain regularities in behaviour that are common to all substances.

SURFACE TENSION

Between a liquid and its corresponding vapour there is a dividing surface that has a measurable tension; work must be done to increase the area of the surface at constant temperature. Hence, in the absence of gravity or during free fall, the equilibrium shape of a volume of liquid is one that has a minimum area—i.e., a sphere. In Earth's field this shape is found only for small drops, for which the gravitational forces, since they are proportional to the volume, are negligible compared with surface forces, which are proportional to the area. The surface tension falls with rising temperature and vanishes at the critical point. There is a similar dividing surface between two immiscible liquids, but this usually has lower tension. It is believed that there is a tension also between a liquid and a solid, though it is not directly measurable because of the rigidity of the solid; it may be inferred, however, under certain assumptions, from the angle of contact between the liquid and the solid (i.e., the angle at which the liquid's surface meets the solid). If this angle is zero, the liquid surface is parallel to the solid surface and is said to wet the solid completely.

MOLECULAR STRUCTURE OF LIQUIDS

For a complete understanding of the liquid state of matter, an understanding of behaviour on the molecular level is necessary. Such behaviour is characterized by two quantities called the intermolecular pair potential function, u, and the radial distribution function, g. The pair potential gives information about the energy due to the interaction of a pair of molecules and is a function of the distance r between their centres. Information about the structure or the distances between pairs of molecules is contained in the radial distribution function. If g and u are known for a substance, macroscopic properties can be calculated.

In an ideal gas—where there are no forces between molecules, and the volume of the molecules is negligible—g is unity, which means that the chance of encountering a second molecule when moving away from a central molecule is independent of position. In a solid, g takes on discrete values at distances that correspond to the locations associated with the solid's crystal structure. Liquids

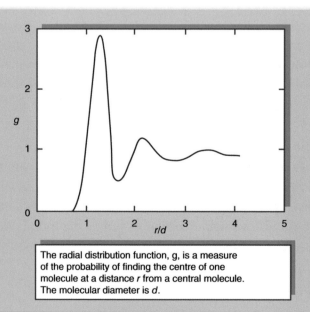

The radial distribution function, g, is a measure of the probability of finding the centre of one molecule at a distance r from a central molecule. The molecular diameter is d.

Radial distribution function for a dense liquid. Copyright Encyclopædia Britannica; rendering for this edition by Rosen Educational Services

possess neither the completely ordered structure of a solid crystal nor the complete randomness of an ideal gas. The structure in a liquid is intermediate to these two extremes—i.e., the molecules in a liquid are free to move about, but there is some order because they remain relatively close to one another.

Although there are an infinite number of possible positions one molecule may assume with respect to another, some are more likely than others. In the radial distribution function for the dense packing typical of liquids, g is a measure of the probability of finding the centre of one molecule at a distance r from the centre of a second molecule. For values of r less than those of the molecular diameter, d, g goes to zero. This is consistent with the fact that two molecules cannot occupy the same space. The most likely location for a second molecule with respect to a central molecule is slightly more than one molecular diameter away, which reflects the fact that in liquids the molecules are packed almost against one another. The second most likely location is a little more than two molecular diameters away, but beyond the third layer preferred locations damp out, and the chance of finding the centre of a molecule becomes independent of position.

The pair potential function, u, is a large positive number for r less than d, assumes a minimum value at the most preferred location, and damps out to zero as r approaches infinity. The large positive value of u corresponds to a strong repulsion, while the minimum corresponds to the net result of repulsive and attractive forces.

There are two methods of measuring the radial distribution function g: first, by X-ray or neutron diffraction from simple fluids and, second, by computer simulation of the molecular structure and motions in a liquid. In the first, the liquid is exposed to a specific, single wavelength (monochromatic) radiation, and the observed results are then subjected to a mathematical treatment known as a Fourier transform.

The second method of obtaining the radial distribution function g supposes that the energy of interaction, u, for the liquid under study is known. A computer model of a liquid is set up in which thousands of molecules are contained within a cube. There are now two methods of proceeding, by Monte Carlo calculation or by what is called molecular dynamics; only the latter is discussed here.

Each molecule is assigned a random position and velocity, and Newton's equations of motion are solved to calculate the path of each molecule in the changing field of all the others. A molecule that leaves the cell is deemed to be replaced by a new one with equal velocity entering through the corresponding point on the opposite wall. After a few collisions per molecule, the distribution of velocities conforms with equations worked out by the Scottish physicist James Clerk Maxwell, and after a longer time the mean positions are those appropriate to the density and mean kinetic energy (i.e., temperature) of the liquid. Functions such as the radial distribution function g can now be evaluated by taking suitable averages as the system evolves in time. Since 1958 such computer experiments have added more to the knowledge of the molecular structure of simple liquids than all the theoretical work of the previous century and continue to be an active area of research for not only pure liquids but liquid mixtures as well.

SPEED OF SOUND AND ELECTRIC PROPERTIES

A sound wave is a series of longitudinal compressions and expansions that travels through a liquid at a speed of about 1 km (0.62 mile) per second, or about three times the speed of sound in air. If the frequency is not too high, the compressions and expansions are adiabatic (i.e., the changes take place without transfer of heat) and reversible. Conduction of energy from the hot (compressed) to the cold (expanded) regions of the liquid introduces irreversible effects, which are dissipative, and thus such conduction leads to the absorption of the sound. A longitudinal compression (in the direction of the wave) is a combination of a uniform compression and a shearing stress (a force that causes one plane of a substance to glide past an adjacent plane). Hence, both bulk and shear viscosity also govern the propagation of sound in a liquid.

If a liquid is placed in a static electric field, the field exerts a force on any free carriers of electric charge in the liquid, and the liquid, therefore, conducts electricity. Such carriers are of two kinds: mobile electrons and ions. The former are present in abundance in liquid metals, which have conductivities that are generally about one-third of the conductivity of the corresponding solid. The decrease in conductivity upon melting arises from the greater disorder of the positive ions in the liquid and hence their greater ability to scatter electrons. The contribution of the ions is small, less than 5 percent in most liquid metals, but it is the sole cause of conductivity in molten salts and in their aqueous solutions. Such conductivities vary widely but are much lower than those of liquid metals.

Nonionic liquids (those composed of molecules that do not dissociate into ions) have negligible conductivities, but they are polarized by an electric field; that is, the liquid develops positive and negative poles and also a dipole moment (which is the product of the pole strength and the distance between the poles) that is oriented against the field, from which the liquid acquires energy. This polarization is of three kinds: electron, atomic, and orientation.

In electron polarization the electrons in each atom are displaced from their usual positions, giving each molecule a small dipole moment. The contribution of electron polarization to the dielectric constant of the liquid is numerically equal to the square root of its refractive index.

The second effect, atomic polarization, arises because there is a relative change in the mean positions of the atomic nuclei within the molecules. This generally small effect is observed at radio frequencies but not at optical, and so it is missing from the refractive index.

The third effect, orientation polarization, occurs with molecules that have permanent dipole moments. These molecules are partially aligned by the field and contribute heavily to the polarization. Thus, the dielectric constant of a nonpolar liquid, such as a hydrocarbon, is about 2, that of a weakly polar liquid, such as chloroform or ethyl ether, about 5, while those of highly polar liquids, such as ethanol and water, range from 25 to 80.

CHAPTER 5
LIQUID SOLUTIONS
AND SOLUBILITY

The ability of liquids to dissolve solids, other liquids, or gases has long been recognized as one of the fundamental phenomena of nature encountered in daily life. The practical importance of solutions and the need to understand their properties have challenged numerous writers since the Ionian philosophers and Aristotle. Many physicists and chemists have devoted themselves to a study of solutions.

A solution is a mixture of two or more chemically distinct substances that is said to be homogeneous on the molecular scale—the composition at any one point in the mixture is the same as that at any other point. This is in contrast to a suspension (or slurry), in which small discontinuous particles are surrounded by a continuous fluid. Although the word *solution* is commonly applied to the liquid state of matter, solutions of solids and gases are also possible. Brass, for example, is a solution of copper and zinc, and air is a solution primarily of oxygen and nitrogen with a few other gases present in relatively small amounts.

The ability of one substance to dissolve another depends always on the chemical nature of the substances, frequently on the temperature, and occasionally on the pressure. Water, for example, readily dissolves methyl alcohol but does not dissolve mercury; it barely dissolves benzene at room temperature but does so increasingly as the temperature rises. While the solubility in water of the gases present in air is extremely small at atmospheric pressure, it becomes appreciable at high pressures where, in many cases, the solubility of a gas is (approximately)

73

proportional to its pressure. Thus, a diver breathes air (four-fifths nitrogen) at a pressure corresponding to the pressure around him, and, as he goes deeper, more air dissolves in his blood. If he ascends rapidly, the solubility of the gases decreases so that they leave his blood suddenly, forming bubbles in the blood vessels. This condition (known as the bends) is extremely painful and may cause death; it can be alleviated by breathing, instead of air, a mixture of helium and oxygen because the solubility of helium in blood is much lower than that of nitrogen.

The solubility of one fluid in another may be complete or partial. Thus, at room temperature water and methyl alcohol mix in all proportions, but 100 grams (3.5 ounces) of water dissolve only 0.07 gram (0.002 ounce) of benzene. Though it is generally supposed that all gases are completely miscible—i.e., mutually soluble in all proportions—this is true only at normal pressures. At high pressures pairs of chemically unlike gases may exhibit only limited miscibility. For example, at 20 °C (68 °F) helium and xenon are completely miscible at pressures below 200 atmospheres but become increasingly immiscible as the pressure rises.

The ability of a liquid to dissolve selectively forms the basis of common separation operations in chemical and related industries. A mixture of two gases, carbon dioxide and nitrogen, can be separated by bringing it into contact with ethanolamine, a liquid solvent that readily dissolves carbon dioxide but barely dissolves nitrogen. In this process, called absorption, the dissolved carbon dioxide is later recovered, and the solvent is made usable again by heating the carbon dioxide-rich solvent, since the solubility of a gas in a liquid usually (but not always) decreases with rising temperature. A similar absorption operation can remove a pollutant such as sulfur dioxide from smokestack gases in a plant using sulfur-containing coal or petroleum as fuel.

The process wherein a dissolved substance is transferred from one liquid to another is called extraction. As an example, phenolic pollutants (organic compounds of the types known as phenol, cresol, and resorcinol) are frequently found in industrial aqueous waste streams, and, since these phenolics are damaging to marine life, it is important to remove them before sending the waste stream back to a lake or river. One such removal technique is to bring the waste stream into contact with a water-insoluble solvent (e.g., an organic liquid such as a high-boiling hydrocarbon) that has a strong affinity for the phenolic pollutant. The solubility of the phenolic in the solvent divided by that in water is called the distribution coefficient, and it is clear that for an efficient extraction process it is desirable to have as large a distribution coefficient as possible.

CLASSES OF SOLUTIONS

Broadly speaking, liquid mixtures can be classified as either solutions of electrolytes or solutions of nonelectrolytes. They can also be divided into endothermic and exothermic solutions based on their chemical reactions.

ELECTROLYTES AND NONELECTROLYTES

Electrolytes are substances that can dissociate into electrically charged particles called ions, while nonelectrolytes consist of molecules that bear no net electric charge. Thus, when ordinary salt (sodium chloride, formula $NaCl$) is dissolved in water, it forms an electrolytic solution, dissociating into positive sodium ions (Na^+) and negative chloride ions (Cl^-), whereas sugar dissolved in water maintains its molecular integrity and does not dissociate. Because of its omnipresence, water is the most common solvent for electrolytes; the ocean is a solution of electrolytes. Electrolyte solutions, however, are also formed by other solvents (such as ammonia and sulfur dioxide) that have a large dielectric constant (a measure of the ability of a fluid to decrease the forces of attraction and repulsion between charged particles). The energy required to separate an ion pair (i.e., one ion of positive charge and one ion of negative charge) varies inversely with the dielectric constant, and, therefore, appreciable dissociation into separate ions occurs only in solvents with large dielectric constants.

Most electrolytes (for example, salts) are nonvolatile, which means that they have essentially no tendency to enter the vapour phase. There are, however, some notable exceptions, such as hydrogen chloride (HCl), which is readily soluble in water, where it forms hydrogen ions (H^+) and chloride ions (Cl^-). At normal temperature and pressure, pure hydrogen chloride is a gas, and, in the absence of water or some other ionizing solvent, hydrogen chloride exists in molecular, rather than ionic, form.

Solutions of electrolytes readily conduct electricity, whereas nonelectrolyte solutions do not. A dilute solution of hydrogen chloride in water is a good electrical conductor, but a dilute solution of hydrogen chloride in a hydrocarbon is a good insulator. Because of the large difference in dielectric constants, hydrogen chloride is ionized in water but not in hydrocarbons.

WEAK ELECTROLYTES

While classification under the heading electrolyte-solution or nonelectrolyte-solution is often useful, some solutions have properties near the boundary between these two broad classes. Although such substances as ordinary salt and hydrogen chloride are strong electrolytes—i.e., they dissociate completely in an ionizing solvent—there are many substances, called weak electrolytes, that dissociate to only a small extent in ionizing solvents. For example, in aqueous solution, acetic acid can dissociate into a positive hydrogen ion and a negative acetate ion (CH_3COO^-), but it does so to a limited extent; in an aqueous solution containing 50 grams (1.8 ounces) acetic acid and 1,000 grams (2.2 pounds) water, less than 1 percent of the acetic acid molecules are dissociated into ions. Therefore, a solution of acetic acid in water exhibits some properties associated with electrolyte solutions (e.g., it is a fair conductor of electricity), but in general terms it is more properly classified as a nonelectrolyte solution. By similar reasoning, an aqueous solution of carbon dioxide is also considered a nonelectrolyte solution even though carbon dioxide and water have a slight tendency to form carbonic acid, which, in turn, dissociates to a small extent to hydrogen ions and bicarbonate ions (HCO_3^-).

ENDOTHERMIC AND EXOTHERMIC SOLUTIONS

When two substances mix to form a solution, heat is either evolved (an exothermic process) or absorbed (an endothermic process); only in the special case of an ideal solution do substances mix without any heat effect. Most simple molecules mix with a small endothermic heat of solution, while exothermic heats of solution are observed when the components interact strongly with one another. An extreme example of an exothermic heat of mixing is provided by adding an aqueous solution of sodium hydroxide, a powerful base, to an aqueous solution of hydrogen chloride, a powerful acid; the hydroxide ions (OH^-) of the base combine with the hydrogen ions of the acid to form water, a highly exothermic reaction that yields 75,300 calories per 100 grams (3.5 ounces) of water formed. In nonelectrolyte solutions, heat effects are usually endothermic and much smaller, often about 100 calories, when roughly equal parts are mixed to form 100 grams of mixture.

Formation of a solution usually is accompanied by a small change in volume. If equal parts of benzene and stannic chloride are mixed, the temperature drops; if the mixture is then heated slightly to bring its temperature back to that of the unmixed liquids, the volume increases by about 2 percent. On the other hand, mixing roughly equal parts of acetone and chloroform produces a small decrease in volume, about 0.2 percent. It frequently happens that mixtures with endothermic heats of mixing expand—i.e., show small increases in volume—while mixtures with exothermic heats of mixing tend to contract.

A large decrease in volume occurs when a gas is dissolved in a liquid. For example, at 0 °C (32 °F) and atmospheric pressure, the volume of 28 grams (1 ounce) of nitrogen gas is 22,400 cubic cm (0.79 cubic feet). When these 28 grams of nitrogen are dissolved in an excess of water, the volume of the water increases only 40 cubic cm (2.4 cubic inches); the decrease in volume accompanying the dissolution of 28 grams of nitrogen in water is therefore 22,360 cubic cm. In this case, it is said that the nitrogen gas has been condensed into a liquid, the word condense meaning "to make dense"—i.e., to decrease the volume.

PROPERTIES OF SOLUTIONS

The properties of liquid solutions have been the subject of thorough study. For instance, the composition of a solution and the proportions of the dissolved and dissolving substances play key roles in a mixture's properties.

COMPOSITION RATIOS

The composition of a liquid solution means the composition of that solution in the bulk—that is, of that part that is not near the surface. The interface between the liquid solution and some other phase (for example, a gas such as air) has a composition that differs, sometimes very much, from that of the bulk. The environment at an interface is significantly different from that throughout the bulk of the liquid, and in a solution the molecules of a particular component may prefer one environment over the other. If the molecules of one component in the solution prefer to be at the interface as opposed to the bulk, it is said that this component is positively adsorbed at the interface.

In aqueous solutions of organic liquids, the organic component is usually positively adsorbed at the solution-air interface; as a result, it is often possible to separate a mixture of an organic solute from water by a process called froth separation. Air is bubbled vigorously into the solution, and a froth is formed. The composition of the froth differs from that of the bulk because the organic solute concentrates at the interfacial region. The froth is mechanically removed and collapsed, and, if further separation is desired, a new froth is generated. The tendency of some dissolved molecules to congregate at the surface has been utilized in water conservation. A certain type of alcohol, when added to water, concentrates at the surface to form a barrier to evaporating water molecules. In warm climates, therefore, water loss by evaporation from lakes can be significantly reduced by introducing a solute that adsorbs positively at the lake-air interface.

The composition of a solution can be expressed in a variety of ways, the simplest of which is the weight fraction, or weight percent; for example, the salt content of seawater is about 3.5 weight percent—i.e., of 100 grams (3.5 ounces) of seawater, 3.5 grams (0.1 ounce) is salt. For a fundamental understanding of solution properties, however, it is often useful to express composition in terms of molecular units such as molecular concentration, molality, or mole fraction.

To understand these terms, it is necessary to define atomic and molecular weights. The atomic weight of elements is a relative figure, with one atom of the carbon-12 isotope being assigned the atomic weight of 12; the atomic weight of hydrogen is then approximately 1, of oxygen approximately 16, and the molecular weight of water (H_2O) 18. The atomic and molecular theory of matter asserts that the atomic weight of any element in grams must contain the same number of atoms as the atomic weight in grams (the gram-atomic weight) of any other element. Thus, two grams of molecular hydrogen (H_2)—its gram-molecular weight—contain the same number of molecules as 18 grams (0.6 ounce) of water or 32 grams (1.1 ounces) of oxygen molecules (O_2). Further, a specified volume of any gas (at low pressure) contains the same number of molecules as the same volume of any other gas at the same temperature and pressure. At standard temperature and pressure (0 °C [32 °F] and one atmosphere) the volume of one gram-molecular weight of any gas has been determined experimentally to be approximately 22.4 litres (23.7 quarts). The number of molecules in this volume of gas, or in the gram-molecular weight of any compound, is called Avogadro's number.

Molarity

Molecular concentration is the number of molecules of a particular component per unit volume. Since the number of molecules in a litre or even a cubic centimetre is enormous, it has become common practice to use what are called molar, rather than molecular, quantities. A mole is the gram-molecular weight of a substance and, therefore, also Avogadro's number of molecules (6.02×10^{23}).

Thus, the number of moles in a sample is the weight of the sample divided by the molecular weight of the substance; it is also the number of molecules in the sample divided by Avogadro's number. Instead of using molecular concentration, it is more convenient to use molar concentration; instead of saying, for example, that the concentration is 12.04×10^{23} molecules per litre, it is simpler to say that it is two moles per litre. Concentration in moles per litre (i.e., molarity) is usually designated by the letter M.

MOLALITY

In electrolyte solutions it is common to distinguish between the solvent (usually water) and the dissolved substance, or solute, which dissociates into ions. For these solutions it is useful to express composition in terms of molality, designated as m, a unit proportional to the number of undissociated solute molecules (or, alternatively, to the number of ions) per 1,000 grams of solvent. The number of molecules or ions in 1,000 grams of solvent usually is very large, so molality is defined as the number of moles per 1,000 grams (2.2 pounds) of solvent.

FORMALITY

Many compounds do not exist in molecular form, either as pure substances or in their solutions. The particles that make up sodium chloride (NaCl), for example, are sodium ions (Na^+) and chloride ions (Cl^-), and, although equal numbers of these two ions are present in any sample of sodium chloride, no Na^+ ion is associated with a particular Cl^- ion to form a neutral molecule having the composition implied by the formula. Therefore, even though the compositions of such compounds are well defined, it would be erroneous to express concentrations of their solutions in terms of molecular weights. A useful concept in cases of this kind is that of the formula weight, defined as the sum of the weights of the atoms in the formula of the compound; thus, the formula weight of sodium chloride is the sum of the atomic weights of sodium and chlorine, 23 plus 35.5, or 58.5, and a solution containing 58.5 grams (2.1 ounces) of sodium chloride per litre is said to have a concentration of one formal, or 1 F.

MOLE FRACTION AND MOLE PERCENTAGE

It often is useful to express the composition of non-electrolyte solutions in terms of mole fraction or mole percentage. In a binary mixture—i.e., a mixture of two components, 1 and 2—there are two mole fractions, x_1 and x_2, which satisfy the relation $x_1 + x_2 = 1$. The mole fraction x_1 is the fraction of molecules of species 1 in the solution, and x_2 is the fraction of molecules of species 2 in the solution. (Mole percentage is the mole fraction multiplied by 100.)

VOLUME FRACTION

The composition of a nonelectrolyte solution containing very large molecules, known as polymers, is most conveniently expressed by the volume fraction (Φ)—i.e., the volume of polymer used to prepare the solution divided by the sum of that volume of polymer and the volume of the solvent.

EQUILIBRIUM PROPERTIES

A quantitative description of liquid-solution properties when the system is in equilibrium is provided by relating the vapour pressure of the solution to its composition. The vapour pressure of a liquid, pure or mixed, is the pressure exerted by those molecules that escape from the liquid to form a separate vapour phase above the liquid. If a quantity of liquid is placed in an evacuated, closed container the volume of which is slightly larger than that of the liquid, most of the container is filled with the liquid, but, immediately above the liquid surface, a vapour phase forms, consisting of molecules that have passed through the liquid surface from liquid to gas; the pressure exerted by that vapour phase is called the vapour (or saturation) pressure. For a pure liquid, this pressure depends only on the temperature, the best-known example being the normal boiling point, which is that temperature at which the vapour pressure is equal to the pressure of the atmosphere. The vapour pressure is one atmosphere at 100 °C (212 °F) for water, at 78.5 °C (173.3 °F) for ethyl alcohol, and at 125.7 °C (258.3 °F) for octane. In a liquid solution, the component with the higher vapour pressure is called the light component, and that with the lower vapour pressure is called the heavy component.

In a liquid mixture, the vapour pressure depends not only on the temperature but also on the composition, and the key problem in understanding the properties of solutions lies in determining this composition dependence. The simplest approximation is to assume that, at constant temperature, the vapour pressure of a solution is a linear function of its composition (i.e., as one increases, so does the other in such proportion that, when the values are plotted, the resulting graph is a straight line). A mixture following this approximation is called an ideal solution.

FUGACITY

In a pure liquid, the vapour generated by its escaping molecules necessarily has the same composition as that of the liquid. In a mixture, however, the composition of the vapour is not the same as that of the liquid; the vapour is richer in that component whose molecules have greater tendency to escape from the liquid phase. This tendency is measured by fugacity, a term derived from the Latin *fugere* ("to escape, to fly away"). The fugacity of a component in a mixture is (essentially) the pressure that the component exerts in the vapour phase when the vapour is in equilibrium with the liquid mixture. (A state of equilibrium is attained when all the properties remain constant in time and there is no net transfer of energy or matter between the vapour and the liquid.) If the vapour phase can be considered to be an ideal gas (i.e., the molecules in the gas phase are assumed to act independently and without any influence on each other), then the fugacity of a component, i, is equal to its partial pressure, which is defined as the product of the total vapour pressure, P, and the vapour-phase mole fraction, y_i. Assuming ideal gas behaviour for the vapour phase, the fugacity ($y_i P$) equals the product of the liquid-phase mole fraction, x_i, the vapour pressure of pure liquid at the same temperature as that of the mixture, P_i°, and the activity coefficient, γ_i. The real concentration of a substance may not be an accurate measure of its effectiveness, because of physical and chemical interactions, in which case an effective concentration must be used, called the activity. The activity is given by the product of the mole fraction x_i and the activity coefficient γ_i. The equation is:

$$y_i P = \gamma_i x_i P_i^\circ. \tag{4}$$

RAOULT'S LAW

In a real solution, the activity coefficient, γ_i, depends on both temperature and composition, but, in an ideal solution, γ_i equals 1 for all components in the mixture. For an ideal binary mixture then, the above equation becomes, for components 1 and 2, $y_1 P = x_1 P_1^\circ$ and $y_2 P = x_2 P_2^\circ$, respectively. Upon adding these equations—recalling that $x_1 + x_2 = 1$ and $y_1 + y_2 = 1$—the total pressure, P, is shown to be expressed by the equation $P = x_1 P_1^\circ + x_2 P_2^\circ = x_1 [P_1^\circ - P_2^\circ] + P_2^\circ$, which is a linear function of x_1.

Assuming $\gamma_1 = \gamma_2 = 1$, equations for $y_1 P$ and $y_2 P$ express what is commonly known as Raoult's law, which states that at constant temperature the partial pressure of a component in a liquid mixture is proportional to its mole fraction in that mixture (i.e., each component exerts a pressure that depends directly on the number of its molecules present). It is unfortunate that the word law is associated with this relation, because only very few mixtures behave according to the equations for ideal binary mixtures. In most cases the activity coefficient, γ_i, is not equal to unity. When γ_i is greater than 1, there are positive deviations from Raoult's law; when γ_i is less than 1, there are negative deviations from Raoult's law.

When the vapour in equilibrium with a liquid mixture has a composition identical to that of the liquid, the mixture is called an azeotrope. It is not possible to separate an azeotropic mixture by fractional distillation because no change in composition is achieved by a series of vaporizations and condensations. Azeotropic mixtures are common. At the azeotropic composition, the total pressure (at constant temperature) is always either a maximum or a minimum with respect to composition, and the boiling temperature (at constant pressure) is always either a minimum or a maximum temperature.

PARTIAL MISCIBILITY

Only pairs of liquids that are completely miscible have been considered so far. Many pairs of liquids, however, are only partially miscible in one another, the degree of miscibility often depending strongly on temperature. In most cases, rising temperature produces enhanced solubility, but this is not always so. For example, at 50 °C (122 °F) the solubility (weight percent) of n-butyl alcohol in water is 6.5 percent, whereas that of water in n-butyl alcohol is 22.4 percent. At 127 °C (261 °F), the upper consolute temperature, complete miscibility is attained: above 127 °C the two liquids mix in all proportions, but below 127 °C they show a miscibility gap. Thus, if *n*-butyl alcohol is added to water at 50 °C, there is only one liquid phase until 6.5 weight percent of the mixture is alcohol; when more alcohol is added, a second liquid phase appears the composition of which is 22.4 weight percent water. When sufficient alcohol is present to make the overall composition 77.6 weight percent alcohol, the first phase disappears, and only one liquid phase remains. A qualitatively different example is the system water-triethylamine, which has a lower consolute temperature at 17 °C (63 °F). Below 17 °C the two liquids are completely miscible, but at higher temperatures they are only partially miscible. Finally, it is possible, although rare, for a binary system to exhibit both upper and lower consolute temperatures. Above 128 °C (262 °F) and below 49 °C (120 °F) butyl glycol and water are completely miscible, but between these temperatures they do not mix in all proportions.

COLLIGATIVE PROPERTIES

Colligative properties depend only on the concentration of the solute, not on the identity of the solute molecules. The concept of an ideal solution, as expressed by Raoult's law, was already well-known during the last quarter of the 19th century, and it provided the early physical chemists with a powerful technique for measuring molecular weights. (Reliable measurements of molecular weights, in turn, provided important evidence for the modern atomic and molecular theory of matter.)

RISE IN BOILING POINT

It was observed that, whenever one component in a binary solution is present in large excess, the partial pressure of that component is correctly predicted by Raoult's law, even though the solution may exhibit departures from ideal behaviour in other respects. When Raoult's law is applied to the solvent of a very dilute solution containing a nonvolatile solute, it is possible to calculate the mole fraction of the solute from an experimental determination of the rise in boiling point that results when the solute is dissolved in the solvent. Since the separate weights of solute and solvent are readily measured, the procedure provides a simple experimental method for the determination of molecular weight. If a weighed amount of a nonvolatile substance, w_2, is dissolved in a weighed amount of a solvent, w_1, at constant pressure, the increase in the boiling temperature, ΔT_{b1}, the gas constant, R (derived from the gas laws), the heat of vaporization of the pure solvent per unit weight, l_1^{vap}, and the boiling temperature of pure solvent, T_{b1}, are related in a simple product of ratios equal to the molecular weight of the solute, M_2. The equation is:

$$M_2 = \left(\frac{RT_{b1}^2}{l_1^{vap}} \right) \left(\frac{w_2}{w_1} \right) \left(\frac{1}{\Delta T_{b1}} \right). \qquad (5)$$

The essence of this technique follows from the observation that, in a dilute solution of a nonvolatile solute, the rise in boiling point is proportional to the number of solute molecules, regardless of their size and mass.

DECREASE IN FREEZING POINT

Another colligative property of solutions is the decrease in the freezing temperature of a solvent that is observed when a small amount of solute is dissolved in that solvent. By reasoning similar to that leading to equation (5), the freezing-point depression, ΔT_f, the freezing temperature of pure solvent, T_{f1}, the heat of fusion (also called the heat of melting) of pure solvent per unit weight, l_1^{fusion}, and the weights of solute and solvent in the solution, w_2 and

w_1, respectively, are so related as to equal the molecular weight of solute, M_2, in the equation

$$M_2 = \left(\frac{RT_{f1}^2}{l_1^{\text{fusion}}}\right)\left(\frac{w_2}{w_1}\right)\left(\frac{1}{\Delta T_f}\right). \qquad (6)$$

A well-known practical application of freezing-point depression is provided by adding antifreeze to the cooling water in an automobile's radiator. Water alone freezes at 0 °C (32 °F), but the freezing temperature decreases appreciably when ethylene glycol is mixed with water.

OSMOTIC PRESSURE

A third colligative property, osmotic pressure, helped to establish the fundamentals of modern physical chemistry and played a particularly important role in the early days of solution theory. Osmosis is especially important in medicine and biology, but in recent years it has also been applied industrially to problems such as the concentration of fruit juices, the desalting of seawater, and the purification of municipal sewage. Osmosis occurs whenever a liquid solution is in contact with a semipermeable membrane—i.e., a thin, porous wall whose porosity is such that some, but not all, of the components in the liquid mixture can pass through the wall. A semipermeable membrane is a selective barrier, and many such barriers are found in plants and animals. Osmosis gives rise to what is known as osmotic pressure in which a container at uniform temperature is divided into two parts by a semipermeable membrane that allows only molecules of component A to pass from the left to the right side; the selective membrane does not allow molecules of component B to pass. Example compounds for A and B might be water and sodium chloride (table salt), respectively.

Molecules of component A are free to pass back and forth through the membrane, but, at equilibrium, when

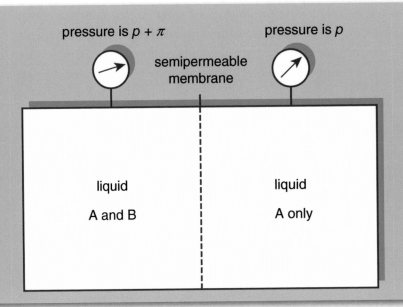

pressure is $p + \pi$

pressure is p

semipermeable membrane

liquid

A and B

liquid

A only

Osmotic pressure π caused by a membrane that allows A to pass but not B. A representative system could consist of water (A) and salt (B). Copyright Encyclopædia Britannica; rendering for this edition by Rosen Educational Services

the fugacity (escaping tendency) of A in the right-hand side the same as that in the left-hand side, there is no net transfer of A from one side to the other. On the left side, the presence of B molecules lowers the fugacity of A, and, therefore, to achieve equal fugacities for A on both sides, some compensating effect is needed on the left side. This compensating effect is an enhanced pressure, designated by π and called osmotic pressure. At equilibrium the pressure in the left side of the container is larger than that in the right side; the difference in pressure is π. In the simplest case, when the concentration of B is small (i.e., A is in excess), the osmotic pressure is the product of the gas constant (R), the absolute temperature (T), and the concentration of B (c_B) in the solution expressed in moles of B per unit volume: $\pi = RTc_B$. Since the osmotic pressure for a dilute solution is proportional to the number of solute molecules, it is a colligative property, and, as a result, osmotic-pressure measurements are often used to determine molecular weights, especially for large molecules such as polymers. When w_B grams of solute B are added to a large amount of solvent A at temperature T, and V is the volume of liquid solvent A in the left side of the container, then the molecular weight of B, M_B, is given by

$$M_B = \frac{w_B RT}{\pi V}.$$ (7)

For sodium chloride in water, c_B is the concentration of the ions, which is twice the concentration of the salt owing to the dissociation of the salt (NaCl) into sodium ions (Na^+) and chloride ions (Cl^-). Thus, for a 3.5 percent sodium chloride solution at 25 °C (77 °F), π is 29 atmospheres, which is the minimum pressure at which a desalination reverse osmosis process can operate.

TRANSPORT PROPERTIES IN SOLUTIONS

Pure fluids have two transport properties that are of primary importance: viscosity and thermal conductivity. Transport properties differ from equilibrium properties in that they reflect not what happens at equilibrium but the speed at which equilibrium is attained. In solutions these two transport properties are also important. In addition, there is a third one, called diffusivity.

VISCOSITY

The viscosity of a fluid (pure or not) is a measure of its ability to resist deformation. If water is poured into a thin vertical tube with a funnel at the top, it flows easily through the tube, but salad oil is difficult to force into the tube. If the oil is heated, however, its flow through the tube is much facilitated. The intrinsic property that is responsible for these phenomena is the viscosity (the "thickness") of the fluid, a property which is often strongly affected by temperature. All fluids (liquid or gas) exhibit viscous behaviour (i.e., all fluids resist deformation to some degree), but the range of viscosity is enormous: the viscosity of air is extremely small, while that of glass is essentially infinite. The viscosity of a solution depends not only on temperature but also on composition. By varying the composition of a petroleum mixture, it is possible to attain a desired viscosity at a particular temperature. This is precisely what the oil companies do when they sell oil to a motorist: in winter, they recommend an oil with lower viscosity than that used in summer, because otherwise, on a cold morning, the viscosity of the lubricating oil may be so high that the car's battery will not be powerful enough to move the lubricated piston.

THERMAL CONDUCTIVITY

The thermal conductivity of a material reflects its ability to transfer heat by conduction. In practical situations both viscosity and thermal conductivity are important, as is illustrated by the contrast between an air mattress and a water bed. Because of its low viscosity, air yields rapidly to an imposed load, and thus the air mattress responds quickly when someone lying on it changes position. Water, because of its higher viscosity, noticeably resists deformation, and someone lying on a water bed experiences a caressing response whenever position is changed. At the same time, since the thermal conductivity as well as the viscosity of water are larger than those of air, the user of a water bed rapidly gets cold unless a heater keeps the water warm. No heater is required by the user of an air mattress because stagnant air is inefficient in removing heat from a warm body.

Composition and temperature affect the thermal conductivity of a solution but, in typical liquid mixtures, the effect on viscosity is much larger than that on thermal conductivity.

DIFFUSIVITY

While viscosity is concerned with the transfer of momentum and thermal conductivity with the transfer of heat, diffusivity is concerned with the transport of molecules in a mixture. If a lump of sugar is put into a cup of coffee, the sugar molecules travel from the surface of the lump into the coffee at a speed determined by the temperature and by the pertinent intermolecular forces. The characteristic property that determines this speed is called diffusivity— i.e., the ability of a molecule to diffuse through a sea of other molecules. Diffusivities in solids are extremely small, and those in liquids are much smaller than those in gases. For this reason, a spoon is used to stir the coffee to speed up the motion of the sugar molecules, but, if the odour of cigarette smoke fills a room, little effort is needed to clear the air—opening the windows for a few minutes is sufficient.

In order to define diffusivity, it is necessary to consider a binary fluid mixture in which the concentration of solute molecules is c_1 at position 1 and c_2 at position 2, which is l centimetres from position 1; if c_1 is larger than c_2, then the concentration gradient (change with respect to distance), given by $(c_2 - c_1)/l$, is a negative number, indicating that molecules of solute spontaneously diffuse from position 1 to position 2. The number of solute molecules that pass through an area of 1 square cm perpendicular to l, per second, is called the flux J (expressed in molecules per second per square centimetre). The diffusivity D is given by the formula

$$D = -\frac{J}{(c_2 - c_1)/l}. \qquad (8)$$

The leading minus sign is introduced because, when the gradient is positive, J is negative, and, by convention, D is a positive number. In binary gaseous mixtures, diffusivity depends only weakly on the composition, and, therefore, to a good approximation, the diffusivity of gas A in gas B is the same as that of gas B in gas A. In liquid systems, however, the diffusivity of solute A in solvent B may be significantly different from that of solute B in solvent A. In a very viscous fluid, molecules cannot rapidly move from one place to another. Therefore, in liquid systems, the diffusivity of solute A depends strongly on the viscosity of solvent B and vice versa. While the letter D is always used for diffusivity, viscosity is commonly given the symbol η: in many liquid solutions it is observed that, as the composition changes (as long as the temperature remains constant), the product $D\eta$ remains nearly the same.

THERMODYNAMICS AND INTERMOLECULAR FORCES IN SOLUTIONS

The properties of solutions depend, essentially, on two characteristics: first, the manner in which the molecules arrange themselves (that is, the geometric array in which the molecules occupy space) and, second, the nature and strength of the forces operating between the molecules.

ENERGY CONSIDERATIONS

The first characteristic is reflected primarily in the thermodynamic quantity S, called entropy, which is a measure of disorder, and the second characteristic is reflected in the thermodynamic quantity H, called enthalpy, which is a measure of potential energy—i.e., the energy that must be supplied to separate all the molecules from one another. Enthalpy minus the product of the absolute temperature T and entropy equals a thermodynamic quantity G, called Gibbs energy (also called free energy):

$$G = H - TS. \tag{9}$$

From the second law of thermodynamics, it can be shown that, at constant temperature and pressure, any spontaneous process is accompanied by a decrease in Gibbs energy. The change in G that results from mixing is designated by ΔG, which, in turn, is related to changes in H and S at constant temperature by the equation

$$\Delta G = \Delta H - T\Delta S. \tag{10}$$

At a fixed temperature and pressure, two substances mix spontaneously whenever ΔG is negative; that is, mixing (either partial or complete) occurs whenever the Gibbs energy of the substances after mixing is less than that before mixing.

The two characteristics that determine solution behaviour, structure and intermolecular forces, are, unfortunately, not independent, because the structure is influenced by the intermolecular forces and because the potential energy of the mixture depends on the structure. Only in limiting cases is it possible, on the one hand, to calculate ΔS (the entropy change upon mixing) from structural considerations alone and, on the other, to calculate ΔH (the enthalpy change of mixing) exclusively from relations describing intermolecular forces. Nevertheless, such calculations have proved to be useful for establishing models that approximate solution behaviour and that serve as guides in interpreting experimental measurements. Solutions for which structural considerations are dominant are called athermal solutions, and those for which the effects of intermolecular forces are more important than those of structure are called regular solutions (see Theories of Solutions: Regular and Athermal Solutions).

EFFECTS OF MOLECULAR STRUCTURE

A variety of forces operate between molecules, and there is a qualitative relation between the properties of a solution and the types of intermolecular forces that operate within it. The volume occupied by a solution is determined primarily by repulsive forces. When two molecules are extremely close to one another, they must necessarily exert a repulsive force on each other since two molecules of finite dimensions cannot occupy the same space; two molecules in very close proximity resist attempts to shorten the distance between them.

At larger distances of separation, molecules may attract or repel each other depending on the sign (plus or minus) and distribution of their electrical charge. Two ions attract one another if the charge on one is positive and that on the other is negative; they repel when both carry charges of the same sign. Forces between ions are called Coulomb forces and are characterized by their long range; the force (F) between two ions is inversely proportional to the square of the distance between them; i.e., F varies as $1/r^2$. Noncoulombic physical forces between molecules decay more rapidly with distance; i.e., in general F varies as $1/rn$, n being larger than 2 for intermolecular forces other than those between ions.

The Coulomb force (F) equals the product of the magnitude of the charge on one ion (e_1) and that on the other

(e_2) divided by the product of the distance squared (r^2) and the dielectric constant (ε):

$$F = \frac{e_1 e_2}{r^2 \varepsilon}. \tag{11}$$

If both e_1 and e_2 are positive, F is positive and the force is repulsive. If either e_1 or e_2 is positive while the other is negative, F is negative and the force is attractive. Coulomb forces are dominant in electrolyte solutions.

MOLECULAR STRUCTURE AND CHARGE DISTRIBUTION

If a molecule has no net electrical charge, its negative charge is equal to its positive charge. The forces experienced by such molecules depend on how the positive and negative charges are arranged in space. If the arrangement is spherically symmetric, the molecule is said to be nonpolar; if there is an excess of positive charge on one end of the molecule and an excess of negative charge on the other, the molecule has a dipole moment (i.e., a measurable tendency to rotate in an electric or magnetic field) and is therefore called polar. The dipole moment (μ) is defined as the product of the magnitude of the charge, e, and the distance separating the positive and negative charges, l: $\mu = el$. Electrical charge is measured in electrostatic units (esu), and the typical charge at one end of a molecule is of the order of 10^{-10} esu; the distance between charges is of the order of 10^{-8} cm. Dipole moments, therefore, usually are measured in debyes (one debye is 10^{-18} esu-cm). For nonpolar molecules, $\mu = 0$.

POLAR MOLECULES

The force F between two polar molecules is directly proportional to the product of the two dipole moments (μ_1 and μ_2) and inversely proportional to the fourth power of the distance between them (r^4): that is, F varies as $\mu_1\mu_2/r^4$. The equation for this relationship contains a constant of proportionality ($F = k\mu_1\mu_2/r^4$), the sign and magnitude of which depend on the mutual orientation of the two dipoles. If the positive end of one faces the negative end of the other, the constant of proportionality is negative (meaning that an attractive force exists), while it is positive (meaning that a repulsive force exists) when the positive end of one faces the positive end of the other. When polar molecules are free to rotate, they tend to favour those orientations that lead to attractive forces. To a first approximation, the force (averaged over all orientations) is inversely proportional to the temperature and to the seventh power of the distance of separation. Mixtures of polar molecules often exhibit only mild deviations from ideality, but mixtures containing polar and nonpolar molecules are frequently strongly nonideal. Because of the qualitative and quantitative differences in intermolecular forces, the molecules segregate: the polar molecules prefer to be with each other, and so do the nonpolar ones. Only at higher temperatures, such that the thermal energy of the molecules offsets the cohesion between identical molecules, do the two liquids mix in all proportions. In mixtures containing both polar and nonpolar components, deviations from Raoult's law diminish as temperature rises.

NONPOLAR MOLECULES

A nonpolar molecule is one whose charge distribution is spherically symmetric when averaged over time; since the charges oscillate, a temporary dipole moment exists at any given instant in a so-called nonpolar molecule. These temporary dipole moments fluctuate rapidly in magnitude and direction, giving rise to intermolecular forces of attraction called London (or dispersion) forces. All molecules, charged or not, polar or not, interact by London forces. To a first approximation, the London force between two molecules is inversely proportional to the seventh power of the distance of separation; it is therefore short-range, decreasing rapidly as one molecule moves away from the other. The London theory indicates that for simple molecules positive deviations from Raoult's law may be expected (i.e., the activity coefficient γ_i is greater than 1, as explained previously). Since the London theory suggests that the attractive forces between unlike simple molecules are smaller than those corresponding to an ideal solution, the escaping tendency of the molecules in solution is larger than that calculated by Raoult's law. As a result, mixing of small nonpolar molecules is endothermic (absorbing heat from the surroundings) and the volume occupied by the liquid solution often exceeds that of the unmixed components — that is, the components expand on mixing.

In addition to the forces listed above, there are so-called induction forces set up when a charged or polar molecule induces a dipole in another molecule; the electric field of the inducing molecule distorts the charge distribution in the other. When a charged molecule induces a dipole in another, the force is always attractive and is inversely proportional to the fifth power of the distance of separation. When a polar molecule induces a dipole in another molecule, the force is also attractive and is inversely proportional to the seventh power of separation. Induction forces are usually small but may make a significant contribution to the energy of a mixture of molecules that are strongly dissimilar.

EFFECTS OF CHEMICAL INTERACTIONS

In many cases the properties of a mixture are determined primarily by forces that are more properly classified as chemical rather than as physical. For example, when dinitrogen pentoxide is dissolved in water, a new substance, nitric acid, is formed; and it is necessary to interpret the behaviour of such a solution in terms of its chemical properties, which, in this case, are more important than its physical properties. This example is an extreme one, and there are many solutions for which the chemical effect is less severe but nevertheless dominant.

HYDROGEN BONDING: ASSOCIATION

This dominance is especially important in those solutions that involve hydrogen bonding. Whenever a solution contains molecules with an electropositive hydrogen atom and with an electronegative atom (such as nitrogen, oxygen, sulfur, or fluorine), hydrogen bonding may occur and, when it does, the properties of the solution are affected profoundly. Hydrogen bonds may form between identical molecules or between dissimilar molecules. For example, methanol (CH_3OH) has an electropositive (electron-attracting) hydrogen atom and also an electronegative (electron-donating) oxygen atom, and therefore two methanol molecules may hydrogen-bond (represented by the dashed line) singly to form the structure

$$CH_3OH \text{----} \overset{\overset{\textstyle H}{|}}{O}CH_3,$$

or in chains to form

Hydrogen bonding between identical molecules is often called association.

HYDROGEN BONDING: SOLVATION

In a mixture of methanol and, say, pyridine (C_5H_5N), hydrogen bonds can also form between the electropositive hydrogen atom in methanol and the electronegative nitrogen atom in pyridine. Hydrogen bonding between dissimilar molecules is an example of a type of interaction known as solvation. Since the extent of association or solvation or both depends on the concentrations of the solution's components, the partial pressure of a component is not even approximately proportional to its mole fraction as given by Raoult's law; therefore, large deviations from Raoult's law are commonly observed in solutions in which hydrogen bonding is extensive. Broadly speaking, association of one component, but not the other, tends to produce positive deviations from Raoult's law, because the associating component hydrogen-bonds to a smaller extent when it is surrounded by other molecules than it does in the pure state. On the other hand, solvation between dissimilar molecules tends to produce negative deviations from Raoult's law.

THEORIES OF SOLUTIONS

The following section treats solutions in a more theoretical manner. Much of the theory of solutions deals with the activity coefficients mentioned above in the discussion of Raoult's law.

ACTIVITY COEFFICIENTS AND EXCESS FUNCTIONS

As has been explained previously, when actual concentrations do not give simple linear relations for the behaviour of a solution, activity coefficients, symbolized by γ_i, are used in expressing deviations from Raoult's law. Activity coefficients are directly related to excess functions, and, in attempting to understand solution behaviour, it is convenient to characterize nonelectrolyte solutions in terms of these functions. In particular, it is useful to distinguish between two types of limiting behaviour: one corresponds to that of a regular solution; the other, to that of an athermal solution (i.e., when components are mixed, no heat is generated or absorbed).

In a binary mixture with mole fractions x_1 and x_2 and activity coefficients γ_1 and γ_2, these quantities can be related to a thermodynamic function designated by GE, called the excess Gibbs (or free) energy. The significance of the word excess lies in the fact that GE is the Gibbs energy of a solution in excess of what it would be if it were ideal.

In a binary solution the two activity coefficients are not independent but are related by an exact differential equation called the Gibbs-Duhem relation. If experimental data at constant temperature are available for γ_1 and γ_2 as a function of composition, it is possible to apply this equation to check the data for thermodynamic consistency: the data are said to be consistent only if they satisfy the Gibbs-Duhem relation. Experimental data that do not satisfy this relation are thermodynamically inconsistent and therefore must be erroneous.

To establish a theory of solutions, it is necessary to construct a theoretical (or semitheoretical) equation for the excess Gibbs energy as a function of absolute temperature (T) and the mole fractions x_1 and x_2. After such an equation has been established, the individual activity coefficients can readily be calculated.

Gibbs energy, by definition, consists of two parts: one part is the enthalpy, which reflects the intermolecular forces between the molecules, which, in turn, are responsible for the heat effects that accompany the mixing process (enthalpy is, in a general sense, a measure of the heat content of a substance); and the other part is the entropy, which reflects the state of disorder (a measure of the random behaviour of particles) in the mixture. The excess Gibbs energy G^E is given by the equation

$$G^E = H^E - TS^E, \tag{12}$$

where H^E is the excess enthalpy and S^E is the excess entropy. The word *excess* means in excess of that which would prevail if the solution were ideal. In the simplest case, both H^E and S^E are zero; in that case the solution is ideal and $\gamma_1 = \gamma_2 = 1$. In the general case, neither H^E nor S^E is zero, but two types of semi-ideal solutions can be designated: in the first, S^E is zero but H^E is not; this is called a regular solution. In the second, H^E is zero but S^E is not; this is called an athermal solution. An ideal solution is both regular and athermal.

REGULAR SOLUTIONS

The word *regular* implies that the molecules mix in a completely random manner, which means that there is no segregation or preference; a given molecule chooses its neighbours with no regard for chemical identity (species 1 or 2). In a regular solution of composition x_1 and x_2, the probability that the neighbour of a given molecule is of species 1 is given by the mole fraction x_1, and the probability that it is of species 2 is given by x_2.

Two liquids form a solution that is approximately regular when the molecules of the two liquids do not differ appreciably in size and there are no strong orienting forces caused by dipoles or hydrogen bonding. In that event, the mixing process can be represented by a lattice model with

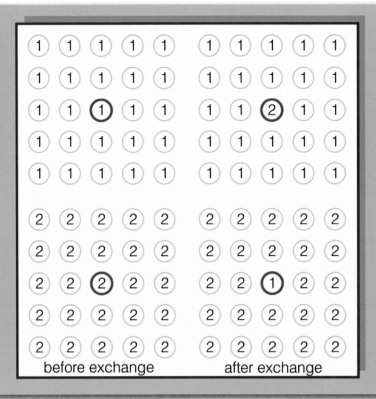

Physical significance of interchange energy. The energy absorbed in the process above is 2ω. Copyright Encyclopædia Britannica; rendering for this edition by Rosen Educational Services

two pure liquids, 1 and 2, and the central molecule of liquid 1 is then interchanged with the central molecule of liquid 2. Before interchange, the potential energy between central molecule 1 and one of its immediate neighbours is Γ_{11}, and that between central molecule 2 and one of its immediate neighbours is Γ_{22}. After interchange, the potential energy between molecule 1 and one of its immediate neighbours is Γ_{12}, and that between molecule 2 and one of its immediate neighbours is also Γ_{12}. The change in energy that accompanies this mixing process is equal to twice the interchange energy (ω), which is equal to the potential energy after mixing less one-half the sum of the potential energies before mixing, the whole multiplied by the number of immediate neighbours, called the coordination number (z), surrounding the two shifted molecules:

$$\omega = z[\Gamma_{12} - \frac{1}{2}(\Gamma_{11} + \Gamma_{22})]. \qquad (13)$$

In this lattice model, z equals 4; but, in three dimensions, z varies between 6 and 12, depending on the lattice geometry. In this simple lattice model, the interchange process occurs without change of volume; thus, in this particular case, the excess enthalpy is the same as the energy change upon mixing. Assuming regular-solution behaviour (i.e., S^E = 0), an equation may be derived relating Gibbs energy, Avogadro's number, interchange energy, and mole fractions. In principle, the interchange energy (ω) may be positive or negative, but, for simple molecules, for which only London forces of attraction are important, ω is positive. The equation obtained from the simple lattice model can be extended semiempirically to apply to mixtures of molecules whose sizes are not nearly the same by using volume fractions instead of mole fractions to express the effect of composition and by introducing the concept of cohesive energy density, which is defined as the potential energy of a liquid divided by its volume. The adjective cohesive is well chosen because it indicates that this energy is associated with the forces that keep the molecules close together in a condensed state. Again restricting attention to nonpolar molecules and assuming a completely random mixture (S^E = 0), an equation may be derived that requires only pure-component properties to predict the excess Gibbs energy (and hence the activity coefficients) of binary mixtures. Because of many simplifying assumptions, this equation does not give consistently accurate results, but in many cases it provides good semiquantitative estimates. The form of the equation is such that the excess Gibbs energy is larger than zero; hence, the equation is not applicable to mixtures that have negative deviations from Raoult's law.

ATHERMAL SOLUTIONS

In a solution in which the molecules of one component are much larger than those of the other, the assumption that the solution is regular (i.e., that $S^E = 0$) no longer provides a reasonable approximation even if the effect of intermolecular forces is neglected. A large flexible molecule (e.g., a chain molecule such as polyethylene) can attain many more configurations when it is surrounded by small molecules than it can when surrounded by other large flexible molecules; the state of disorder in such a solution is therefore much larger than that of a regular solution in which $S^E = 0$. A solution of very large molecules (i.e., polymers) in an ordinary liquid solvent is analogous to a mixture of cooked spaghetti (representing the polymers) and tomato sauce (the solvent). When there is a large amount of sauce and relatively little spaghetti, each piece of spaghetti is free to exist in many different shapes; this freedom, however, becomes restricted as the number of spaghetti pieces rises and the amount of sauce available for each strand declines. The excess entropy then is determined primarily by the freedom that the spaghetti has in the tomato sauce mixture relative to the freedom it has in the absence of sauce.

Regular solutions and athermal solutions represent limiting cases; real solutions are neither regular nor athermal. For real solutions it has been proposed to calculate G^E by combining the equations derived separately for regular solutions and for athermal solutions, but, in view of the restrictive and mutually inconsistent assumptions that were made in deriving these two equations, the proposal has met with only limited success.

ASSOCIATED AND SOLVATED SOLUTIONS

For those solutions in which there are strong intermolecular forces due to large dipole moments, hydrogen bonding, or complex formation, equations based on fundamental molecular theory cannot be applied, but it is frequently useful to apply a chemical treatment—i.e., to describe the liquid mixture in terms of association and solvation, by assuming the existence of a variety of distinct chemical species in chemical equilibrium with one another. For example, there is much experimental evidence for association in acetic acid, in which most of the molecules dimerize; i.e., two single acetic acid molecules, called monomers, combine to form a new molecule, called a dimer, through hydrogen bonding. When acetic acid is dissolved in a solvent such as benzene, the extent of dimerization of acetic acid depends on the temperature and on the total concentration of acetic acid in the solution. The escaping tendency (vapour pressure) of a monomer is much greater than that of a dimer, and it is thus possible to explain the variation of activity coefficient with composition for acetic acid in benzene; the activity coefficient of acetic acid in an excess of benzene is large because, under these conditions, acetic acid is primarily in the monomeric state, whereas pure acetic acid is almost completely dimerized. In the acetic acid–benzene system, association of acetic acid molecules produces positive deviations from Raoult's law.

When a solvent and a solute molecule link together with weak bonds, the process is called solvation. For example, in the system acetone-chloroform, a hydrogen bond is formed between the hydrogen atom in chloroform and the oxygen atom in acetone. In this case, hydrogen bonding depresses the escaping tendencies of both components, producing negative deviations from Raoult's law.

While hydrogen bonding is frequently encountered in solutions, there are many other examples of weak chemical-bond formation between dissimilar molecules. The formation of such weak bonds is called complex formation—that is, formation of a new chemical species, called a complex, which is held together by weak forces that are chemical in nature rather than physical. Such complexes usually exist only in solution; because of their low stability, they cannot, in general, be isolated. The ability of molecules to form complexes has a strong effect on solution behaviour. For example, the solubility of a sparingly soluble species can be much increased by complex formation: the solubility of silver chloride in water is extremely small since silver chloride dissociates only slightly to silver ion and chloride ion; however, when a small quantity of ammonia is added, solubility rises dramatically because of the reaction of six molecules of ammonia with one silver ion to form the complex ion $Ag(NH_3)_6^+$. By tying up silver ions and forcing extensive dissociation of molecular silver chloride, the ammonia pulls silver chloride into aqueous solution.

In recent years there has been much interest in the use of computers to generate theoretical expressions for the activity coefficients of solutions. In many cases the calculations have been restricted to model systems, in particular to mixtures of hard-sphere (envisioned as billiard balls) molecules—i.e., idealized molecules that have finite size but no forces of attraction. These calculations have produced a better understanding of the structure of simple liquid solutions since the manner in which nonpolar and non-hydrogen-bonding molecules arrange themselves in space is determined primarily by their size and shape and only secondarily by their attractive intermolecular forces. The results obtained for hard-sphere molecules can be extended to real molecules by applying corrections required for attractive forces and for the "softness" of the molecules—i.e., the ability of molecules to interpenetrate (overlap) at high temperatures. While practical results are still severely limited and while the amount of required computer calculation is large even for simple binary systems, there is good reason to believe that advances in the theory of solution will increasingly depend on computerized, as opposed to analytical, models.

SOLUTIONS OF ELECTROLYTES

Near the end of the 19th century, the properties of electrolyte solutions were investigated extensively by the early workers in physical chemistry. A suggestion of Svante August Arrhenius, a Swedish chemist, that salts of strong acids and bases (for example, sodium chloride) are completely dissociated into ions when in aqueous solution received strong support from electrical-conductivity measurements and from molecular-weight studies (freezing-point depression, boiling-point elevation, and osmotic pressure). These studies showed that the number of solute particles was larger than it would be if no dissociation occurred. For example, a 0.001 molal solution of a uni-univalent electrolyte (one in which each ion has a valence, or charge, of 1, and, when dissociated, two ions are produced) such as sodium chloride, Na^+Cl^-, exhibits colligative properties corresponding to a nonelectrolyte solution whose molality is 0.002. The colligative properties of a 0.001 molal solution of a univalent-divalent electrolyte (yielding three ions) such as magnesium bromide, $Mg^{2+}Br_2^-$, correspond to those of a nonelectrolyte solution with a molality of 0.003.

At somewhat higher concentrations the experimental data showed some inconsistencies with Arrhenius's dissociation theory, and initially these were ascribed to incomplete, or partial, dissociation. In the years 1920–30, however, it was shown that these inconsistencies could be explained by electrostatic interactions (Coulomb forces) of the ions in solution. The current view of electrolyte solutions is that, in water at normal temperatures, the salts of strong acids and strong bases are completely dissociated into ions at all concentrations up to the solubility limit. At high concentrations Coulombic interactions may cause the formation of ion pairs, which implies that the ions are not dispersed uniformly in the solution but have a tendency to form two-ion aggregates in which a positive ion seeks the close proximity of a negative ion and vice versa. While the theory of dilute electrolyte solutions is well advanced, no adequate theory exists for concentrated electrolyte solutions primarily because of the long-range Coulomb forces that dominate in ionic solutions.

The equilibrium properties of electrolyte solutions can be studied experimentally by electrochemical measurements, freezing-point depressions, solubility determinations, osmotic pressures, or measurements of vapour pressure. Most electrolytes, such as salts, are nonvolatile at ordinary temperature, and, in that event, the vapour pressure exerted by the solution is the same as the partial pressure of the solvent. The activity coefficient of the solvent can, therefore, be found from total-pressure measurements, and, using the Gibbs-Duhem equation, it is then possible to calculate the activity coefficient of the electrolyte solute. This activity coefficient is designated by $\gamma_{\pm}$ to indicate that it is a mean activity coefficient for the positive and negative ions. Since it is impossible to isolate positive ions and negative ions into separate containers, it is not possible to determine individual activity coefficients for the positive ions and for the negative ions. The mean activity coefficient $\gamma_{\pm}$ is so defined that it approaches a value of unity at very low molality where the ions are so far apart that they exert negligible influence on one another.

For small concentrations of electrolyte, the theory of Peter Debye, a Dutch-born American physical chemist, and Erich Hückel, a German chemist, relates $\gamma_{\pm}$ to the ionic strength, which is the sum of the products of the concentration of each ion (in moles per litre) and the square of its charge. The equation predicts that $\gamma_{\pm}$ decreases with rising ionic strength in agreement with experiment at very low ionic strength. At higher ionic strength, however, $\gamma_{\pm}$ rises, and in some cases $\gamma_{\pm}$ is greater than 1. The derivation of the Debye-Hückel theory clearly shows that it is limited to low concentrations. Many attempts have been made to extend the Debye-Hückel equation to higher electrolyte concentrations. One of the more successful attempts is based on the idea that the ions are solvated, which means that every ion is surrounded by a tight-fitting shell of solvent molecules.

The concept of solvation is often used to explain properties of aqueous solutions; one well-known property is the salting-out effect, in which the solubility of a nonelectrolyte in water is decreased when electrolyte is added. For example, the solubility of ethyl ether in water at 25 °C (77 °F) is 0.91 mole percent, but, in an aqueous solution containing 15 weight percent sodium chloride, it is only 0.13 mole percent. This decrease in solubility can be explained by postulating that some of the water molecules cannot participate in the dissolution of the ether because they are tightly held (solvated) by sodium and chloride ions.

Electrolyte solutions have long been of interest in industry since many common inorganic chemicals are directly obtained, or else separated, by crystallization from aqueous solution. Further, many important chemical and metallurgical products (e.g., aluminum) are obtained or refined by electrochemical processes that occur in liquid solution. In recent years there has been renewed interest in electrolyte solutions because of their relevance to fuel cells as a possible source of power for automobiles.

The properties of electrolyte solutions also have large importance in physiology. Many molecules that occur in biological systems bear electric charges; a large molecule that has a positive electric charge at one end and a negative charge at the other is called a zwitterion. Very large molecules, such as those of proteins, may have numerous positive and negative charges; such molecules are called polyelectrolytes. In solution, the conformation (i.e., the three-dimensional structure) of a large, charged molecule is strongly dependent on the ionic strength of the dissolving medium. For example, depending on the nature and concentration of salts present in the solvent, a polyelectrolyte molecule may coagulate into a ball, it may stretch out like a rod, or it may form a coil or helix. The conformation, in turn, is closely related to the molecule's physiological function. As a result, improved understanding of the properties of electrolyte solutions has direct consequences in molecular biology and medicine.

SOLUBILITIES OF SOLIDS AND GASES

Since the dissolution of one substance in another can occur only if there is a decrease in the Gibbs energy, it follows that, generally speaking, gases and solids do not dissolve in liquids as readily as do other liquids. To understand this, the dissolution of a solid can be visualized as occurring in two steps. In the first, the pure solid is melted at constant temperature to a pure liquid. In the second, that liquid is dissolved at constant temperature in the solvent. Similarly, the dissolution of a gas can be divided at some fixed pressure into two parts, the first corresponding to constant-temperature condensation of the pure gas to a liquid and the second to constant-temperature mixing of that liquid with solvent. In many cases, the pure liquids (obtained by melting or by condensation) may be hypothetical (i.e., unstable and, therefore, physically unobtainable), but usually their properties can be estimated by reasonable extrapolations.

It is found that the change in Gibbs energy corresponding to the first step is positive and, hence, in opposition to the change needed for dissolution. For example, at -10 °C (14 °F), ice is more stable than water, and, at 110 °C (230 °F) and one atmosphere, steam is more stable than water. Therefore, the Gibbs energy of melting ice at -10 °C is positive, and the Gibbs energy of condensing steam at one atmosphere and 110 °C is also positive. For the second step, however, the change in Gibbs energy is negative; its magnitude depends on the equilibrium composition of the mixture. Owing to the positive Gibbs energy change that accompanies the first step, there is a barrier that makes it more difficult to dissolve solids and gases as compared with liquids.

For gases at normal pressures, the positive Gibbs energy of condensation increases with rising temperature, but, for solids, the positive Gibbs energy of melting decreases with rising temperature. For example, the change in energy, ΔG, of condensing steam at one atmosphere is larger at 120 °C (248 °F) than it is at 110 °C, while the change in energy of melting ice at -5 °C (23 °F) is smaller than it is at -10 °C. Thus, as temperature rises, the barrier becomes larger for gases but lower for solids, and therefore, with few exceptions, the solubility of a solid rises while the solubility of a gas falls as the temperature is raised.

For solids, the positive Gibbs energy "barrier" depends on the melting temperature. If the melting temperature is much higher than the temperature of the solution, the barrier is large, shrinking to zero when the melting temperature and solution temperature become identical.

The solubilities of the common gases hydrogen, nitrogen, methane, and carbon dioxide, as well as the solubility of (solid) naphthalene in a few typical solvents, illustrate the qualitative rule that "like dissolves like"; thus naphthalene, an aromatic hydrocarbon, dissolves more readily in another aromatic hydrocarbon such as benzene than it does in a chlorinated solvent such as carbon tetrachloride or in a hydrogen-bonded solvent such as methyl alcohol. By similar reasoning, the gas methane, a paraffinic hydrocarbon, dissolves more readily in another paraffin such as hexane than it does in water. In all three solvents, the gas hydrogen (which boils at -252.5 °C [-422.5 °F]) is less soluble than nitrogen (which boils at a higher temperature, -195.8 °C [-320.4 °F]).

While exceptions may occur at very high pressures, the solubility of a gas in a liquid generally rises as the pressure of that gas increases. When the pressure of the gas is much larger than the vapour pressure of the solvent, the solubility is often proportional to the pressure. This proportionality is consistent with Henry's law, which states that, if the gas phase is ideal, the solubility x_2 of gas 2 in solvent 1 is equal to the partial pressure (the vapour-phase mole fraction y_2 times the total pressure P—i.e., $y_2 P$) divided by a temperature-dependent constant, $H_{2,1}$ (called Henry's constant), which is determined to a large extent by the intermolecular forces between solute 2 and solvent 1:

$$x_2 = \frac{y_2 P}{H_{2,1}}.$$

When the vapour pressure of solvent 1 is small compared with the total pressure, the vapour-phase mole fraction of gas 2 is approximately one, and the solubility of the gas is proportional to the total pressure.

CHAPTER 6
CRYSTALLINE SOLIDS AND LIQUID CRYSTALS

Solids are one of the three basic states of matter, the others being liquids and gases. (Sometimes plasmas, or ionized gases, are considered a fourth state of matter.) A solid forms from liquid or gas because the energy of atoms decreases when the atoms take up a relatively ordered, three-dimensional structure.

Solids exhibit certain characteristics that distinguish them from liquids and gases. All solids have, for example, the ability to resist forces applied either perpendicular or parallel to a surface (i.e., normal or shear loads, respectively). Such properties depend on the properties of the atoms that form the solid, on the way those atoms are arranged, and on the forces between them.

Solids are generally divided into three broad classes—crystalline, noncrystalline (amorphous), and quasicrystalline. Crystalline solids have a very high degree of order in a periodic atomic arrangement. Practically all metals and many other minerals, such as common table salt (sodium chloride), belong to this class. Noncrystalline solids are those in which atoms and molecules are not organized in a definite lattice pattern. They include glasses, plastics, and gels. Quasicrystalline solids display novel symmetries in which the atoms are arranged in quasiperiodic fashion—i.e., in patterns that do not repeat at regular intervals. They exhibit symmetries, such as five-fold symmetry, that are forbidden in ordinary crystals. Quasicrystal structures are common in alloys in which aluminum is combined with another metal, such as iron, cobalt, or nickel.

Some molecules may exist in the liquid crystal state, which is intermediate to the crystalline solid and liquid states. Liquid crystals flow like liquids yet display a certain degree of the symmetry characteristic of crystalline solids.

Four principal types of atomic bonds are found in crystalline solids: metallic, ionic, covalent, and molecular. Metals and their alloys are characterized in the main by their high electrical and thermal conductivity, which arise from the migration of free electrons; free electrons also influence how the atoms bond. Ionic crystals are aggregates of charged ions. These salts commonly exhibit ionic conductivity, which increases with temperature. Covalent crystals are hard, frequently brittle materials such as diamond, silicon, and silicon carbide. In the simpler, monatomic types (e.g., diamond), each atom is surrounded by a number of atoms equal to its valence. Molecular crystals are substances that have relatively weak intermolecular binding, such as dry ice (solidified carbon dioxide), solid forms of the rare gases (e.g., argon, krypton, and xenon), and crystals of numerous organic compounds.

Various alloys, salts, covalent crystals, and molecular crystals that are good electrical insulators at low temperature become conductors at elevated temperatures, conductivity increasing rapidly with temperature. Materials of this type are called semiconductors. Their electrical conductivity is generally low when compared with that of such metals as copper, silver, or aluminum.

BASIC UNITS OF SOLIDS

The definition of a solid appears obvious; a solid is generally thought of as being hard and firm. Upon inspection, however, the definition becomes less straightforward. A cube of butter, for example, is hard after being stored in a refrigerator and is clearly a solid. After remaining on the kitchen counter for a day, the same cube becomes quite soft, and it is unclear if the butter should still be considered a solid. Many crystals behave like butter in that they are hard at low temperatures but soft at higher temperatures. They are called solids at all temperatures below their melting point. A possible definition of a solid is an object that retains its shape if left undisturbed. The pertinent issue is how long the object keeps its shape. A highly viscous fluid retains its shape for an hour but not a year. A solid must keep its shape longer than that.

The basic units of solids are either atoms or atoms that have combined into molecules. The electrons of an atom move in orbits that form a shell structure around the nucleus. The shells are filled in a systematic order, with each shell accommodating only a small number of electrons. Different atoms have different numbers of electrons, which are distributed in a characteristic electronic structure of filled and partially filled shells. The arrangement of an atom's electrons determines its chemical properties. The properties of solids are usually predictable from the properties of their constituent atoms and molecules, and the different shell structures of atoms are therefore responsible for the diversity of solids.

All occupied shells of the argon (Ar) atom, for example, are filled, resulting in a spherical atomic shape. In solid argon the atoms are arranged according to the closest packing of these spheres. The iron (Fe) atom, in contrast, has one electron shell that is only partially filled, giving the atom a net magnetic moment. Thus, crystalline iron is a magnet. The covalent bond between two carbon (C) atoms is the strongest bond found in nature. This strong bond is responsible for making diamond the hardest solid.

LONG- AND SHORT-RANGE ORDER

A solid is crystalline if it has long-range order. Once the positions of an atom and its neighbours are known at one point, the place of each atom is known precisely throughout the crystal. Most liquids lack long-range order, although many have short-range order. Short range is defined as the first- or second-nearest neighbours of an atom. In many liquids the first-neighbour atoms are arranged in the same structure as in the corresponding solid phase. At distances that are many atoms away, however, the positions of the atoms become uncorrelated. These fluids, such as water, have short-range order but lack long-range order. Certain liquids may have short-range order in one direction and long-range order in another direction; these special substances are called liquid crystals. Solid crystals have both short-range order and long-range order.

Solids that have short-range order but lack long-range order are called amorphous. Almost any material can be made amorphous by rapid solidification from the melt (molten state). This condition is unstable, and the solid will crystallize in time. If the timescale for crystallization is years, then the amorphous state appears stable. Glasses are an example of amorphous solids. In crystalline silicon (Si) each atom is tetrahedrally bonded to four neighbours. In amorphous silicon (a-Si) the same short-range order exists, but the bond directions become changed at distances farther away from any atom. Amorphous silicon is a type of glass. Quasicrystals are another type of solid that lack long-range order.

Most solid materials found in nature exist in polycrystalline form rather than as a single crystal. They are actually composed of millions of grains (small crystals) packed together to fill all space. Each individual grain has a different orientation from its neighbours. Although long-range order exists within one grain, at the boundary between grains, the ordering changes direction. A typical piece of iron or copper (Cu) is polycrystalline. Single crystals of metals are soft and malleable, while polycrystalline metals are harder and stronger and are more useful industrially. Most polycrystalline materials can be made into large single crystals after extended heat treatment. In the past blacksmiths would heat a piece of metal to make it malleable: heat makes a few grains grow large by incorporating smaller ones. The smiths would bend the softened metal into shape and then pound it awhile; the pounding would make it polycrystalline again, increasing its strength.

CATEGORIES OF CRYSTALS

Crystals are classified in general categories, such as insulators, metals, semiconductors, and molecular solids. A single crystal of an insulator is usually transparent and resembles a piece of glass. Metals are shiny unless they have rusted. Semiconductors are sometimes shiny and sometimes transparent but are never rusty. Many crystals can be classified as a single type of solid, while others have intermediate behaviour. Cadmium sulfide (CdS) can be prepared in pure form and is an excellent insulator; when impurities are added to cadmium sulfide, it becomes an interesting semiconductor. Bismuth (Bi) appears to be a metal, but the number of electrons available for electrical conduction is similar to that of semiconductors. In fact, bismuth is called a semimetal. Molecular solids are usually crystals formed from molecules or polymers. They can be insulating, semiconducting, or metallic, depending on the type of molecules in the crystal. New molecules are continuously being synthesized, and many are made into crystals. The number of different crystals is enormous.

STRUCTURE

Crystals can be grown under moderate conditions from all 92 naturally occurring elements except helium, and helium can be crystallized at low temperatures by using 25 atmospheres of pressure. Binary crystals are composed of two elements. There are thousands of binary crystals; some examples are sodium chloride (NaCl), alumina (Al_2O_3), and ice (H_2O). Crystals can also be formed with three or more elements.

THE UNIT CELL

A basic concept in crystal structures is the unit cell. It is the smallest unit of volume that permits identical cells to be stacked together to fill all space. By repeating the pattern of the unit cell over and over in all directions, the entire crystal lattice can be constructed. A cube is the simplest

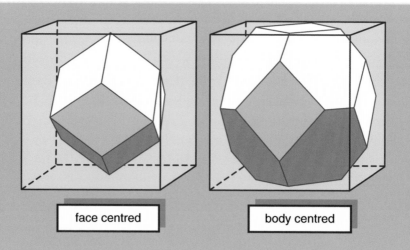

face centred

body centred

Unit cells for face-centred and body-centred cubic lattices. Copyright Encyclopædia Britannica; rendering for this edition by Rosen Educational Services

example of a unit cell. Two other examples are the face-centred cubic lattice and the body-centred cubic lattice.

There are only a few different unit-cell shapes, so many different crystals share a single unit-cell type. An important characteristic of a unit cell is the number of atoms it contains. The total number of atoms in the entire crystal is the number in each cell multiplied by the number of unit cells. Copper and aluminum (Al) each have one atom per unit cell, while zinc (Zn) and sodium chloride have two. Most crystals have only a few atoms per unit cell, but there are some exceptions. Crystals of polymers, for example, have thousands of atoms in each unit cell.

STRUCTURES OF METALS

The elements are found in a variety of crystal packing arrangements. The most common lattice structures for metals are those obtained by stacking the atomic spheres into the most compact arrangement. There are two such possible periodic arrangements. In each, the first layer has the atoms packed into a plane-triangular lattice in which every atom has six immediate neighbours. The second layer has the same plane-triangular structure; the atoms sit in the holes formed by the first layer. The first layer has two equivalent sets of holes, but the atoms of the second layer can occupy only one set. The third layer, labeled C, has the same structure, but there are two choices for selecting the holes that the atoms will occupy. The third layer can be placed over the atoms of the first layer, generating an alternate layer sequence $ABABAB$ . . . , which is called the hexagonal closest-packed (hcp) structure. Cadmium and zinc crystallize with this structure.

The second possibility is to place the atoms of the third layer over those of neither of the first two but instead over

The atoms of the second layer (black, or *B*) sit in the holes formed by the atoms of the first layer (labeled *A*). If the atoms of the third layer are placed in positions labeled *C* and the structure is repeated (*ABCABC*...), the face-centred cubic lattice is formed. If the third layer is placed directly over the atoms of the first layer (*A*) and the structure is repeated (*ABABAB*...), the hexagonal closest-packed arrangement is obtained.

Stacking of spheres in closest-packed arrangements. Copyright Encyclopædia Britannica; rendering for this edition by Rosen Educational Services

the set of holes in the first layer that remains unoccupied. The fourth layer is placed over the first, and so there is a three-layer repetition *ABCABCABC* . . . , which is called the face-centred cubic (fcc), or cubic-closest-packed, lattice. Copper, silver (Ag), and gold (Au) crystallize in fcc lattices. In the hcp and the fcc structures the spheres fill 74 percent of the volume, which represents the closest possible packing of spheres. Each atom has 12 neighbours. The number of atoms in a unit cell is two for hcp structures and one for fcc. There are 32 metals that have the hcp lattice and 26 with the fcc. Another possible arrangement is the body-centred cubic (bcc) lattice, in which each atom has eight neighbours arranged at the corners of a cube. For example, the cesium chloride (CsCl) structure is a cubic arrangement. If all atoms in this structure are of the same species, it is a bcc lattice. The spheres occupy 68 percent of the volume. There are 23 metals with the bcc arrangement. The sum of these three numbers (32 + 26 + 23) exceeds the number of elements that form metals (63), since some elements are found in two or three of these structures.

The fcc structure is also found for crystals of the rare gas solids neon (Ne), argon (Ar), krypton (Kr), and xenon (Xe). Their melting temperatures at atmospheric pressure are: Ne, 24.6 K (-248.5 °C, or -415.4 °F); Ar, 83.8 K (-189.4 °C, or -308.8 °F); Kr, 115.8 K (-157.4 °C, or -251.2 °F); and Xe, 161.4 K (-111.8 °C, or -169.2 °F).

STRUCTURES OF NONMETALLIC ELEMENTS

The elements in the fourth row of the periodic table—carbon, silicon, germanium (Ge), and a-tin (a-Sn)—prefer covalent bonding. Carbon has several possible crystal structures. Each atom in the covalent bond has four first-neighbours, which are at the corners of a tetrahedron. This arrangement is called the diamond lattice. There are two atoms in a unit cell, which is fcc. Large crystals of diamond are valuable gemstones. The crystal has other interesting properties; it has the highest sound velocity of any solid and is the best conductor of heat. Besides diamond, the other common form of carbon is graphite, which is a layered material. Each carbon atom has three coplanar near neighbours, forming an arrangement called the honeycomb lattice. Three-dimensional graphite crystals are obtained by stacking similar layers.

Another form of crystalline carbon is based on a molecule with 60 carbon atoms called buckminsterfullerene (C_{60}). The molecular shape is spherical. Each carbon is bonded to three neighbours, as in graphite, and the spherical shape is achieved by a mixture of 12 rings with five sides and 20 rings with six sides. Similar structures were first visualized by the American architect R. Buckminster Fuller for geodesic domes. The C_{60} molecules, also called buckyballs, are quite strong and almost incompressible. Crystals are formed such that the balls are arranged in an fcc lattice with a one-nanometre spacing between the centres of adjacent balls. The similar C_{70} molecule has the shape of a rugby ball; C_{70} molecules also form an fcc crystal when stacked together. The solid fullerenes form molecular crystals, with weak binding—provided by van der Waals interactions—between the molecules.

Many elements form diatomic gases: hydrogen (H), oxygen (O), nitrogen (N), fluorine (F), chlorine (Cl), bromine (Br), and iodine (I). When cooled to low temperature, they form solids of diatomic molecules. Nitrogen has the hcp structure, while oxygen has a more complex structure.

The most interesting crystal structures are those of elements that are neither metallic, covalent, nor diatomic. Although boron (B) and sulfur (S) have several different crystal structures, each has one arrangement in which it is usually found. Twelve boron atoms form a molecule in the shape of an icosahedron. Crystals are formed by stacking the molecules. The β-rhombohedral structure of boron

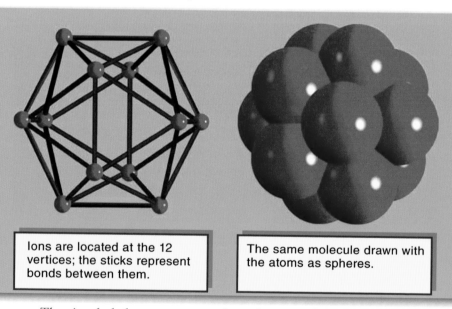

Ions are located at the 12 vertices; the sticks represent bonds between them.

The same molecule drawn with the atoms as spheres.

The icosahedral arrangement of a boron molecule. Copyright Encyclopædia Britannica; rendering for this edition by Rosen Educational Services

CRYSTALLINE SOLIDS AND LIQUID CRYSTALS

has seven of these icosahedral molecules in each unit cell, giving a total of 84 atoms. Molecules of sulfur are usually arranged in rings; the most common ring has eight atoms. The typical structure is a-sulfur, which has 16 molecules per unit cell, or 128 atoms. In the common crystals of selenium (Se) and tellurium (Te), the atoms are arranged in helical chains, which stack like cordwood. However, selenium also makes eight-atom rings, similar to sulfur, and forms crystals from them. Sulfur also makes helical chains, similar to selenium, and stacks them together into crystals.

STRUCTURES OF BINARY CRYSTALS

Binary crystals are found in many structures. Some pairs of elements form more than one structure. At room temperature, cadmium sulfide may crystallize either in the zinc blende or wurtzite structure. Alumina also has two possible structures at room temperature, a-alumina (corundum) and β-alumina. Other binary crystals exhibit different structures at different temperatures. Among the most complex crystals are those of silicon dioxide (SiO_2), which has seven different structures at various temperatures and pressures; the most common of these structures is quartz. Some pairs of elements form several different crystals in which the ions have different chemical valences. Cadmium (Cd) and phosphorus (P) form the crystals Cd_3P_2, CdP_2, CdP_4, Cd_7P_{10}, and Cd_6P_7. Only in the first case are the ions assigned the expected chemical valences of Cd^{2+} and P^{3-}.

Among the binary crystals, the easiest structures to visualize are those with equal numbers of the two types of atoms. The structure of sodium chloride is based on a cube. To construct the lattice, the sodium and chlorine atoms are placed on alternate corners of a cube, and the

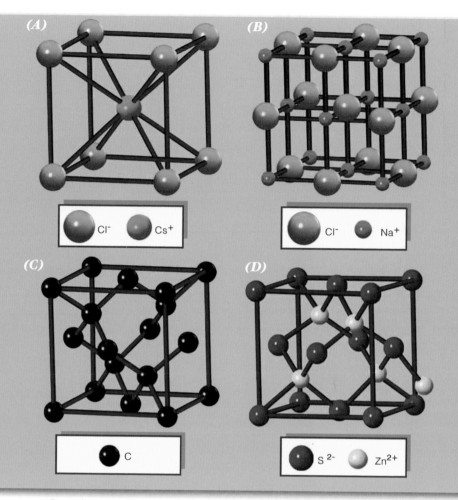

Crystal structures. There is an equal number of the two types of ions in the unit cell of the (A) cesium chloride, (B) sodium chloride, and (D) zinc blende arrangements. The diamond arrangement is shown in (C). If both atoms are identical in (A), the structure is body-centred cubic. Copyright Encyclopædia Britannica; rendering for this edition by Rosen Educational Services

structure is repeated. The structure of the sodium atoms alone, or the chlorine atoms alone, is fcc and defines the unit cell. The sodium chloride structure thus is made up of two interpenetrating fcc lattices. The cesium chloride lattice is based on the bcc structure; every other atom is cesium or chlorine. In this case, the unit cell is a cube. The third important structure for AB (binary) lattices is zinc blende. It is based on the diamond structure, where every other atom is A or B. Many binary semiconductors have this structure, including those with one atom from the third (boron, aluminum, gallium [Ga], or indium [In]) and one from the fifth (nitrogen, phosphorus, arsenic [As], or antimony [Sb]) column of the periodic table (GaAs, InP, etc.). Most of the chalcogenides (O, S, Se, Te) of cadmium and zinc (CdTe, ZnSe, ZnTe, etc.) also have the zinc blende structure. The mineral zinc blende is ZnS; its unit cell is also fcc. The wurtzite structure is based on the hcp lattice, where every other atom is A or B. These four structures comprise most of the binary crystals with equal numbers of cations and anions.

The fullerene molecule forms binary crystals $M_x C_{60}$ with alkali atoms, where M is potassium (K), rubidium (Rb), or cesium (Cs). The fullerene molecules retain their spherical shape, and the alkali atoms sit between them. The subscript x can take on several values. A compound with $x = 6$ (e.g., $K_6 C_{60}$) is an insulator with the fullerenes in a bcc structure. The case $x = 4$ is an insulator with the body-centred tetragonal structure, while the case $x = 3$ is a metal with the fullerenes in an fcc structure. $K_3 C_{60}$, $Rb_3 C_{60}$, and $Cs_3 C_{60}$ are superconductors at low temperatures.

ALLOYS

Alloys are solid mixtures of atoms with metallic properties. The definition includes both amorphous and crystalline solids. Although many pairs of elements will mix together as solids, many pairs will not. Almost all chemical entities can be mixed in liquid form. But cooling a liquid to form a solid often results in phase separation; a polycrystalline material is obtained in which each grain is purely one atom or the other. Extremely rapid cooling can produce an amorphous alloy. Some pairs of elements form alloys that are metallic crystals. They have useful properties that differ from those exhibited by the pure elements. For example, alloying makes a metal stronger; for this reason alloys of gold, rather than the pure metal, are used in jewelry.

Atoms tend to form crystalline alloys when they are of similar size. The sizes of atoms are not easy to define, however, because atoms are not rigid objects with sharp boundaries. The outer part of an atom is composed of electrons in bound orbits; the average number of electrons decreases gradually with increasing distance from the nucleus. There is no point that can be assigned as the precise radius of the atom. Scientists have discovered, however, that each atom in a solid has a characteristic radius that determines its preferred separation from neighbouring atoms. For most types of atom this radius is constant, even in different solids. An empirical radius is assigned to each atom for bonding considerations, which leads to the concept of atomic size. Atoms readily make crystalline alloys when the radii of the two types of atoms agree to within roughly 15 percent.

Two kinds of ordering are found in crystalline alloys. Most alloys at low temperature are binary crystals with perfect ordering. An example is the alloy of copper and zinc. Copper is fcc, whereas zinc is hcp. A 50-percent-zinc–50-percent-copper alloy has a different structure—β-brass. At low temperatures it has the cesium chloride structure: a bcc lattice with alternating atoms of copper and zinc and a cubic unit cell. If the temperature is raised above 470 °C (878 °F), however, a phase transition to another crystalline state occurs. The ordering at high temperature is also bcc, but now each site has equal probability of having a copper or zinc atom. The two types of atoms randomly occupy each site, but there is still long-range order. At all temperatures, thousands of atoms away from a site, the location of the atom site can be predicted with certainty. At temperatures below 470 °C one also knows whether that site will be occupied by a copper or zinc atom, while above 470 °C there is an equal likelihood of finding either atom. The high-temperature phase is crystalline but disordered. The disorder phase is obtained through a partial melting, not into a liquid state but into a less ordered one. This behaviour is typical of metal alloys. Other common alloys are steel, an alloy of iron and carbon; stainless steel, an alloy of iron, nickel (Ni), and chromium (Cr); pewter and solder, alloys of tin and lead (Pb); and britannia metal, an alloy of tin, antimony, and copper.

CRYSTAL DEFECTS

A crystal is never perfect; a variety of imperfections can mar the ordering. A defect is a small imperfection affecting a few atoms. The simplest type of defect is a missing atom and is called a vacancy. Since all atoms occupy space, extra atoms cannot be located at the lattice sites of other atoms, but they can be found between them; such atoms are called interstitials. Thermal vibrations may cause an atom to leave its original crystal site and move into a nearby interstitial site, creating a vacancy-interstitial pair. Vacancies and interstitials are the types of defects found in a pure crystal. In another defect, called an impurity, an atom is present that is different from the host crystal atoms. Impurities may either occupy interstitial spaces or substitute for a host atom in its lattice site.

There is no sharp distinction between an alloy and a crystal with many impurities. An alloy results when a sufficient number of impurities are added that are soluble in the host metal. However, most elements are not soluble in most crystals. Crystals generally can tolerate a few impurities per million host atoms. If too many impurities of the insoluble variety are added, they coalesce to form their own small crystallite. These inclusions are called precipitates and constitute a large defect.

Germanium is a common impurity in silicon. It prefers the same tetrahedral bonding as silicon and readily substitutes for silicon atoms. Similarly, silicon is a common impurity in germanium. No large crystal can be made without impurities; the purest large crystal ever grown was made of germanium. It had about 10^{10} impurities in each cubic centimetre of material, which is less than one impurity for each trillion atoms.

Impurities often make crystals more useful. In the absence of impurities, a-alumina is colourless. Iron and titanium impurities impart to it a blue colour, and the resulting gem-quality mineral is known as sapphire. Chromium impurities are responsible for the red colour characteristic of rubies, the other gem of a-alumina. Pure semiconductors rarely conduct electricity well at room temperatures. Their ability to conduct electricity is caused by impurities. Such impurities are deliberately added to silicon in the manufacture of integrated circuits. In fluorescent lamps the visible light is emitted by impurities in the phosphors (luminescent materials).

Other imperfections in crystals involve many atoms. Twinning is a special type of grain boundary defect, in which a crystal is joined to its mirror image. Another kind of imperfection is a dislocation, which is a line defect that may run the length of the crystal. One of the many types of dislocations is due to an extra plane of atoms that is inserted somewhere in the crystal structure. Another type is called an edge dislocation. This line defect occurs when there is a missing row of atoms. In the figure the crystal arrangement is perfect on the top and on the bottom. The

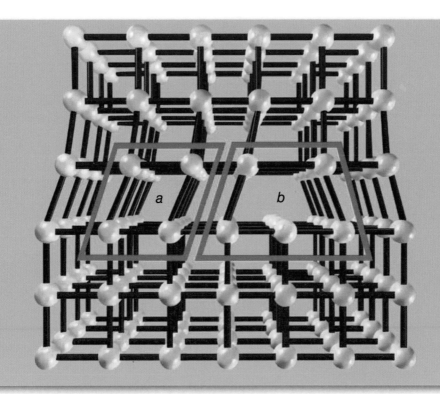

Crystalline lattice defect. An edge dislocation occurs when there is a missing row of atoms as shown in region b. Region a is strained. Copyright Encyclopædia Britannica; rendering for this edition by Rosen Educational Services

defect is the row of atoms missing from region *b*. This mistake runs in a line that is perpendicular to the page and places a strain on region *a*.

Dislocations are formed when a crystal is grown, and great care must be taken to produce a crystal free of them. Dislocations are stable and will exist for years. They relieve mechanical stress. If one presses on a crystal, it will accommodate the induced stress by growing dislocations at the surface, which gradually move inward. Dislocations make a crystal mechanically harder. When a metal bar is cold-worked by rolling or hammering, dislocations and grain boundaries are introduced; this causes the hardening.

DETERMINATION OF CRYSTAL STRUCTURES

Crystal structures are determined by scattering experiments using a portion of the crystal as the target. A beam of particles is sent toward the target, and upon impact some of the particles scatter from the crystal and ricochet in various directions. A measurement of the scattered particles provides raw data, which is then computer-processed to give a picture of the atomic arrangements. The positions are then inferred from the computer-analyzed data.

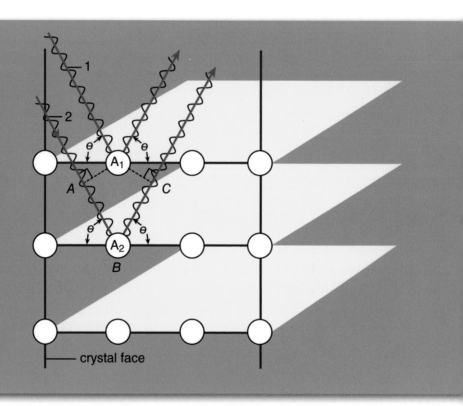

Incident rays (1 and 2) at angle θ on the planes of atoms in a crystal. Rays reinforce if their difference in path length (AB + BC) is an integer times the wavelength of the X ray. Copyright Encyclopædia Britannica; rendering for this edition by Rosen Educational Services

Max von Laue first suggested in 1912 that this measurement could be done using X rays, which are electromagnetic radiation of very high frequency. High frequencies are needed because these waves have a short wavelength. Von Laue realized that atoms have a spacing of only a few angstroms (1 angstrom [Å] is 10^{-10} metre, or 3.94×10^{-9} inch). In order to measure atomic arrangements, the particles scattering from the target must also have a wavelength of a few angstroms. X rays are required when the beam consists of electromagnetic radiation. The X rays only scatter in certain directions, and there are many X rays associated with each direction. The scattered particles appear in spots corresponding to locations where the scattering from each identical atom produces an outgoing wave that has all the wavelengths in phase. The scattering from an atom A_2 further in the crystal has a longer path than that from atom A_1. If this additional path has a length $(AB + BC)$ that is an exact multiple of the wavelength, then the two outgoing waves are in phase and reinforce each other. If the scattering angle is changed slightly, the waves no longer add coherently and begin to cancel one another. Combining the scattered radiation from all the atoms in the crystal causes all the outgoing waves to add coherently in certain directions and produce a strong signal in the scattered wave. If the extra path length $(AB + BC)$ is five wavelengths, for example, the spot appears in one place. If it is six wavelengths, the spot is elsewhere. Thus, the different spots correspond to the different multiples of the wavelength of the X ray. The measurement produces two types of information: the directions of the spots and their intensity. This information is insufficient to deduce the exact crystal structure, however, as there is no algorithm by which the computer can go directly from the data to the structure. The crystallographer must propose various structures and compute how they would scatter the X rays. The theoretical results are compared with the measured one, and the theoretical arrangement is chosen that best fits the data. Although this procedure is fast when there are only a few atoms in a unit cell, it may take months or years for complex structures. Some protein molecules, for instance, have hundreds of atoms. Crystals of the proteins are grown, and X rays are used to measure the structure. The goal is to determine how the atoms are arranged in the protein, rather than how the proteins are arranged in the crystal.

Beams of neutrons may also be used to measure crystal structure. The beam of neutrons is obtained by drilling a hole in the side of a nuclear reactor. The energetic neutrons created in nuclear fission escape through the hole. The motion of elementary particles is governed by quantum, or wave, mechanics. Each neutron has a wavelength that depends on its momentum. The scattering directions are determined by the wavelength, as is the case with X rays. The wavelengths for neutrons from a reactor are suitable for measuring crystal structures.

X rays and neutrons provide the basis for two competing technologies in crystallography. Although they are similar in principle, the two methods have some differences. X rays scatter from the electrons in the atoms so that more electrons result in more scattering. X rays easily detect atoms of high atomic number, which have many electrons, but cannot readily locate atoms with few electrons. In hydrogen-bonded crystals, X rays do not detect the protons at all. Neutrons, on the other hand, scatter from the atomic nucleus. They scatter readily from protons and are excellent for determining the structure of hydrogen-bonded solids. One drawback to this method is that some nuclei absorb neutrons completely, and there is little scattering from these targets.

Beams of electrons can also be used to measure crystal structure, because energetic electrons have a wavelength that is suitable for such measurements. The problem with electrons is that they scatter strongly from atoms. Proper interpretation of the experimental results requires that an electron scatter only from one atom and leave the crystal without scattering again. Low-energy electrons scatter many times, and the interpretation must reflect this. Low-energy electron diffraction (LEED) is a technique in which a beam of electrons is directed toward the surface. The scattered electrons that reflect backward from the surface are measured. They scatter many times before leaving backward but mainly leave in a few directions that appear as "spots" in the measurements. An analysis of the varied spots gives information on the crystalline arrangement. Because the electrons are scattered strongly by the atoms in the first few layers of the surface, the measurement gives only the arrangements of atoms in these layers. It is assumed that the same structure is repeated throughout the crystal. Another scattering experiment involves electrons of extremely high energy. The scattering rate decreases as the energy of the electron increases, so that very energetic electrons usually scatter only once. Various electron microscopes are constructed on this principle.

TYPES OF BONDS

The properties of a solid can usually be predicted from the valence and bonding preferences of its constituent atoms. Four main bonding types are discussed here: ionic, covalent, metallic, and molecular. Hydrogen-bonded solids, such as ice, make up another category that is important in a few crystals. There are many examples of solids that have a single bonding type, while other solids have a mixture of types, such as covalent and metallic or covalent and ionic.

IONIC BONDS

Sodium chloride exhibits ionic bonding. The sodium atom has a single electron in its outermost shell, while chlorine needs one electron to fill its outer shell. Sodium donates one electron to chlorine, forming a sodium ion (Na^+) and a chlorine ion (Cl^-). Each ion thus attains a closed outer shell of electrons and takes on a spherical shape. In addition to having filled shells and a spherical shape, the ions of an ionic solid have integer valence. An ion with positive valence is called a cation. In an ionic solid the cations are surrounded by ions with negative valence, called anions. Similarly, each anion is surrounded by cations. Since opposite charges attract, the preferred bonding occurs when each ion has as many neighbours as possible, consistent with the ion radii. Six or eight nearest neighbours are typical; the number depends on the size of the ions and not on the bond angles. The alkali halide crystals are binaries of the AH type, where A is an alkali ion (lithium [Li], sodium, potassium, rubidium, or cesium) and H is a halide ion (fluorine, chlorine, bromine, or iodine). The crystals have ionic bonding, and each ion has six or eight neighbours. Metal ions in the alkaline earth series (magnesium [Mg], calcium [Ca], barium [Ba], and strontium [Sr]) have two electrons in their outer shells and form divalent cations in ionic crystals. The chalcogenides (oxygen, sulfur, selenium, and tellurium) need two electrons to fill their outer p-shell. (Electron shells are divided into subshells, designated as s, p, d, f, g, and so forth. Each subshell is divided further into orbitals.) Two electrons are transferred from the cations to the anions, leaving each with a closed shell. The alkaline earth chalcogenides form ionic binary crystals such as barium oxide (BaO), calcium sulfide (CaS), barium selenide (BaSe), or strontium oxide (SrO). They have the same structure as sodium chloride, with each atom having six neighbours. Oxygen can be combined with various cations to form a large number of ionically bonded solids.

COVALENT BONDS

Silicon, carbon, germanium, and a few other elements form covalently bonded solids. In these elements there are four electrons in the outer sp-shell, which is half filled. (The sp-shell is a hybrid formed from one s and one p subshell.) In the covalent bond an atom shares one valence (outer-shell) electron with each of its four nearest neighbour atoms. The bonds are highly directional and prefer a tetrahedral arrangement. A covalent bond is formed by two electrons — one from each atom — located in orbitals between the ions. Insulators, in contrast, have all their electrons within shells inside the atoms.

The perpetual spin of an electron is an important aspect of the covalent bond. From a vantage point above the spinning particle, counterclockwise rotation is designated spin-up, while clockwise rotation is spin-down. A fundamental law of quantum physics is the Pauli exclusion principle, which states that no two electrons can occupy the same point in space at the same time with the same direction of spin. In a covalent bond two electrons occupy the same small volume of space (i.e., the same orbital) at all times, so they must have opposite spin: one up and one down. The exclusion principle is then satisfied, and the resulting bond is strong.

In graphite the carbon atoms are arranged in parallel sheets, and each atom has only three near neighbours. The covalent bonds between adjacent carbons within each layer are quite strong and are called σ bonds. The fourth valence electron in carbon has its orbital perpendicular to the plane. This orbital bonds weakly with the similar orbitals on all three neighbours, forming π bonds. The four bonds for each carbon atom in the graphite structure are not arranged in a tetrahedron; three are in a plane. The planar arrangement results in strong bonding, although not as strong as the bonding in the diamond configuration. The bonding between layers is quite weak and arises from the van der Waals interaction; there is much slippage parallel to the layers. Diamond and graphite form an interesting contrast: diamond is the hardest material in nature and is used as an abrasive, while graphite is used as a lubricant.

Besides the elemental semiconductors, such as silicon and germanium, some binary crystals are covalently bonded. Gallium has three electrons in the outer shell, while arsenic lacks three. Gallium arsenide (GaAs) could be formed as an insulator by transferring three electrons from gallium to arsenic; however, this does not occur. Instead, the bonding is more covalent, and gallium arsenide is a covalent semiconductor. The outer shells of the gallium atoms contribute three electrons, and those of the arsenic atoms contribute five, providing the eight electrons needed for four covalent bonds. The centres of the bonds are not at the midpoint between the ions but are shifted slightly toward the arsenic. Such bonding is typical of the III–V semiconductors—i.e., those consisting of one element from the third column of the periodic table and one from the fifth column. Elements from the third column (boron, aluminum, gallium, and indium) contribute three electrons, while the fifth-column elements (nitrogen, phosphorus, arsenic, and antimony) contribute five electrons. All III–V semiconductors are covalently bonded and typically have the zinc blende structure with four neighbours per atom. Most common semiconductors favour this arrangement.

The factor that determines whether a binary crystal will act as an insulator or a semiconductor is the valence of its constituent atoms. Ions that donate or accept one or two valence electrons form insulators. Those that have three to five valence electrons tend to have covalent bonds and form semiconductors. There are exceptions to these rules, however, as is the case with the IV–VI semiconductors such as lead sulfide. Heavier elements from the fourth column of the periodic table (germanium, tin, and lead) combine with the chalcogenides from the sixth row to form good binary semiconductors such as germanium telluride (GeTe) or tin sulfide (SnS). They have the sodium chloride structure, where each atom has six neighbours. Although not tetrahedrally bonded, they are good semiconductors.

Filled atomic shells with d-orbitals have an important role in covalent bonding. Electrons in atomic orbits have angular momentum (L), which is quantized in integer (n) multiples of Planck's constant h: $L = nh$. Electron orbitals with $n = 0$ are called s-states, with $n = 1$ are p-states, and with $n = 2$ are d-states. Silver and copper ions have one valence electron outside their closed shells. The outermost filled shell is a d-state and affects the bonding. Eight binary crystals are formed from the copper and silver halides. Three (AgF, AgCl, AgBr) have the sodium chloride structure with six neighbours. The other five (AgI, CuF, CuCl, CuBr, CuI) have the zinc blende structure with four neighbours. The bonding in this group of solids is on the borderline between covalent and ionic, since the crystals prefer both types of bonds. The alkali metal halides exhibit somewhat different behaviour. The alkali metals are also monovalent cations, but their halides are strictly ionic. The difference in bonding between the alkali metals on the one hand and silver and copper on the other hand is that silver and copper have filled d-shells while the alkalis have filled p-shells. Since the d-shells are filled, they do not covalently bond. This group of electrons is, however, highly polarizable, which influences the bonding of the valence electrons. Similar behaviour is found for zinc and cadmium, which have two valence electrons outside a filled d-shell. They form binary crystals with the chalcogenides, which have tetrahedral bonding. In this case the covalent bonding seems to be preferred over the ionic bond. In contrast, the alkaline earth chalcogenides, which are also divalent, have outer p-shells and are ionic. The zinc and cadmium chalcogenides are covalent, as the outer d-shell electrons of the two cations favour covalent bonding.

METALLIC BONDS

Metallic bonds fall into two categories. The first is the case in which the valence electrons are from the sp-shells of the metal ions; this bonding is quite weak. In the second category the valence electrons are from partially filled d-shells, and this bonding is quite strong. The d-bonds dominate when both types of bonding are present.

The simple metals are bonded with sp-electrons. The electrons of these metal atoms are in filled atomic shells except for a few electrons that are in unfilled sp-shells. The electrons from the unfilled shells are detached from the metal ion and are free to wander throughout the crystal. They are called conduction electrons, since they are responsible for the electrical conductivity of metals. Although the conduction electrons may roam anywhere in the crystal, they are distributed uniformly throughout the entire solid. Any large imbalance of charge is prevented by the strong electrical attraction between the negative electrons and the positive ions, plus the strong repulsion between electrons. The phrase electron correlation describes the correlated movements of the electrons; the motion of each electron depends on the positions of neighbouring electrons. Electrons have strong short-range order with one another. Correlation ensures that each unit cell in the crystal has, on the average, the number of electrons needed to cancel the positive charge of the cation so that the unit cell is electrically neutral.

Cohesive energy is the energy gained by arranging the atoms in a crystalline state, as compared with the gas state. Insulators and semiconductors have large cohesive energies; these solids are bound together strongly and have good mechanical strength. Metals with electrons in sp-bonds have very small cohesive energies. This type of metallic bond is weak; the crystals are barely held together. Single crystals of simple metals such as sodium are mechanically weak. At room temperature the crystals have the mechanical consistency of warm butter. Special care must be used in handling these crystals, because they are easily distorted. Metals such as magnesium or aluminum must be alloyed or polycrystalline to have any mechanical strength. Although the simple metals are found in a variety of structures, most are in one of the three closest-packed structures: fcc, bcc, and hcp. Theoretical calculations show that the cohesive energy of a given metal is almost the same in each of the different crystal arrangements; therefore, crystal arrangements are unimportant in metals bound with electrons from sp-shells.

A different type of metallic bonding is found in transition metals, which are metals whose atoms are characterized by unfilled d-shells. The d-orbitals are more tightly bound to an ion than the sp-orbitals. Electrons in d-shells do not wander away from the ion. The d-orbitals form a covalent bond with the d-orbitals on the neighbouring atoms. The bonding of d-orbitals does not occur in a tetrahedral arrangement but has a different directional preference. In metals the bonds from d-orbitals are not completely filled with electrons. This situation is different from the tetrahedral bonds in semiconductors, which are filled with eight electrons. In transition metals the covalent bonds formed with the d-electrons are much stronger than the weak bonds made with the sp-electrons of simple metals. The cohesive energy is much larger in transition metals. Titanium, iron, and tungsten, for example, have exceptional mechanical strength. Crystal arrangements are important in the behaviour of the transition metals and occur in the close-packed fcc, bcc, or hcp arrangements.

MOLECULAR BINDING

The Dutch physicist Johannes D. van der Waals first proposed the force that binds molecular solids. Any two atoms or molecules have a force of attraction (F) that varies according to the inverse seventh power of the distance R between the centres of the atoms or molecules: $F = -C/R^7$, where C is a constant. The force, known as the van der Waals force, declines rapidly with the distance R and is quite weak. If the atoms or molecules have a net charge, there is a strong force whose strength varies according to Coulomb's law as the inverse second power of the separation distance: $F = -C'/R^2$, where C' is a constant. This force provides the binding in ionic crystals and some of the binding in metals. Coulomb's law does not apply to atoms or molecules without a net charge. Molecules with a dipole moment, such as water, have a strong attractive force owing to the interactions between the dipoles. For atoms and molecules with neither net charges nor dipole moments, the van der Waals force provides the crystal binding. The force of gravity also acts between neutral atoms and molecules, but it is far too weak to bind molecules into crystals.

The van der Waals force is caused by quantum fluctuations. Two neighbouring atoms that are each fluctuating can lower their joint energy by correlating their fluctuations. The van der Waals force arises from correlations in their dipole fluctuations. Electrons bound in atomic orbits are in constant motion around the nucleus, and the distribution of charges in the atom changes constantly as the electrons move, owing to quantum fluctuations. One fluctuation might produce a momentary electric dipole moment (i.e., a separation of charges) on an atom if a majority of its electrons are on one side of the nucleus. The dipole moment creates an electric field on a neighbouring atom; this field will induce a dipole moment on the second atom. The two dipoles attract one another via the van der Waals interaction. Since the force depends on the inverse seventh power of the distance, it declines rapidly with increasing distance. Atoms have a typical radius of one to three angstroms. The van der Waals force binds atoms and molecules within a few angstroms of each other; beyond that distance the force is negligible. Although weak, the van der Waals force is always present and is important in cases where the other forces are absent.

Hydrogen is rarely found as a single atom. Instead it forms diatomic molecules (H_2), which are gaseous at room temperature. At lower temperatures the hydrogen becomes a liquid and at about 20 K turns into a solid. The molecule retains its identity in the liquid and solid states. The solid exists as a molecular crystal of covalently bound H_2 molecules. The molecules attract one another by van der Waals forces, which provide the crystal binding. Helium, the second element in the periodic table, has two electrons, which constitute a filled atomic shell. In its liquid and solid states, the helium atoms are bound together by van der Waals forces. In fact, all the rare gases (helium, neon, argon, krypton, and xenon) are molecular crystals with the binding provided by van der Waals forces.

Many organic molecules form crystals where the molecules are bound by van der Waals forces. In methane (CH_4), a central carbon makes a covalent bond with each hydrogen atom, forming a tetrahedron. In crystalline methane the molecules are arranged in the fcc structure. Benzene (C_6H_6) has the carbon atoms in a hexagonal ring; each carbon has three coplanar σ bonds, as in graphite, where two bonds are with neighbouring carbon atoms and the third bond is with a hydrogen atom. Crystalline benzene has four molecules per unit cell in a complex arrangement. Fullerene and the rare gas atoms are spherical, and the crystalline arrangement corresponds to the closest packing of spheres. Most organic molecules, however, are not spherical and display irregular shapes. For odd-shaped molecules, the van der Waals interaction depends on the rotational orientation of the two molecules. In order to maximize the force, the molecules in the crystal have unusual arrangements, as in the case of benzene.

HYDROGEN BONDING

Hydrogen bonding is important in a few crystals, notably in ice. With its lone electron, a hydrogen atom usually forms a single covalent bond with an electronegative atom. In the hydrogen bond the atom is ionized to a proton. The proton sits between two anions and joins them. Hydrogen bonding occurs with only the most electronegative ions: nitrogen, oxygen, and fluorine. In water the hydrogen links pairs of oxygen ions. Water is found in many different crystal structures, but they all have the feature that the hydrogen atoms sit between pairs of oxygen. Another hydrogen-bonded solid is hydrogen fluoride (HF), in which the hydrogen atom (proton) links pairs of fluorines.

CRYSTAL GROWTH

The earliest crystal grower was nature. Many excellent crystals of minerals formed in the geologic past are found in mines and caves throughout the world. Most precious and semiprecious stones are well-formed crystals. Early efforts to produce synthetic crystals were concentrated on making gems. Synthetic ruby was grown by the French scientist Marc Antoine Augustin Gaudin in 1873. Since about 1950 scientists have learned to grow in the laboratory crystals of quality equal or superior to those found in nature. New techniques for growth are continually being developed, and crystals with three or more atoms per unit cell are continually being discovered.

VAPOUR GROWTH

Crystals can be grown from a vapour when the molecules of the gas attach themselves to a surface and move into the crystal arrangement. Several important conditions must be met for this to occur. At constant temperature and equilibrium conditions, the average number of molecules in the gas and solid states is constant; molecules leave the gas and attach to the surface at the same rate that they leave the surface to become gas molecules. For crystals to grow, the gas-solid chemical system must be in a nonequilibrium state such that there are too many gaseous molecules for the conditions of pressure and temperature. This state is called supersaturation. Molecules are more prone to leave the gas than to rejoin it, so they become deposited on the surface of the container. Supersaturation can be induced by maintaining the crystal at a lower temperature than the gas. A critical stage in the growth of a crystal is seeding, in which a small piece of crystal of the proper structure and orientation, called a seed, is introduced into the container. The gas molecules find the seed a more favourable surface than the walls and preferentially deposit there. Once the molecule is on the surface of the seed, it wanders around this surface to find the preferred site for attachment. Growth proceeds one molecule at a time and one layer at a time. The process is slow; it takes days to grow a small crystal. Crystals are grown at temperatures well below the melting point to reduce the density of defects. The advantage of vapour growth is that very pure crystals can be grown by this method, while the disadvantage is that it is slow.

Most clouds in the atmosphere are ice crystals that form by vapour growth from water molecules. Most raindrops are crystals as they begin descending but thaw during their fall to Earth. Seeding for rain—accomplished by dropping silver iodide crystals from airplanes—is known to induce precipitation. In the laboratory, vapour growth is usually accomplished by flowing a supersaturated gas over a seed crystal. Quite often a chemical reaction at the surface is needed to deposit the atoms. Crystals of silicon can be grown by flowing chlorosilane ($SiCl_4$) and hydrogen (H_2) over a seed crystal of silicon. Hydrogen acts as the buffer gas by controlling the temperature and rate of flow. The molecules dissociate on the surface in a chemical reaction that forms hydrogen chloride (HCl) molecules. Hydrogen chloride molecules leave the surface, while silicon atoms remain to grow into a crystal. Binary crystals such as gallium arsenide (GaAs) are grown by a similar method. One process employs gallium chloride (GaCl) as the gallium carrier. Arsenic is provided by molecules such as arsenous chloride ($AsCl_3$), arsine (AsH_3), or As_4 (yellow arsenic). These molecules, with hydrogen as the buffer gas, grow crystals of gallium arsenide while forming gas molecules such as gallium trichloride ($GaCl_3$) and hydrogen chloride. Trimethylgallium, $(CH_3)_3Ga$, is another molecule that can be used to deliver gallium to the surface.

GROWTH FROM SOLUTION

Large single crystals may be grown from solution. In this technique the seed crystal is immersed in a solvent that contains typically about 10–30 percent of the desired solute. The choice of solvent usually depends on the solubility of the solute. The temperature and pH (a measure of acidity or basicity) of the solution must be well controlled. The method is faster than vapour growth, because there is a higher concentration of molecules at the surface in a liquid as compared to a gas, but it is still relatively slow.

GROWTH FROM THE MELT

This method is the most basic. A gas is cooled until it becomes a liquid, which is then cooled further until it becomes a solid. Polycrystalline solids are typically produced by this method unless special techniques are employed. In any case, the temperature must be controlled carefully. Large crystals can be grown rapidly from the liquid elements using a popular method invented in 1918 by the Polish scientist Jan Czochralski and called crystal pulling. One attaches a seed crystal to the bottom of a vertical arm such that the seed is barely in contact with the material at the surface of the melt. The arm is raised slowly, and a crystal grows underneath at the interface between the crystal and the melt. Usually the crystal is rotated slowly, so that inhomogeneities in the liquid are not replicated in the crystal. Large-diameter crystals of silicon are grown in this way for use as computer chips. Based on measurements of the weight of the crystal during the pulling process, computer-controlled apparatuses can vary the pulling rate to produce any desired diameter.

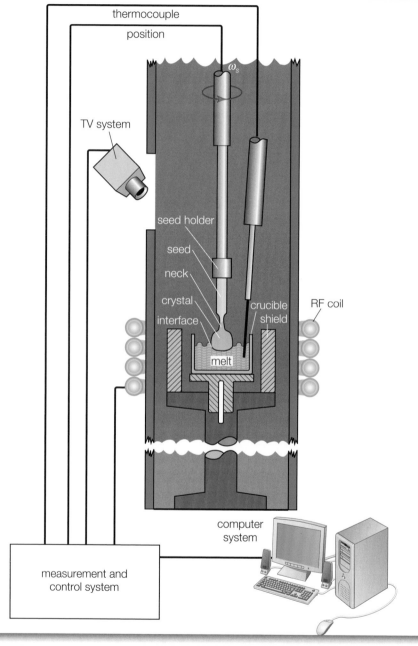

Crystal pulling using the Czochralski method. A schematic view of a modern apparatus. Copyright Encyclopædia Britannica; rendering for this edition by Rosen Educational Services

Crystal pulling is the least expensive way to grow large amounts of pure crystal. The original seed is on the right tip. Binary crystals can also be pulled; for example, synthetic sapphire crystals can be pulled from molten alumina. Special care is required to grow binary and other multicomponent crystals; the temperature must be precisely controlled because such crystals may be grown only at a single, extremely high temperature. The melt has a tendency to be inhomogeneous, since the two liquids may try to separate by gravity.

The Bridgman method (named after the American scientist Percy Williams Bridgman) is also widely used for growing large single crystals. The molten material is put into a crucible, often of silica, which has a cylindrical shape with a conical lower end. Heaters maintain the molten state. As the crucible is slowly lowered into a cooler region, a crystal starts growing in the conical tip. The crucible is lowered at a rate that matches the growth of the crystal, so that the interface between crystal and melt is always at the same temperature. The rate of moving the crucible depends on the temperature and the material. When done successfully, the entire molten material in the crucible grows into a single large crystal. One disadvantage of the method is that excess impurities are pushed out of the crystal during growth. A layer of impurities grows at the interface between melt and solid as this surface moves up the melt, and the impurities become concentrated in the higher part of the crystal.

Epitaxy is the technique of growing a crystal, layer by layer, on the atomically flat surface of another crystal. In homoepitaxy a crystal is grown on a substrate of the same material. Silicon layers of different impurity content, for example, are grown on silicon substrates in the manufacture of computer chips. Heteroepitaxy, on the other hand, is the growth of one crystal on the substrate of another. Silicon substrates are often used since they are readily available in atomically smooth form. Many different semi-conductor crystals can be grown on silicon, such as gallium arsenide, germanium, cadmium telluride (CdTe), and lead telluride (PbTe). Any flat substrate can be used for epitaxy, however, and insulators such as rock salt (NaCl) and magnesium oxide (MgO) are also used.

Molecular-beam epitaxy, commonly abbreviated as MBE, is a form of vapour growth. The field began when the American scientist John Read Arthur reported in 1968 that gallium arsenide could be grown by sending a beam of gallium atoms and arsenic molecules toward the flat surface of a crystal of the molecule. The amount of gas molecules can be controlled to grow just one layer, or just two, or any desired amount. This method is slow, since molecular beams have low densities of atoms. Chemical vapour deposition (CVD) is another form of epitaxy that makes use of the vapour growth technique. Also known as vapour-phase epitaxy (VPE), it is much faster than MBE since the atoms are delivered in a flowing gas rather than in a molecular beam. Synthetic diamonds are grown by CVD. Rapid growth occurs when methane (CH_4) is mixed with atomic hydrogen gas, which serves as a catalyst. Methane dissociates on a heated surface of diamond. The carbon remains on the surface, and the hydrogen leaves as a molecule. Growth rates are several micrometres (1 micrometre is equal to 0.00004 inch) per hour. At that rate, a stone 1 cm (0.4 inch) thick is grown in 18 weeks. CVD diamonds are of poor quality as gemstones but are important electronic materials. Because hydrogen is found in nature as a molecule rather than as a single atom, making atomic hydrogen gas is the major expense in growing CVD diamonds. Liquid-phase epitaxy (LPE) uses the solution method to grow crystals on a substrate. The substrate is placed in a solution with a saturated concentration of solute. This technique is used to grow many crystals employed in modern electronics and optoelectronic devices, such as gallium arsenide, gallium aluminum arsenide, and gallium phosphide.

An important concern in successful epitaxy is matching lattice distances. If the spacing between atoms in the substrate is close to that of the top crystal, then that crystal will grow well; a small difference in lattice distance can be accommodated as the top crystal grows. When the lattice distances are different, however, the top crystal becomes deformed, since structural defects such as dislocations appear. Although few crystals share the same lattice distance, a number of examples are known. Aluminum arsenide and gallium arsenide have the same crystal structure and the same lattice parameters to within 0.1 percent; they grow excellent crystals on one another. Such materials, known as superlattices, have a repeated structure of n layers of GaAs, m layers of AlAs, n layers of GaAs, m layers of AlAs, and so forth. Superlattices represent artificially created structures that are thermodynamically stable; they have many applications in the modern electronics industry. Another lattice-matched epitaxial system is mercury telluride (HgTe) and cadmium telluride (CdTe). These two semiconductors form a continuous semiconductor alloy $Cd_xHg_{1-x}Te$, where x is any number between 0 and 1. This alloy is used as a detector of infrared radiation and is incorporated in particular in night-vision goggles.

DENDRITIC GROWTH

At slow rates of crystal growth, the interface between melt and solid remains planar, and growth occurs uniformly across the surface. At faster rates of crystal growth, instabilities are more likely to occur; this leads to dendritic growth. Solidification releases excess energy in the form of heat at the interface between solid and melt. At slow growth rates, the heat leaves the surface by diffusion. Rapid growth creates more heat, which is dissipated by convection (liquid flow) when diffusion is too slow. Convection breaks the planar symmetry so that crystal growth develops along columns, or "fingers," rather than along planes. Each crystal has certain directions in which growth is fastest, and dendrites grow in these directions. As the columns grow larger, their surfaces become flatter and more unstable. This feather or tree structure is characteristic of dendritic growth. Snowflakes are an example of crystals that result from dendritic growth.

LIQUID CRYSTALS

Liquid crystals blend the structures and properties of the normally disparate liquid and crystalline solid states. Liquids can flow, for example, while solids cannot, and crystalline solids possess special symmetry properties that liquids lack. Ordinary solids melt into ordinary liquids as the temperature increases—e.g., ice melts into liquid water. Some solids actually melt twice or more as temperature rises. Between the crystalline solid at low temperatures and the ordinary liquid state at high temperatures lies an intermediate state, the liquid crystal. Liquid crystals share with liquids the ability to flow but also display symmetries inherited from crystalline solids. The resulting combination of liquid and solid properties allows important applications of liquid crystals in the displays of such devices as wristwatches, calculators, portable computers, and flat-screen televisions.

STRUCTURE AND SYMMETRY

Crystals exhibit special symmetries when they slide in certain directions or rotate through certain angles. These symmetries can be compared to those encountered when walking in a straight line through empty space. Regardless of the direction or distance of each step, the view remains the same, as there are no landmarks by which to measure one's progress. This is called continuous translational symmetry because all positions look identical. A crystal lattice breaks the continuous translational symmetry of free space; starting at one molecule there is a finite distance to travel before reaching the next. Some translational symmetry is present, however, because, by moving the proper distance in the proper direction, one is guaranteed to locate additional molecules on repeated excursions. This property is called discrete translational periodicity. Real, three-dimensional crystals display translational periodicity in three independent directions.

Rotational symmetries can be considered in a similar fashion. From one point in empty space, the view is the same regardless of which direction one looks. There is continuous rotational symmetry—namely, the symmetry of a perfect sphere. In a crystal, however, the distance to the nearest molecule from any given molecule depends on the direction taken. Furthermore, the molecules themselves may have shapes that are less symmetric than a sphere. A crystal possesses a certain discrete set of angles of rotation that leave the appearance unchanged. The continuous rotational symmetry of empty space is broken, and only a discrete symmetry exists. Broken rotational symmetry influences many important properties of crystals. Their resistance to compression, for example, may vary according to the direction along which one squeezes the crystal. Transparent crystals, such as quartz, may exhibit an optical property known as birefringence. When a light ray passes through a birefringent crystal, it is bent, or refracted, at an angle depending on the direction of the light and also its polarization, so that the single ray is broken up into two

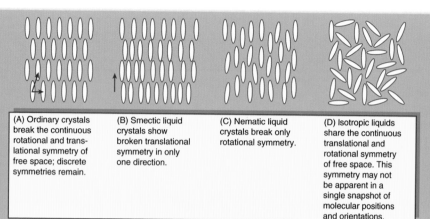

| (A) Ordinary crystals break the continuous rotational and trans-lational symmetry of free space; discrete symmetries remain. | (B) Smectic liquid crystals show broken translational symmetry in only one direction. | (C) Nematic liquid crystals break only rotational symmetry. | (D) Isotropic liquids share the continuous translational and rotational symmetry of free space. This symmetry may not be apparent in a single snapshot of molecular positions and orientations. |

Arrangements of molecules. Copyright Encyclopædia Britannica; rendering for this edition by Rosen Educational Services

polarized rays. This is why one sees a double image when looking through such crystals.

In a liquid, all the molecules sit in random positions with random orientations. This does not mean that there is less symmetry than in the crystal, however. All positions are actually equivalent to one another, and likewise all orientations are equivalent, because in a liquid the molecules are in constant motion. At one instant the molecules in the liquid may occupy specific positions and orientations, but a moment later the molecules will move to previously empty points in space. Likewise, at one instant a molecule points in one direction, and the next instant it points in another. Liquids share the homogeneity and isotropy of empty space; they have continuous translational and rotational symmetries. No form of matter has greater symmetry.

As a general rule, molecules solidify into crystal lattices with low symmetry at low temperatures. Both translational and rotational symmetries are discrete. At high temperatures, after melting, liquids have high symmetry.

Translational and rotational symmetries are continuous. High temperatures provide molecules with the energy needed for motion. The mobility disorders the crystal and raises its symmetry. Low temperatures limit motion and the possible molecular arrangements. As a result, molecules remain relatively immobile in low-energy, low-symmetry configurations.

SYMMETRIES OF LIQUID CRYSTALS

Liquid crystals, sometimes called mesophases, occupy the middle ground between crystalline solids and ordinary liquids with regard to symmetry, energy, and properties. Not all molecules have liquid crystal phases. Water molecules, for example, melt directly from solid crystalline ice into liquid water. The most widely studied liquid-crystal-forming molecules are elongated, rodlike molecules, rather like grains of rice in shape (but far smaller in size). A popular example is the molecule p-azoxyanisole (PAA):

$$CH_3-O-\langle\!\!\!\bigcirc\!\!\!\rangle-N=N-\langle\!\!\!\bigcirc\!\!\!\rangle-O-CH_3$$
$$|$$
$$O$$

Typical liquid crystal structures include the smectic and the nematic (this nomenclature was invented in the 1920s by the French scientist Georges Friedel). The smectic phase differs from the solid phase in that translational symmetry is discrete in one direction and continuous in the remaining two.

In the nematic phase all translational symmetries are continuous. The molecule positions are disordered in all directions. Their orientations are all alike, however, so that the rotational symmetry remains discrete. The orientation of the long axis of a nematic molecule is called its director.

THE BRITANNICA GUIDE TO MATTER

It was noted earlier that, as temperature decreases, matter tends to evolve from highly disordered states with continuous symmetries toward ordered states with discrete symmetries. This can occur through a sequence of symmetry-breaking phase transitions. As a substance in the liquid state is reduced in temperature, rotational symmetry breaking creates the nematic liquid crystal state in which molecules are aligned along a common axis. Their directors are all nearly parallel. At lower temperatures continuous translational symmetries break into discrete symmetries. There are three independent directions for translational symmetry. When continuous translational symmetry is broken along only one direction, the smectic liquid crystal is obtained. At temperatures sufficiently low to break continuous translational symmetry in all directions, the ordinary crystal is formed.

The mechanism by which liquid crystalline order is favoured can be illustrated through an analogy between molecules and grains of rice. Collisions of molecules require energy, so the greater the energy, the greater the tolerance for collisions. If rice grains are poured into a pan, they fall at random positions and orientations and tend to jam up against their neighbours. This is similar to the liquid state. After the pan is shaken to allow the rice grains to readjust their positions, the neighbouring grains tend to line up. The alignment is not perfect across the sample owing to defects, which also can occur in nematic liquid crystals. When all grains align, they have greater freedom to move before hitting a neighbour than they have when they are disordered. This produces the nematic phase. The freedom to move is primarily in the direction of molecular alignment, as sideways motion quickly results in collision with a neighbour. Layering the grains enhances sideways motion. This

156

produces the smectic phase. In the smectic phase some molecules have ample free volume to move in, while others are tightly packed. The lowest-energy arrangement shares the free volume equitably among molecules. Each molecular environment matches all others, and the structure is a crystal.

There is a great variety of liquid crystalline structures known in addition to those described so far. Continuous in-plane rotational symmetry, present within smectic-A layers, is broken in the hexatic-B phase, but a proliferation of dislocations maintains continuous translational symmetry within its layers. A similar relationship holds between smectic-C and smectic-F. Crystal-B and crystal-G have molecular positions on regular crystal lattice sites, with long axes of molecules (directors) aligned, but allow rotation of molecules about their directors. These are the so-called plastic crystals. There also are crystals in the discotic phase, consisting of disk-shaped molecules, and the columnar phases, in which translational symmetry is broken in not one but two spatial directions, leaving liquidlike order only along columns. In general, crystals in the isotropic liquid and nematic phases are expected at high temperatures, while many of the other phases mentioned here are expected at low temperatures.

LIQUID CRYSTAL COMPOUNDS

Liquid-crystal-forming compounds are widespread and quite diverse. Soap can form a type of smectic known as a lamellar phase, also called neat soap. In this case it is important to recognize that soap molecules have a dual chemical nature. One end of the molecule (the hydrocarbon tail) is attracted to oil, while the other end (the polar head) attaches itself to water. When soap is placed in water, the hydrocarbon tails cluster together, while the polar heads adjoin the water. Small numbers of soap molecules form spherical or rodlike micelles, which float freely in the water, while concentrated solutions create bilayers, which stack along some direction just like smectic layers. Indeed, the name smectic is derived from the Greek word for soap. The slippery feeling caused by soap reflects the ease with which the layers slide across one another.

Many biological materials form liquid crystals. Myelin, a fatty material extracted from nerve cells, was the first intensively studied liquid crystal. The tobacco mosaic virus, with its rodlike shape, forms a nematic phase. In cholesterol the nematic phase is modified to a cholesteric phase characterized by continuous rotation of the direction of molecular alignment. An intrinsic twist of the cholesterol molecule, rather like the twist of the threads of a screw, causes this rotation. Since the molecular orientation rotates steadily, there is a characteristic distance after which the orientation repeats itself. This distance is frequently comparable to the wavelength of visible light, so brilliant colour effects result from the diffraction of light by these materials.

Perhaps the first description of a liquid crystal occurred in the story *The Narrative of Arthur Gordon Pym*, by Edgar Allan Poe:

> *I am at a loss to give a distinct idea of the nature of this liquid, and cannot do so without many words. Although it flowed with rapidity in all declivities where common water would do so, yet never, except when falling in a cascade, had it the customary appearance of limpidity.... At first sight, and especially in cases where little declivity was found, it bore resemblance, as regards consistency, to a thick infusion of gum Arabic in common water. But this was only the least remarkable of its*

extraordinary qualities. It was not colourless, nor was it of any one uniform colour—presenting to the eye, as it flowed, every possible shade of purple, like the hues of a changeable silk. . . . Upon collecting a basinful, and allowing it to settle thoroughly, we perceived that the whole mass of liquid was made up of a number of distinct veins, each of a distinct hue; that these veins did not commingle; and that their cohesion was perfect in regard to their own particles among themselves, and imperfect in regard to neighbouring veins. Upon passing the blade of a knife athwart the veins, the water closed over it immediately, as with us, and also, in withdrawing it, all traces of the passage of the knife were instantly obliterated. If, however, the blade was passed down accurately between two veins, a perfect separation was effected, which the power of cohesion did not immediately rectify.

The liquid described in this passage is human blood. In its usual state within the human body, blood is an ordinary disordered isotropic fluid. The disklike shape of red blood cells, however, favours liquid crystallinity at certain concentrations and temperatures.

OPTICAL PROPERTIES

An understanding of the principal technological applications of liquid crystals requires a knowledge of their optical properties. In particular, liquid crystals alter the polarization of light passing through them.

EFFECT OF LIQUID CRYSTALS ON POLARIZED LIGHT

Light waves are actually waves in electric and magnetic fields. The direction of the electric field is the polarization of the light wave. A polarizing filter selects a single component of polarized light to pass through while absorbing all other components of incoming waves. If a second polarizing filter is placed above the first but with its polarization axis rotated by 90°, no light can pass through because the polarization passed by the first filter is precisely the polarization blocked by the second filter. When optically active materials, such as liquid crystals, are placed between polarizing filters crossed in this manner, some light may get through, because the intervening material changes the polarization of the light. If the nematic director is not aligned with either of the polarizing filters, polarized light passing through the first filter becomes partially polarized along the nematic director. This component of light in turn possesses a component

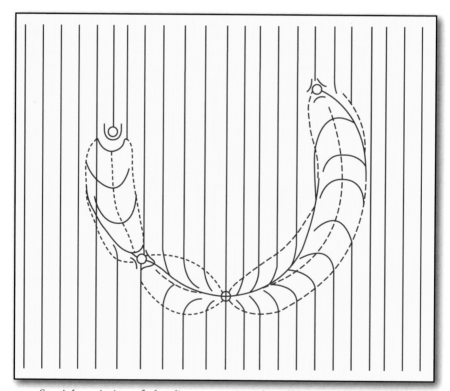

Spatial variation of the director causing threadlike images. Copyright Encyclopædia Britannica; rendering for this edition by Rosen Educational Services

aligned with the top polarizing filter, so a fraction of the incoming light passes through the entire assembly. The amount of light passing through is largest when the nematic director is positioned at a $45°$ angle from both filters. The light is fully blocked when the director lies parallel to one filter or the other.

During the last decades of the 19th century, pioneering investigators of liquid crystals, such as the German physicist Otto Lehmann and the Austrian botanist Friedrich Reinitzer, equipped ordinary microscopes with pairs of polarizing filters to obtain images of nematic and smectic phases. Spatial variation in the alignment of the nematic director causes spatial variation in light intensity. Since the nematic is defined by having all directors nearly parallel to one another, the images arise from defects in the nematic structure. The directors may rotate or bend around defect lines. The resulting threadlike images inspired the name nematic, which is based on the Greek word for thread. The layered smectic structure causes layering of defects.

Nonuniformity in director alignment may be induced artificially. The surfaces of a glass container can be coated with a material that, when rubbed in the proper direction, forces the director to lie perpendicular or parallel to the wall adjacent to a nematic liquid crystal. The orientation forced by one wall need not be consistent with that forced by another wall; this situation causes the director orientation to vary in between the walls. The nematic must compromise its preference for all directors to be parallel to one another with the inconsistent orienting forces of the container walls. In doing so, the liquid crystal may take on a twisted alignment across the container. Electric or magnetic fields provide an alternate means of influencing the orientation of the nematic directors. Molecules may prefer to align so that their director is, say, parallel to an applied electric field.

USE OF LIQUID CRYSTALS AS OPTOELECTRONIC DISPLAYS

Optical behaviour and orienting fields underlie the important contemporary use of liquid crystals as optoelectronic displays. Consider, for example, the twisted-nematic cell. The polarizer surfaces are coated and rubbed so that the nematic will align with the polarizing axis. The two polarizers are crossed, forcing the nematic to rotate between them. The rotation is slow and smooth, assuming a 90° twist across the cell. Light passing through the first polarizer is aligned with the bottom of the nematic layer. As the nematic twists, it rotates the polarization of the light so that, as the light leaves the top of the nematic layer, its polarization is rotated by 90° from that at the bottom. The new polarization is just right for passing through the top filter, and so light travels unhindered through the assembly.

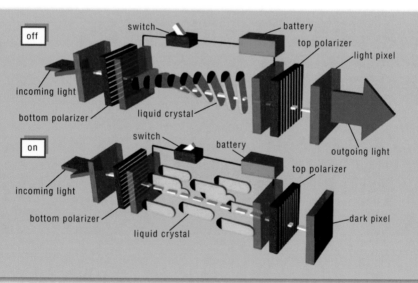

A twisted-nematic cell. (A) The assembly is transparent to light in the absence of an electric field. (B) An applied field destroys the twist of the nematic, rendering the assembly opaque. Copyright Encyclopædia Britannica; rendering for this edition by Rosen Educational Services

If an electric field is applied in the direction of light propagation, the liquid crystal directors align with the orienting field, so they are no longer parallel to the light passing though the bottom polarizer. They are no longer capable of rotating this polarization through the 90° needed to allow the light to emerge from the top polarizer. Although this assembly is transparent when no field is applied, it becomes opaque when the field is present. A grid of such assemblies placed side by side may be used to display images. If one turns on the electric field attached to the parts of the grid that lie where the image is to appear, these points will turn black while the remaining points of the grid stay white. The resulting patchwork of dark and light creates the image on the display. In a wristwatch, calculator, or computer these may be simply numbers or letters, and in a television the images may be detailed pictures. Switching the electric fields on or off will cause the picture to move, just as ordinary television pictures display an ever-changing stream of electrically encoded images.

CHAPTER 7

AMORPHOUS SOLIDS
AND QUASICRYSTALS

A morphous solids are any noncrystalline solid in which the atoms and molecules are not organized in a definite lattice pattern. Such solids include glass, plastic, and gel.

Quasicrystals are matter formed atomically in a manner somewhere between the amorphous solids of glasses (special forms of metals and other minerals, as well as common glass) and the precise pattern of crystals. Like crystals, quasicrystals contain an ordered structure, but the patterns are subtle and do not recur at precisely regular intervals. Rather, quasicrystals appear to be formed from two different structures assembled in a nonrepeating array, the three-dimensional equivalent of a tile floor made from two shapes of tile and having an orientational order but no repetition.

AMORPHOUS SOLIDS

Solids and liquids are both forms of condensed matter; both are composed of atoms in close proximity to each other. But their properties are, of course, enormously different. While a solid material has both a well-defined volume and a well-defined shape, a liquid has a well-defined volume but a shape that depends on the shape of the container. Stated differently, a solid exhibits resistance to shear stress while a liquid does not. Externally applied forces can twist or bend or distort a solid's shape, but (provided the forces have not exceeded the solid's elastic limit) it "springs back" to its original shape when the forces are removed. A liquid flows under the action of an external force; it does not hold its shape. These macroscopic characteristics constitute the essential distinctions: a liquid flows, lacks a definite shape (though its volume is definite), and cannot withstand a shear stress; a solid does not flow, has a definite shape, and exhibits elastic stiffness against shear stress.

On an atomic level, these macroscopic distinctions arise from a basic difference in the nature of the atomic motion. Atoms in a solid are not mobile. Each atom stays close to one point in space, although the atom is not stationary but instead oscillates rapidly about this fixed point (the higher the temperature, the faster it oscillates). The fixed point can be viewed as a time-averaged centre of gravity of the rapidly jiggling atom. The spatial arrangement of these fixed points constitutes the solid's durable atomic-scale structure. In contrast, a liquid possesses no enduring arrangement of atoms. Atoms in a liquid are mobile and continually wander throughout the material.

DISTINCTION BETWEEN CRYSTALLINE AND AMORPHOUS SOLIDS

There are two main classes of solids: crystalline and amorphous. What distinguishes them from one another is the nature of their atomic-scale structure. Atomic positions in a crystal exhibit a property called long-range order or translational periodicity; positions repeat in space in a regular array. In an amorphous solid, translational periodicity is absent. There is no long-range order. The atoms are not randomly distributed in space, however, as they are in the gas. In certain glasses, for example, each atom has three nearest-neighbour atoms at the same distance (called the chemical bond length) from it, just as in a corresponding crystal.

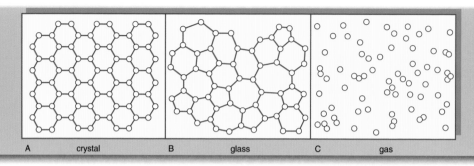

The atomic arrangements in (A) a crystalline solid, (B) an amorphous solid, and (C) a gas. Copyright Encyclopædia Britannica; rendering for this edition by Rosen Educational Services

All solids, both crystalline and amorphous, exhibit short-range (atomic-scale) order. Thus, the term *amorphous*, literally "without form or structure," is actually a misnomer in the context of the standard expression amorphous solid. The well-defined short-range order is a consequence of the chemical bonding between atoms, which is responsible for holding the solid together.

In addition to the terms *amorphous solid* and *glass*, other terms in use include *noncrystalline solid* and *vitreous solid*. *Amorphous solid* and *noncrystalline solid* are more general terms, while *glass* and *vitreous solid* have historically been reserved for an amorphous solid prepared by rapid cooling (quenching) of a melt.

There are two types of scenarios that can occur when cooling causes a given number of atoms to condense from the gas phase into the liquid phase and then into the solid phase. In the discussion that follows, the temperature T_b is the boiling point, T_f is the freezing (or melting) point, and T_g is the glass transition temperature. In scenario 1 the liquid freezes at T_f into a crystalline solid, with an abrupt discontinuity in volume. When cooling occurs slowly, this is usually what happens. At sufficiently high cooling rates, however, most materials display a different behaviour and follow scenario 2 to the solid state. T_f is bypassed, and the liquid state persists until the lower temperature T_g is reached and the second solidification scenario is realized. In a narrow temperature range near T_g, the glass transition occurs: the liquid freezes into an amorphous solid with no abrupt discontinuity in volume.

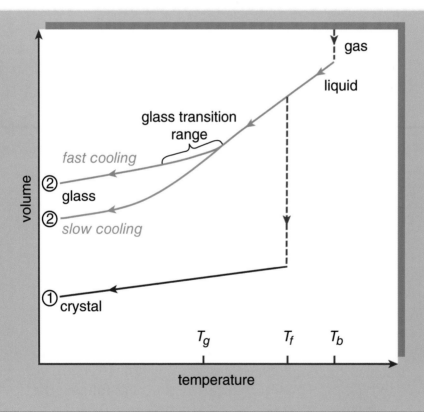

The two general cooling paths by which a group of atoms can condense. Route 1 is the path to the crystalline state; route 2 is the rapid-quench path to the amorphous solid state. Copyright Encyclopædia Britannica; rendering for this edition by Rosen Educational Services

The glass transition temperature T_g is not as sharply defined as T_f; T_g shifts downward slightly when the cooling rate is reduced. The reason for this phenomenon is the steep temperature dependence of the molecular response time. When the temperature is lowered below T_g, the response time for molecular rearrangement becomes much larger than experimentally accessible times, so that liquidlike mobility disappears and the atomic configuration becomes frozen into a set of fixed positions to which the atoms are tied.

Some textbooks erroneously describe glasses as undercooled viscous liquids, but this is actually incorrect. In scenario 2, it is the portion lying between T_f and T_g that is correctly associated with the description of the material as an undercooled liquid (undercooled meaning that its temperature is below T_f). But below T_g, in the glass phase, it is a bona fide solid (exhibiting such properties as elastic stiffness against shear).

PREPARATION OF AMORPHOUS SOLIDS

It was once thought that relatively few materials could be prepared as amorphous solids, and such materials (notably, oxide glasses and organic polymers) were called glass-forming solids. It is now known that the amorphous solid state is almost a universal property of condensable matter. The glass transition temperatures of every class of chemical bonding type span a wide range.

Glass formation is a matter of bypassing crystallization. The channel to the crystalline state is evaded by quickly crossing the temperature interval between T_f and T_g. Nearly all materials can, if cooled quickly enough, be prepared as amorphous solids. The definition of "quickly enough" varies enormously from material to material. The four techniques for preparing amorphous solids—slow cooling, moderate quenching, rapid splat quenching, and condensation from the gas phase—are not fundamentally different from those used for preparing crystalline solids; the key is simply to quench the sample quickly enough to form the glass, rather than slowly enough to form the crystal. The quench rate increases greatly from left to right in the figure.

MELT QUENCHING

Preparation of metallic glasses requires a quite rapid quench. The technique called splat quenching can quench a droplet of a molten metal roughly 1,000 °C (1,800 °F) in one millisecond, producing a thin film of metal that is an amorphous solid. In enormous contrast to this, the silicate glass that forms the rigid ribbed disk of the Hale telescope of the Palomar Observatory near San Diego, California, was prepared by cooling (over a comparable temperature drop) during a time interval of eight months. The great difference in the quench rates needed for arriving at the amorphous solid state (the quench rates here differ by a factor of 3×10^{10}) is a dramatic demonstration of the difference in the glass-forming tendency of silicate glasses (very high) and metallic glasses (very low).

The required quench rate for glass formation can vary significantly within a family of related materials that differ from one another in chemical composition. Consider the representative behaviour for a binary (two-component) system, gold-silicon. Here x specifies the fraction of atoms that are silicon atoms, and $Au_{1-x}Si_x$ denotes a particular material in this family of materials. (Au is the chemical symbol for gold, Si is the symbol for silicon, and, for example, $Au_{0.8}Si_{0.2}$ denotes a material containing 20 percent silicon atoms and 80 percent gold atoms.) In a diagram of the composition dependence of the freezing point T_f, there is a deep cusp near the composition $x = 0.2$.

Near this special composition, as at a in the figure, a liquid is much more readily quenched than is a liquid at a distant composition such as b. To reach the glass phase, the liquid must be cooled from above T_f to below the glass transition temperature T_g without crystallizing. Throughout the temperature interval from T_f down to T_g, the liquid is at risk vis-à-vis crystallization. Since this dangerous interval is much longer at b than at a, a faster quench rate is needed for glass formation at b than at a.

Similar diagrams exist for many binary systems. For example, in the oxide system CaO-Al_2O_3, in which the two end-member compositions ($x = 0$ and $x = 1$) correspond to pure calcium oxide (CaO) and pure aluminum oxide (Al_2O_3), there is a deep minimum in the T_f-versus-x curve near the middle of the composition range. Although neither calcium oxide nor aluminum oxide readily forms a glass, glasses are easily formed from mixed compositions; for reasons related to this, many oxide glasses have complex chemical compositions.

VAPOUR CONDENSATION TECHNIQUES

In the gold-silicon system, at compositions far from the cusp, glasses cannot be formed by melt quenching—even by the rapid splat-quench technique. Amorphous solids can still be prepared by dispensing with the liquid phase completely and constructing a thin solid film in atom-by-atom fashion from the gas phase. In the simplest of these vapour-condensation techniques, a vapour stream, formed within a vacuum chamber by thermal evaporation of a sample of the material to be deposited, impinges on the surface of a cold substrate. The atoms condense on the cold surface and, under a range of conditions (usually a high rate of deposition and a low substrate temperature), an amorphous solid is formed as a thin film. Pure silicon can be prepared as an amorphous solid in this manner. Variations of the method include using an electron beam to vapourize the source or using the plasma-induced decomposition of a molecular species. The latter technique is used to deposit amorphous silicon from gaseous silane (SiH_4). Among the amorphous solids those that normally require vapour-condensation methods for their preparation are silicon (Si), germanium (Ge), water (H_2O), and the elemental metallic glasses iron (Fe), cobalt (Co), and bismuth (Bi).

OTHER PREPARATION TECHNIQUES

Numerous other methods exist for preparing amorphous solids, and new methods are continually invented. In melt spinning, a jet of molten metal is propelled against the moving surface of a cold, rotating copper cylinder. A solid film of metallic glass is spun off as a continuous ribbon at a speed that can exceed 1 km per minute. In laser glazing, a brief intense laser pulse melts a tiny spot, which is swiftly quenched by the surrounding material into a glass. In sol-gel synthesis, small molecules in a liquid solution chemically link up with each other, forming a disordered network. It is possible to take a crystalline solid and convert it into an amorphous solid by bombarding it with high-kinetic-energy ions. Under certain conditions of composition and temperature, interdiffusion (mixing on an atomic scale) between crystalline layers can produce an amorphous phase. Pyrolysis and electrolysis are other methods that can be used.

ATOMIC-SCALE STRUCTURE

The absence of long-range order is the defining characteristic of the atomic arrangement in amorphous solids.

However, because of the absence in glasses of long parallel rows and flat parallel planes of atoms, it is extremely difficult to determine details of the atomic arrangement with the structure-probing techniques (such as X-ray diffraction) that are so successful for crystals. For glasses the information obtained from such structure-probing experiments is contained in a curve called the radial distribution function (RDF).

THE RADIAL DISTRIBUTION FUNCTION

The significance of the RDF is that it gives the probability of neighbouring atoms being located at various distances from an average atom. Imagine an RDF graph, with the horizontal axis specifying the distance from a given atom and the vertical axis proportional to the average number of atoms found at each distance. (The distance scale is expressed in angstrom units; one angstrom equals 10^{-8} cm.) The curve for crystalline germanium (c-Ge) would display sharp peaks over the full range shown, corresponding to well-defined shells of neighbouring atoms at specific distances, which arise from the long-range regularity of the crystal's atomic arrangement. Amorphous germanium (a-Ge) would exhibit a close-in sharp peak corresponding to the nearest-neighbour atoms (there are four nearest neighbours in both c-Ge and a-Ge), but at larger distances the undulations in the RDF curve would become washed out owing to the absence of long-range order. The first, sharp, nearest-neighbour peak in a-Ge would be identical to the corresponding peak in c-Ge, showing that the short-range order in the amorphous form of solid germanium is as well-defined as it is in the crystalline form.

The detailed shape of the a-Ge RDF curve is the input used in the difficult task of developing a model for the atomic arrangement in amorphous germanium. The normal procedure is to construct a model of the structure and then to calculate from the model's atomic positions a theoretical RDF curve. This calculated RDF is then compared to the experimental curve (which provides the definitive test of the validity of the model). Computer-assisted refinements are then made in the model in order to improve the agreement between the model-dependent theoretical RDF and the experimentally observed RDF. This program has been successfully carried out for many amorphous solids, so there is now much that is known about their atomic-scale structure. In contrast to the complete information available for crystals, however, the structural knowledge of glasses still contains gaps.

MODELS OF ATOMIC SCALE STRUCTURES

Amorphous solids, like crystalline solids, exhibit a wide variety of atomic-scale structures. Most of these can be recognized as falling within one or another of three broad classes of structure associated with the following models: (1) the continuous random-network model, applicable to covalently bonded glasses, such as amorphous silicon and the oxide glasses, (2) the random-coil model, applicable to the many polymer-chain organic glasses, such as polystyrene, and (3) the random close-packing model, applicable to metallic glasses, such as $Au_{0.8}Si_{0.2}$ gold-silicon. These are the names in conventional use for the models. Although each of them contains the word random, the well-defined short-range order means that they are not random in the sense that the structure of a gas is random.

The continuous random-network model clearly demonstrates how short-range order for an amorphous solid like glass is compatible with the absence of long-range order. At the bridging oxygen atoms, the bond angles have some flexibility, so it is easy to continue the network. Common oxide glasses are chemically more complex than SiO_2. Chemical species such as phosphorus and

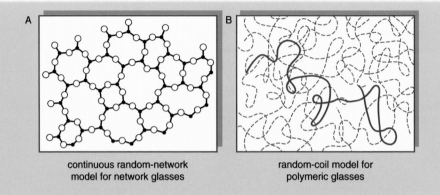

Two basic models for the atomic-scale structure of amorphous solids. Copyright Encyclopædia Britannica; rendering for this edition by Rosen Educational Services

germanium, which (like silicon) enter into the structure of the network by forming strong chemical bonds with oxygen atoms, are called network formers. Chemical species such as sodium and calcium, which do not bond directly to the network but which simply sit (in ionic form) within its interstitial holes, are called network modifiers.

A large fraction of the everyday materials called plastics are amorphous solids composed of long-chain molecules known as polymers. Each polymer chain has a backbone consisting of a string of many (up to roughly 100,000) carbon atoms bonded to each other. These organic polymeric glasses are present in innumerable familiar molded products (e.g., pens, tires, toys, appliance bodies, building materials, and automobile and airplane parts). The random-coil model, first proposed in 1949 by P.J. Flory (who later received a Nobel Prize in Chemistry for his pioneering work on polymers), is the established structural model for this important class of amorphous solids. As schematically sketched in the figure, the structure consists of intermeshed, entangled polymer chains.

The chain configurations are well-defined, statistically, by a mathematical trajectory called a three-dimensional random walk.

The third important structural model, the random close-packing model for metallic glasses, is difficult to illustrate with a simple diagram. Roughly speaking, it is similar to the structure that arises when a bunch of marbles are swiftly scrunched together in a paper bag.

PROPERTIES OF OXIDE GLASSES

The wide range of the properties of glasses depends on their composition, and special effects result from the presence of various modifying agents in certain basic glass-forming materials.

One of the most important glass formers is silica (SiO_2). Pure crystalline silica melts at 1,710 °C (1,980 °F). In pure form, silica glass exhibits such properties as low thermal expansion, high softening temperatures, and excellent chemical and electrical resistance. In pure form it is relatively transparent over a wide range of wavelengths to visible and ultraviolet light and to ultrasonic waves.

The high viscosity and melting temperature of silica glass are affected by the presence or absence of other materials. For example, if certain materials called fluxes are added, the most important being soda (Na_2O), both viscosity and melting temperature can be reduced. If too much soda is added, the resulting glass is readily attacked by water, but, if there are suitable amounts of stabilizing oxides, such as lime (CaO) and magnesia (MgO), the glass becomes more durable. Most commercial glass has a soda-lime-silica composition and is produced in vast quantities for plate and sheet glass, containers, and lightbulbs.

In soda-lime-silica glasses, if lime is replaced by lead oxide (PbO) and if potash (K_2O) is used as a partial replacement for soda, lead-alkali-silicate glasses result that have lower softening points than lime glasses. The refractive indices, dispersive powers, and electrical resistance of these glasses are generally much greater than those of soda-lime-silica glasses.

Boric oxide (B_2O_3), itself a glass former, acts as a flux (i.e., lowers the working temperature) when present in silica and forms borosilicate glass, and the substitution of small percentages of alkali and alumina increases the chemical stability. It also exhibits low thermal expansion, high dielectric strength, and high softening temperature.

Aluminosilicate glasses find applications similar to those of borosilicates, but the former can stand higher operating temperatures; glasses with relatively high alumina contents and no boric oxide are exceptionally resistant to alkalies.

The above glasses all have silica as the glass former. With other glass formers, glasses have special properties. For example, if boric oxide is present, X rays are transmitted and rare-earth glasses will exhibit low dispersion and a high refractive index. Phosphate glasses (used as optical glasses) based on phosphorus pentoxide (P_2O_5) are highly resistant to hydrofluoric acid and act as efficient heat absorbers when iron oxide is added.

PROPERTIES AND APPLICATIONS OF AMORPHOUS SOLIDS

The following sections discuss technological applications of amorphous solids in connection with the properties that make those applications possible. It is important to understand that, although differences do exist between the properties of amorphous and crystalline solids, it is nevertheless broadly true that amorphous solids exhibit essentially the full range of properties and phenomena exhibited by crystalline solids. There are amorphous-solid metals, semiconductors, and insulators; there are transparent glasses and opaque glasses; and there are superconducting amorphous solids and ferromagnetic amorphous solids.

Some of the general differences between the properties of crystals and glasses, in addition to the fundamental one of the glass transition, are noted here. The atomic-scale disorder present in a metallic glass causes its electrical conductivity to be lower than the conductivity of the corresponding crystalline metal, because the structural disorder impedes the motion of the mobile electrons that make up the electrical current. (This lower electrical conductivity for the amorphous metal can be an advantage in some situations.) For a similar reason, the thermal conductivity of an insulating glass is lower than that of the corresponding crystalline insulator; glasses thus make good thermal insulators. Crystals and glasses also differ systematically in their optical spectra, which are the curves that describe the wavelength dependence of the degree to which the solid absorbs infrared, visible, or ultraviolet light. Although the overall spectra are often similar, crystal spectra typically exhibit sharp peaks and other features that specifically arise as a consequence of the long-range order of the crystal's atomic-scale structure. These sharp features are absent in the optical spectra of amorphous solids.

The continuous liquid-to-solid transition near T_g, the glass transition, has a profound significance in connection with classical applications of glasses. While crystallization abruptly transforms a mobile, low-viscosity liquid to a crystalline solid at T_f, near T_g the liquid viscosity increases continuously through a large range in the transformation to an amorphous solid. Viscosity, expressed in units of poise, is often used to specify characteristic working temperatures in the processing of the liquid precursors of various oxide glasses. A poise is the centimetre-gram-second (cgs) unit of viscosity. It expresses the force needed to maintain a unit velocity difference between parallel plates separated by 1 cm of fluid: 1 poise equals 1 dyne-second per square cm. Molten glass may have a viscosity of 10^{13} poise (similar to honey on a cold day), and it quickly gets stiffer when cooled since the viscosity steeply increases with decreasing temperature. The ability to "tune" the viscosity of the melt (by changing temperature) allows glass to be conveniently processed and worked into desired shapes; glassblowing is a classic example of the usefulness of this widely exploited property.

Some amorphous solids have important technological uses. Window glass is a centuries-old technology, but others blossomed during the second half of the 20th century. A significant theme in the uses of amorphous solids is their role in applications calling for large-area sheets or films. Amorphous solids often have great advantages over crystalline solids in such applications, since their use avoids the functional problems associated with polycrystallinity or the expense of preparing large single crystals. Thus, while it would be prohibitively expensive to fabricate large windows out of crystalline SiO_2 (quartz), it is practical to do so using SiO_2-based silicate glasses.

TRANSPARENT GLASSES

The terms *glass* and *window glass* are often used interchangeably in everyday language, so familiar is this ancient architectural application of amorphous solids. Not only are oxide glasses, such as those used for window glass and fibre-optic waveguides, excellent for letting light in, they are also good for keeping cold out, because (as mentioned above) they are efficient thermal insulators.

Another technological application of amorphous solids represents a modern development that carries the property of optical transparency to a phenomenal level. The transparency of the extraordinarily pure glasses that have been developed for fibre-optic telecommunications is so great that, at certain wavelengths, light can pass through 1 km (0.6 mile) of glass and still retain 95 percent of its original intensity.

Glass fibres (transmitting optical signals) are now doing what copper wires (transmitting electrical signals) once did and are doing it more efficiently: carrying telephone messages around the planet. Digital electrical pulses produced by encoding of the voice-driven electrical signal are converted into light pulses by a semiconductor laser coupled to one end of the optical fibre. The signal is then transmitted over a long length of fibre as a stream of light pulses. At the far end it is converted back into electrical pulses and then into sound.

The glass fibre is somewhat thinner than a human hair. The simplest type has a central core of ultratransparent glass surrounded by a coaxial cladding of a glass having a lower refractive index, n. This ensures that light rays propagating within the core, at small angles relative to the fibre axis, do not leak out but instead are 100 percent reflected at the core-cladding interface by the optical effect known as total internal reflection.

The great advantage provided by the substitution of light-transmitting fibres of ultratransparent oxide glass for electricity-transmitting wires of crystalline copper is that a single optical fibre can carry many more simultaneous conversations than can a thick cable packed with copper wires. This is the case because light waves oscillate at enormously high frequencies (about 2×10^{14} cycles per second for the infrared light generally used for fibre-optic telecommunications). This allows the light-wave signal carrier to be modulated at very high frequencies and to transmit a high volume of information traffic. Fibre-optic communications have greatly expanded the information-transmitting capacity of the world's telecommunications networks.

POLYMERIC STRUCTURAL MATERIALS

Polystyrene is a prototypical example of a polymeric glass. These glasses make up a broad class of lightweight structural materials important in the automotive, aerospace, and construction industries. These materials are also ubiquitous in everyday experience as plastic molded objects. The quantity of polymer materials produced each year, measured in terms of volume, exceeds the quantity of steel produced.

Polystyrene is among the most important of the thermoplastic materials that, when heated (to the vicinity of the glass transition temperature), soften and flow controllably, enabling them to be processed at high speeds and on a large scale in the manufacture of molded products. The chemical formula of a polystyrene chain may be written as $(CH_2CHC_6H_5)_N$. The building block (inside the parentheses) consists of two backbone carbon atoms to which three hydrogen atoms and one phenyl (C_6H_5) ring are bonded as side groups. The polymerization index N reaches values above 10^5. Polystyrene is a purely hydrocarbon polymer (i.e., it contains only hydrogen and carbon); most organic polymers contain additional chemical components.

AMORPHOUS SEMICONDUCTORS IN ELECTRONICS

Amorphous semiconductors, in the form of thin films, are important in applications requiring large areas of electronically active material. The first electronic application of amorphous semiconductors to occur on a large scale was in xerography (or electrostatic imaging), the process that provides the basis of plain-paper copiers. Amorphous selenium (Se) and, later, amorphous arsenic selenide (As_2Se_3) were used to form the thin-film, large-area photoconducting element that lies at the heart of the xerographic process. The photoconductor, which is an electrical insulator in the absence of light but which conducts electricity when illuminated, is exposed to an image of the document to be copied. Throughout the world—in offices, libraries, schools, and so forth—the xerographic process makes billions of copies every day. This process is also widely used in laser printers, in which the photoconductor is exposed to a digitally controlled on-and-off laser beam that is raster scanned (like the electron beam in a television tube) over the photoconductor surface.

Although still in use, selenium and arsenic selenide have been joined by other amorphous materials in this important technology. Polymeric organic glasses, in the form of thin films, are now used in multilayer photoconductor configurations in which the light is absorbed in one layer and electrical charge is transported through an adjacent layer. Both layers are formed of amorphous polymer films, and these photoreceptors can be made in the form of flexible belts.

Amorphous silicon thin films are used in solar cells that power handheld calculators. This important amorphous semiconductor is also used as the image sensor in facsimile ("fax") machines, and it serves as the photoreceptor in some xerographic copiers. All these applications exploit the ability of amorphous silicon to be vapour-deposited in the form of large-area thin films. The practical form of this amorphous semiconductor is not pure silicon but a silicon-hydrogen alloy containing 10 percent hydrogen.

The key role played by hydrogen, in what is now called hydrogenated amorphous silicon, emerged in a scientific puzzle that took years to solve. Stated briefly, hydrogen eliminates the electronic defects that are intrinsic to pure amorphous silicon.

Hydrogenated amorphous silicon also is used in high-resolution flat-panel displays for computer monitors and for television screens. In such applications the large-area amorphous-semiconductor thin film is etched into an array of many tiny units, each of which forms the active element of a transistor that electronically turns on or off a small pixel (picture element) of a liquid-crystal display.

MAGNETIC GLASSES

Some metallic glasses have magnetic properties. These are typically iron-rich amorphous solids with compositions such as $Fe_{0.8}B_{0.2}$ iron-boron and $Fe_{0.8}B_{0.1}Si_{0.1}$ iron-boron-silicon. They are readily formed as long metallic glass ribbons by melt spinning or as wide sheets by planar flow casting. Ferromagnetic glasses are mechanically hard materials, but they are magnetically soft, meaning that they are easily magnetized by small magnetic fields. Also, because of their disordered atomic-scale structure, they have higher electrical resistance than conventional (crystalline) magnetic materials.

The three attributes of ease of manufacture, magnetic softness, and high electrical resistance make magnetic glasses extremely suitable for use in the magnetic cores of electrical power transformers. High electrical resistance (which arises here as a direct consequence of amorphicity) is a crucial property in this application, because it minimizes unwanted electrical eddy currents and cuts down on power losses. For these reasons, sheets of iron-based magnetic glasses are used as transformer-core laminations in electrical power applications.

Thin films of magnetic glass are finding use in many other applications. These include magnetic recording media for audio and video digital recording, as well as recording heads used with magnetic disks.

QUASICRYSTALS

Although when first discovered such structures surprised the scientific community, it now appears that quasicrystals rank among the most common structures in alloys of aluminum with such metals as iron, cobalt, or nickel. While no major commercial applications yet exploit properties of the quasicrystalline state directly, quasicrystals form in compounds noted for their high strength and light weight, suggesting potential applications in aerospace and other industries.

STRUCTURE AND SYMMETRY

Dan Shechtman, a researcher from Technion, a part of the Israel Institute of Technology, and his colleagues at the National Bureau of Standards (now the National Institute of Standards and Technology) in Gaithersburg, Maryland, discovered quasicrystals in 1984. A research program of the U.S. Air Force sponsored their investigation of the metallurgical properties of aluminum-iron and aluminum-manganese alloys. Shechtman and his coworkers mixed aluminum and manganese in a roughly six-to-one proportion and heated the mixture until it melted. The mixture was then rapidly cooled back into the solid state by dropping the liquid onto a cold spinning wheel, a process known as melt spinning. When the solidified alloy was examined using an electron microscope, a novel structure was revealed. It exhibited fivefold symmetry, which is forbidden in crystals, and long-range order, which is lacking in amorphous solids. Its order, therefore, was neither amorphous nor crystalline. Many other alloys with these same features have subsequently been produced.

MICROSCOPIC IMAGES OF QUASICRYSTALLINE STRUCTURES

The electron microscope has played a significant role in the investigation of quasicrystals. It is a versatile tool that can probe many important aspects of the structure of matter. Low-resolution scanning electron microscopy magnifies the shapes of individual grains. Symmetries of solid grains often reflect the internal symmetries of the underlying atomic positions. Grains of salt, for example, take cubical shapes consistent with the cubic symmetries of their crystal lattices. Quasicrystalline aluminum-copper-iron has been imaged using a scanning electron microscope, revealing the pentagonal dodecahedral shape of the grains. Its 12 faces are regular pentagons, with axes of fivefold rotational symmetry passing through them. That is to say, rotations about this axis by 72° leave the appearance of the grain unchanged. In a full 360° rotation the grain will repeat itself in appearance five times, once every 72°. There are also axes of twofold rotational symmetry passing through the edges and axes of threefold rotational symmetry passing through the vertices. This is also known as icosahedral symmetry because the icosahedron is the geometric dual of the pentagonal dodecahedron. At the centre of each face on an icosahedron, the dodecahedron places a vertex, and vice versa. The symmetry of a pentagonal dodecahedron or icosahedron is not among the symmetries of any crystal structure, yet this is the symmetry that was revealed in the electron microscope image of the aluminum-manganese alloy produced by Shechtman and his colleagues.

High-resolution electron microscopy magnifies to such a great degree that patterns of atomic positions may be determined. In ordinary crystals such a lattice image reveals regularly spaced rows of atoms. Regular spacing implies spatial periodicity in the placement of atoms. The angles between rows indicate rotational symmetries of the atomic positions. In a high-resolution electron microscope image of quasicrystalline aluminum-manganese-silicon, parallel rows occur in five sets, rotated from one another by 72°, confirming that the fivefold symmetry suggested by the shape of the pentagonal dodecahedron grain reflects a fivefold symmetry in the actual placement of atoms.

TRANSLATIONAL PERIODICITY AND SYMMETRY

Fivefold symmetry axes are forbidden in ordinary crystals, while other axes, such as sixfold axes, are allowed. The reason is that translational periodicity, which is characteristic

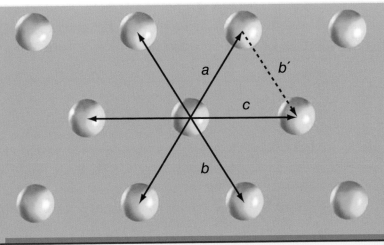

Arrows indicate translational symmetries of the lattice. Combining two symmetries (*a* and *b*) produces a third (*c*).

Hexagonal lattice of atomic sites. Copyright Encyclopædia Britannica; rendering for this edition by Rosen Educational Services

of crystal lattices, cannot be present in structures with fivefold symmetry. A triangular array of atoms has axes of sixfold rotational symmetry passing through each atomic position. Arrows drawn from a specific atom can represent the translational symmetries of this crystalline structure. That is, if the entire array of atoms is displaced along one of these arrows, all new atomic positions coincide with the locations of other atoms prior to the displacement.

Such a displacement of atoms that leaves atomic positions invariant is called a symmetry of the crystal. If two different symmetries are combined such that the structure is first displaced along arrow a and then along arrow b, the net result is equivalent to a displacement along arrow c, which itself must be a symmetry of the structure. Again, atomic sites coincide before and after the displacement. Repeated displacements along the same arrow demonstrate the translational periodicity of the crystal.

A pentagonal atomic arrangement exhibits fivefold rotational symmetry but lacks the translational symmetries that must be present in a crystalline structure. Now,

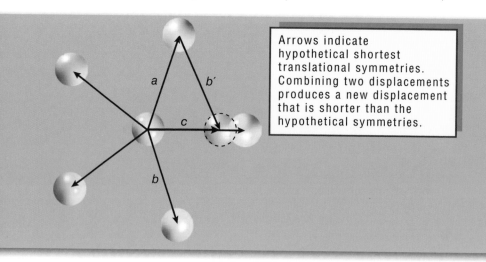

Arrows indicate hypothetical shortest translational symmetries. Combining two displacements produces a new displacement that is shorter than the hypothetical symmetries.

Pentagonal arrangement of atoms. Copyright Encyclopædia Britannica; rendering for this edition by Rosen Educational Services

as before, consider the combinations of two symmetries a and b with the net result c. The length of c is smaller than either a or b by a factor $\tau = (5 + 1)/2$, which is known as the golden mean. The new atomic position does not coincide with a previous atomic position, indicating that the structure does not exhibit translational periodicity. Therefore, an array of atoms may not simultaneously display fivefold rotational symmetry and translational periodicity, for, if it did, there would be no lower limit to the spacing between atoms.

In fact, the compatibility of translational periodicity with sixfold rotational symmetry is a remarkable accident, for translational periodicity is not possible with most rotational symmetries. The only allowed symmetry axes in periodic crystals are twofold, threefold, fourfold, and sixfold. All others are forbidden owing to the lack of minimum interatomic separation. In particular, fivefold, eightfold, tenfold, and twelvefold axes cannot exist in crystals. These symmetries are mentioned in particular because they have been reported in quasicrystalline alloys.

Since a high-resolution electron microscope image of aluminum-manganese-silicon quasicrystal clearly reveals an axis of fivefold symmetry, it may be concluded that the arrangement of atoms lacks translational periodicity. That, in itself, is no great surprise, for many materials lack translational periodicity. Amorphous metals, for example, are frequently produced by the same melt-spinning process that was employed in the discovery of quasicrystals. Amorphous metals have no discrete rotational symmetries, however, and high-resolution electron microscope images reveal no rows of atoms. The arrangement of atoms in a quasicrystal displays a property called long-range order, which is lacking in amorphous metals. Long-range order permits rows of atoms to span the image and maintains

agreement of row orientations. Ordinary crystal structures display long-range order. Strict rules govern the
relative placement of atoms at remote locations in solids
with long-range order.

Electron diffraction confirms the presence of long-
range order in both crystals and quasicrystals. Quantum
mechanics predicts that particles such as electrons move
through space as if they were waves, in the same manner
that light travels. When light waves strike a diffraction
grating, they are diffracted. White light breaks up into a
rainbow, while monochromatic light breaks up into discrete sharp spots. Similarly, when electrons strike evenly
spaced rows of atoms within a crystalline solid, they break
up into a set of bright spots known as Bragg diffraction
peaks. Symmetrical arrangements of spots reveal axes of
rotational symmetry in the crystal, and spacings between
the discrete spots relate inversely to translational periodic-
ities. Amorphous metals contain only diffuse rings in their
diffraction patterns since long-range coherence in atomic
positions is required to achieve sharp diffraction spots.

The electron diffraction pattern of quasicrystalline
aluminum-manganese published by Shechtman and his
coworkers has the following features: rings of 10 bright
spots indicate axes of fivefold symmetry, and rings of
six bright spots indicate axes of threefold symmetry.
The twofold symmetry axes are self-evident. The angles
between these axes, indicated on the figure, agree with
the geometry of the icosahedron. The very existence of
spots at all indicates long-range order in atomic positions. Recalling the earlier result that fivefold symmetry
axes are forbidden in crystalline materials, a paradox is
presented by quasicrystals. They have long-range order
in their atomic positions, but they must lack spatial
periodicity.

Three views of the icosahedral symmetry of quasicrystalline aluminum-manganese. Top view is along the fivefold symmetry axis. The centre view, rotating by 37.38°, reveals the threefold axis, and (bottom left) rotating by 58.29° reveals the twofold axis. Copyright Encyclopædia Britannica; rendering for this edition by Rosen Educational Services

QUASIPERIODICITY

Dov Levine and Paul Steinhardt, physicists at the University of Pennsylvania, proposed a resolution of this apparent conflict. They suggested that the translational order of atoms in quasicrystalline alloys might be quasiperiodic rather than periodic. Quasiperiodic patterns share certain characteristics with periodic patterns. In particular, both are deterministic—that is, rules exist that specify the entire pattern. These rules create long-range order. Both periodic and quasiperiodic patterns have diffraction patterns consisting entirely of Bragg peaks. The difference between quasiperiodicity and periodicity is that a quasiperiodic pattern never repeats itself. There are no translational symmetries, and, consequently, there is no minimum spacing between Bragg peaks. Although the peaks are discrete, they fill the diffraction pattern densely.

The most well-known quasiperiodic pattern may be the Fibonacci sequence, discovered during the Middle Ages in the course of studies conducted on rabbit reproduction. Consider the following rules for birth and maturation of rabbits. Start with a single mature rabbit (denoted by the symbol L for large) and a baby rabbit (denoted by S for small). In each generation every L rabbit gives birth to a new S rabbit, while each preexisting S rabbit matures into an L rabbit. A table of rabbit sequences may be established as follows. Start with an L and an S side by side along a line. Replace the L with LS and the S with L to obtain LSL and repeat the procedure. The numbers of rabbits present after each generation are the Fibonacci numbers. The population grows exponentially over time, with the population of each generation approaching τ (the golden mean) multiplied by the population of the previous generation. The sequence of L and S symbols forms a quasiperiodic pattern. It has no subunit that repeats itself periodically. In contrast, a periodic sequence such as LSLLSLLSLLSLLSL . . . has a fundamental unit (LSL) that is precisely repeated at equal intervals. In crystallography such a repeated unit is called a unit cell. Quasiperiodic sequences have no unit cell of finite size. Any portion of the Fibonacci sequence is repeated infinitely often, but at intervals that are not periodic. These intervals themselves form a Fibonacci sequence.

An example of a two-dimensional pattern that combines fivefold rotational symmetry with quasiperiodic translational order is the Penrose pattern, discovered by the English mathematical physicist Roger Penrose. The diffraction pattern of such a sequence closely resembles those of quasicrystalline aluminum-manganese. The rhombic tiles are arranged in sets of parallel rows; the shaded tiles represent one such set, or family. Five families of parallel rows are present in the figure, with 72° angles

The plane is covered by rhombuses (deformed squares). Tiles with parallel edges lie in rows (shaded) separated by large (L) and small (S) intervals.

A Penrose tiling. Copyright Encyclopædia Britannica; rendering for this edition by Rosen Educational Services

between the families, although only one of the five has been shaded. Within a family the spacings between rows are either large (L) or small (S), as labeled in the margin. The ratio of widths of the large rows to the small rows is equal to the golden mean τ, and the quasiperiodic sequence of large and small follows the Fibonacci sequence.

Levine's and Steinhardt's proposal that quasicrystals possess quasiperiodic translational order can be examined in terms of a high-resolution electron micrograph. The rows of bright spots are separated by small and large intervals. As in the Penrose pattern, the length of the large interval divided by the length of the small one equals the golden mean, and the sequence of large and small reproduces the Fibonacci sequence. Levine's and Steinhardt's proposal appears consistent with the electron diffraction results. The origin of the name quasicrystals arises from the fact that these materials have quasiperiodic translational order, as opposed to the periodic order of ordinary crystals.

SYMMETRIES OBSERVED IN QUASICRYSTALS

Consider quasicrystals with the symmetry of an icosahedron. Icosahedral quasicrystals occur in many intermetallic compounds, including aluminum-copper-iron, aluminum-manganese-palladium, aluminum-magnesium-zinc, and aluminum-copper-lithium. Other crystallographically forbidden symmetries have been observed as well. These include decagonal symmetry, which exhibits tenfold rotational symmetry within two-dimensional atomic layers but ordinary translational periodicity perpendicular to these layers. Decagonal symmetry has been found in the compounds aluminum-copper-cobalt and aluminum-nickel-cobalt. Structures that are periodic in two dimensions but follow a Fibonacci sequence in the remaining third dimension occur in aluminum-copper-nickel.

All the compounds named thus far contain aluminum. Indeed, it appears that aluminum is unusually prone to quasicrystal formation, but there do exist icosahedral quasicrystals without it. Some, like gallium-magnesium-zinc, simply substitute the chemically similar element gallium for aluminum. Others, like titanium-manganese, appear chemically unrelated to aluminum-based compounds. Furthermore, some quasicrystals such as chromium-nickel-silicon and vanadium-nickel-silicon display octagonal and dodecagonal structures with eightfold or twelvefold symmetry, respectively, within layers and translational periodicity perpendicular to the layers.

THE ORIGIN OF QUASICRYSTALLINE ORDER

The origin of quasicrystalline order remains in question. No proven explanation clarifies why a material favours crystallographically forbidden rotational symmetry and translational quasiperiodicity when at nearby compositions it forms more conventional crystal structures. The American chemist Linus Pauling noted that these related crystalline structures frequently contain icosahedral motifs within their unit cells, which are then repeated periodically. Pauling proposed that quasicrystals are really ordinary crystalline materials caught out of equilibrium by a type of crystal defect called twinning, in which unit cells are attached at angles defined by these icosahedral motifs. While this may be a reasonable model for rapidly cooled alloys such as Shechtman's original aluminum-manganese, other compounds, such as aluminum-copper-iron, possess quasicrystalline structures in thermodynamic equilibrium. These quasicrystals can be grown slowly and carefully using techniques for growth of high-quality conventional crystals. The more slowly the quasicrystal grows, the more perfect will be its rotational symmetry and quasiperiodicity. Measuring the sharpness of diffraction pattern spots shows perfect ordering on length scales of at least 30,000 angstroms in these carefully prepared quasicrystals. Twinning cannot account for such long-range order.

Levine and Steinhardt proposed that matching rules, such as those Penrose discovered to determine proper placement of his tiles to fill the plane quasiperiodically, may force the atoms into predefined, low-energy locations. Such a mechanism cannot be the complete explanation, though, since the compound forms ordinary crystalline structures at nearby compositions and temperatures. Indeed, it appears that, when quasicrystals are thermo-dynamically stable phases, it is only over a limited range of temperatures close to the melting point. At lower temperatures they transform into ordinary crystal structures. Thermodynamics predicts that the stable structure is the one that minimizes the free energy, defined as the ordinary energy minus the product of the temperature and the entropy. It is likely that entropy (a measure of fluctuations around an ideal structure) must be considered in addition to energy to explain stability of quasicrystals.

PROPERTIES

Along with their novel structures and symmetries, quasi-crystals are expected to exhibit unusual properties. Both their elastic and their electronic behaviour distinguish quasicrystals from ordinary crystalline metals. Elastic response may be studied by measuring the speed of sound waves propagating through the metal. Sound speeds usually vary depending on the direction of propagation relative to axes of high rotational symmetry. Because the icosahedron has such high symmetry—it is closer to a sphere than is, for instance, a cube—the sound speeds turn out to be independent of the direction of propagation.

Longitudinal sound waves (with displacements parallel to the direction of propagation) have speeds different from transverse waves (with displacements perpendicular to the direction of propagation), as is the case for all matter. Because the sound speeds do not depend on direction of propagation, only two elastic constants are required to specify acoustic properties of icosahedral quasicrystals. In contrast, cubic crystals require three elastic constants, and lower-symmetry crystals require up to 21 constants.

ELASTIC PROPERTIES

As a consequence of the translational quasiperiodicity, there exists a second type of elastic deformation beyond the ordinary sound wave, or phonon. Known as phasons, these elastic deformations correspond to rearrangements of the relative atomic positions. Removal of a phason requires adjusting positions of all atoms within a row of atoms in a quasicrystalline structure. At low temperatures motion of atoms within the solid is difficult, and phason strain may be easily frozen into the quasicrystal, limiting its perfection. At high temperatures, close to the melting point, phasons continually fluctuate, and atoms jump from place to place.

ELECTRIC PROPERTIES

The electric properties of quasicrystals have proved to be rather unusual. Unlike their constituent elements, which tend to be good electrical conductors, quasicrystals conduct electricity poorly. For alloys of aluminum-copper-ruthenium these conductivities differ by as much as a factor of 100. As the perfection of the quasicrystalline order grows, the conductivity drops. Such behaviour is consistent with the appearance of a gap in the electronic density of states at the Fermi surface, which is the energy level separating filled electronic states from empty ones.

Since it is only Fermi-surface electrons that carry current, a vanishingly small density of such electronic states leads to low electrical conductivities in semiconductors and insulators. Such a gap in the density of states may also play a role in explaining the formation of quasicrystalline structures. This is known as the Hume-Rothery rule for alloy formation. Since the Fermi-surface electrons are the highest-energy electrons, diminishing the number of such electrons may lower the overall energy.

MECHANICAL PROPERTIES

The mechanical properties of quasicrystals are especially significant because the desire to develop a material that exhibited these properties motivated the investigators who discovered quasicrystals. Mechanical properties also relate to their first potential practical applications. Quasicrystals are exceptionally brittle. They have few dislocations, and those present have low mobility. Since metals bend by creating and moving dislocations, the near absence of dislocation motion causes brittleness. On the positive side, the difficulty of moving dislocations makes quasicrystals extremely hard. They strongly resist deformation. This makes them excellent candidates for high-strength surface coatings. Indeed, the first successful application of quasicrystals was as a surface treatment for aluminum frying pans.

CHAPTER 8
PLASMA

A plasma is an electrically conducting medium in which there are roughly equal numbers of positively and negatively charged particles, produced when the atoms in a gas become ionized. It is sometimes referred to as the fourth state of matter, distinct from the solid, liquid, and gaseous states.

The negative charge is usually carried by electrons, each of which has one unit of negative charge. The positive charge is typically carried by atoms or molecules that are missing those same electrons. In some rare but interesting cases, electrons missing from one type of atom or molecule become attached to another component, resulting in a plasma containing both positive and negative ions. The most extreme case of this type occurs when small but macroscopic dust particles become charged in a state referred to as a dusty plasma. The uniqueness of the plasma state is due to the importance of electric and magnetic forces that act on a plasma in addition to such forces as gravity that affect all forms of matter. Since these electromagnetic forces can act at large distances, a plasma will act collectively much like a fluid even when the particles seldom collide with one another.

Nearly all the visible matter in the universe exists in the plasma state, occurring predominantly in this form in the Sun and stars and in interplanetary and interstellar space. Auroras, lightning, and welding arcs are also plasmas; plasmas exist in neon and fluorescent tubes, in the crystal structure of metallic solids, and in many other phenomena and objects. Earth itself is immersed in a tenuous plasma called the solar wind and is surrounded by a dense plasma called the ionosphere.

A plasma may be produced in the laboratory by heating a gas to an extremely high temperature, which causes such vigorous collisions between its atoms and molecules that electrons are ripped free, yielding the requisite electrons and ions. A similar process occurs inside stars. In space the dominant plasma formation process is photoionization, wherein photons from sunlight or starlight are absorbed by an existing gas, causing electrons to be emitted. Since the Sun and stars shine continuously, virtually all the matter becomes ionized in such cases, and the plasma is said to be fully ionized. This need not be the case, however, for a plasma may be only partially ionized. A completely ionized hydrogen plasma, consisting solely of electrons and protons (hydrogen nuclei), is the most elementary plasma.

THE DEVELOPMENT OF PLASMA PHYSICS

The modern concept of the plasma state is of recent origin, dating back only to the early 1950s. Its history is interwoven with many disciplines. Three basic fields of study made unique early contributions to the development of plasma physics as a discipline: electric discharges, magnetohydrodynamics (in which a conducting fluid such as mercury is studied), and kinetic theory.

Interest in electric-discharge phenomena may be traced back to the beginning of the 18th century, with three English physicists—Michael Faraday in the 1830s and Joseph John Thomson and John Sealy Edward Townsend at the turn of the 19th century—laying the foundations of the present understanding of the phenomena. Irving Langmuir introduced the term *plasma* in

1923 while investigating electric discharges. In 1929 he and Lewi Tonks, another physicist working in the United States, used the term to designate those regions of a discharge in which certain periodic variations of the negatively charged electrons could occur. They called these oscillations plasma oscillations, their behaviour suggesting that of a jellylike substance. Not until 1952, however, when two other American physicists, David Bohm and David Pines, first considered the collective behaviour of electrons in metals as distinct from that in ionized gases, was the general applicability of the concept of a plasma fully appreciated.

The collective behaviour of charged particles in magnetic fields and the concept of a conducting fluid are implicit in magnetohydrodynamic studies, the foundations of which were laid in the early and middle 1800s by Faraday and André-Marie Ampère of France. Not until the 1930s, however, when new solar and geophysical phenomena were being discovered, were many of the basic problems of the mutual interaction between ionized gases and magnetic fields considered. In 1942 Hannes Alfvén, a Swedish physicist, introduced the concept of magnetohydrodynamic waves. This contribution, along with his further studies of space plasmas, led to Alfvén's receipt of the Nobel Prize for Physics in 1970.

These two separate approaches—the study of electric discharges and the study of the behaviour of conducting fluids in magnetic fields—were unified by the introduction of the kinetic theory of the plasma state. This theory states that plasma, like gas, consists of particles in random motion, whose interactions can be through long-range electromagnetic forces as well as via collisions. In 1905 the Dutch physicist Hendrik Antoon Lorentz applied the kinetic equation for atoms (the formulation by the Austrian physicist Ludwig Eduard Boltzmann) to the behaviour of

David Bohm. Keystone/Hulton Archive/Getty Images

electrons in metals. Various physicists and mathematicians in the 1930s and '40s further developed the plasma kinetic theory to a high degree of sophistication. Since the early 1950s interest has increasingly focused on the plasma state itself. Space exploration, the development of electronic devices, a growing awareness of the importance of magnetic fields in astrophysical phenomena, and the quest for controlled thermonuclear (nuclear fusion) power reactors all have stimulated such interest. Many problems remain unsolved in space plasma physics research, owing to the complexity of the phenomena. For example, descriptions of the solar wind must include not only equations dealing with the effects of gravity, temperature, and pressure as needed in atmospheric science but also the equations of the Scottish physicist James Clerk Maxwell, which are needed to describe the electromagnetic field.

PLASMA OSCILLATIONS AND PARAMETERS

Just as a lightweight cork in water will bob up and down about its rest position, any general displacement of light electrons as a group with respect to the positive ions in a plasma leads to the oscillation of the electrons as a whole about an equilibrium state. In the case of the cork, the restoring force is provided by gravity; in plasma oscillations, it is provided by the electric force. These movements are the plasma oscillations that were studied by Langmuir and Tonks. Analogously, just as buoyancy effects guide water waves, plasma oscillations are related to waves in the electron component of the plasma called Langmuir waves. Wavelike phenomena play a critical role in the behaviour of plasmas.

The time τ required for an oscillation of this type is the most important temporal parameter in a plasma. The main spatial parameter is the Debye length, h, which is the distance traveled by the average thermal electron in time $\tau/2\pi$. A plasma can be defined in terms of these parameters as a partially or fully ionized gas that satisfies the following criteria: (1) a constituent electron may complete many plasma oscillations before it collides with either an ion or one of the other heavy constituents, (2) inside each sphere with a radius equal to the Debye length, there are many particles, and (3) the plasma itself is much larger than the Debye length in every dimension.

Another important temporal parameter is the time between collisions of particles. In any gas, separate collision frequencies are defined for collisions between all different particle types. The total collision frequency for a particular species is the weighted sum of all the separate frequencies. Two basic types of collision may occur: elastic and inelastic. In an elastic collision, the total kinetic energy of all the particles participating in the collision is the same before and after the event. In an inelastic collision, a fraction of the kinetic energy is transferred to the internal energy of the colliding particles. In an atom, for example, the electrons have certain allowed (discrete) energies and are said to be bound. During a collision, a bound electron may be excited— that is, raised from a low to a high energy state. This can occur, however, only by the expenditure of kinetic energy and only if the kinetic energy exceeds the difference between the two energy states. If the energy is sufficient, a bound electron may be excited to such a high level that it becomes a free electron, and the atom is said to be ionized; the minimum, or threshold, energy required to free an electron is called the ionization energy. Inelastic collisions may also occur with positive ions unless all the electrons have been stripped away. In general, only collisions of electrons and photons (quanta of electromagnetic radiation) with atoms and ions are significant in these inelastic collisions; ionization by a photon is called photoionization.

A molecule has additional discrete energy states, which may be excited by particle or photon collisions. At sufficiently high energies of interaction, the molecule can dissociate into atoms or into atoms and atomic ions. As in the case of atoms, collision of electrons and photons with molecules may cause ionization, producing molecular ions. In general, the reaction rate for inelastic collisions is similar to that of chemical reactions. At sufficiently high temperatures, the atoms are stripped of all electrons and become bare atomic nuclei. Finally, at temperatures of about 1,000,000 K or greater, nuclear reactions can occur—another form of inelastic collisions. When such reactions lead to the formation of heavier elements, the process is called thermonuclear fusion; mass is transmuted, and kinetic energy is gained instead of lost.

All sources of energy now existing on the Earth can be traced in one way or another to the nuclear fusion reactions inside the Sun or some long-extinct star. In such energy sources, gravity controls and confines the fusion process. The high temperatures required for the nuclear fusion reactions that take place in a hydrogen, or thermonuclear, bomb are attained by first igniting an atomic bomb, which produces a fission chain reaction. One of the great challenges of humankind is to create these high temperatures in a controlled manner and to harness the energy of nuclear fusion. This is the great practical goal of plasma physics—to produce nuclear fusion on the Earth. Confinement schemes devised by scientists use magnetic fields or the inertia of an implosion to guide and control the hot plasma.

BASIC PLASMA PHYSICS

Apart from solid-state plasmas, such as those in metallic crystals, plasmas do not usually occur naturally at the surface of the Earth. For laboratory experiments and technological applications, plasmas therefore must be produced artificially. Because the atoms of such alkalies as potassium, sodium, and cesium possess low ionization energies, plasmas may be produced from these by the direct application of heat at temperatures of about 3,000 K. In most gases, however, before any significant degree of ionization is achieved, temperatures in the neighbourhood of 10,000 K are required. A convenient unit for measuring temperature in the study of plasmas is the electron volt (eV), which is the energy gained by an electron in vacuum when it is accelerated across one volt of electric potential. The temperature, W, measured in electron volts is given by $W = T/12,000$ when T is expressed in kelvins. The temperatures required for self-ionization thus range from 2.5 to 8 electron volts, since such values are typical of the energy needed to remove one electron from an atom or molecule.

PLASMA FORMATION

Because all substances melt at temperatures far below that level, no container yet built can withstand an external application of the heat necessary to form a plasma; therefore, any heating must be supplied internally. One technique is to apply an electric field to the gas to accelerate and scatter any free electrons, thereby heating the plasma. This type of ohmic heating is similar to the method in which free electrons in the heating element of an electric oven heat the coil. Because of their small energy loss in elastic collisions, electrons can be raised to much higher temperatures than other particles. For plasma formation a sufficiently high electric field must be applied, its exact value depending on geometry and the gas pressure. The electric field may be set up via electrodes or by transformer action, in which the electric field is induced by a changing magnetic field. Laboratory temperatures of about 10 million K, or 8 kiloelectron volts (keV), with electron densities of about 10^{19} per cubic metre have been achieved by the transformer method. The temperature is eventually limited by energy losses to the outside environment. Extremely high temperatures, but relatively low-density plasmas, have been produced by the separate injection of ions and electrons into a mirror system (a plasma device using a particular arrangement of magnetic fields for containment). Other methods have used the high temperatures that develop behind a wave that is moving much faster than sound to produce what is called a shock front; lasers have also been employed.

Natural plasma heating and ionization occur in analogous ways. In a lightning-induced plasma, the electric current carried by the stroke heats the atmosphere in the same manner as in the ohmic heating technique described above. In solar and stellar plasmas the heating is internal and caused by nuclear fusion reactions. In the solar corona, the heating occurs because of waves that propagate from the surface into the Sun's atmosphere, heating the plasma much like shock-wave heating in laboratory plasmas. In the ionosphere, ionization is accomplished not through heating of the plasma but rather by the flux of energetic photons from the Sun. Far-ultraviolet rays and X rays from the Sun have enough energy to ionize atoms in Earth's atmosphere. Some of the energy also goes into heating the gas, with the result that the upper atmosphere, called the thermosphere, is quite hot.

Lightning flashes over a high-rise building in Kuala Lumpur. Plasma is produced when the electric current in a lightning bolt heats the atmosphere. Saeed Khan/AFP/Getty Images

These processes protect Earth from energetic photons much as the ozone layer protects terrestrial life-forms from lower-energy ultraviolet light. The typical temperature 300 km (200 miles) above Earth's surface is 1,200 K (900 °C, or 1,700 °F), or about 0.1 eV. Although it is quite warm compared with the surface of the Earth, this temperature is too low to create self-ionization. When the Sun sets with respect to the ionosphere, the source of ionization ceases, and the lower portion of the ionosphere reverts to its nonplasma state. Some ions, in particular singly charged oxygen (O^+), live long enough that some plasma remains until the next sunrise. In the case of an aurora, a plasma is created in the nighttime or daytime atmosphere when beams of electrons are accelerated to hundreds or thousands of electron volts and smash into the atmosphere.

METHODS OF DESCRIBING PLASMA PHENOMENA

The behaviour of a plasma may be described at different levels. If collisions are relatively infrequent, it is useful to consider the motions of individual particles. In most plasmas of interest, a magnetic field exerts a force on a charged particle only if the particle is moving, the force being at right angles to both the direction of the field and the direction of particle motion. In a uniform magnetic field (B), a charged particle gyrates about a line of force. The centre of the orbit is called the guiding centre. The particle may also have a component of velocity parallel to the magnetic field and so traces out a helix in a uniform magnetic field. If a uniform electric field (E) is applied at right angles to the direction of the magnetic field, the guiding centre drifts with a uniform velocity of magnitude equal to the ratio of the electric to the magnetic field (E/B), at right angles to both the electric and magnetic fields. A particle starting from rest in such fields follows the same cycloidal path a dot on the rim of a rolling wheel follows. Although the "wheel" radius and its sense of rotation vary for different particles, the guiding centre moves at the same E/B velocity, independent of the particle's charge and mass. Should the electric field change with time, the problem would become even more complex. If, however, such an alternating electric field varies at the same frequency as the cyclotron frequency (i.e., the rate of gyration), the guiding centre will remain stationary, and the particle will be forced to travel in an ever-expanding orbit. This phenomenon is called cyclotron resonance and is the basis of the cyclotron particle accelerator.

The motion of a particle about its guiding centre constitutes a circular current. As such, the motion produces a dipole magnetic field not unlike that produced by a simple bar magnet. Thus, a moving charge not only interacts with magnetic fields but also produces them. The direction of the magnetic field produced by a moving particle, however, depends both on whether the particle is positively or negatively charged and on the direction of its motion. If the motion of the charged particles is completely random, the net associated magnetic field is zero. On the other hand, if charges of different sign have an average relative velocity (i.e., if an electric current flows), then a net magnetic field over and above any externally applied field exists. The magnetic interaction between charged particles is therefore of a collective, rather than of an individual, particle nature.

At a higher level of description than that of the single particle, kinetic equations of the Boltzmann type are used. Such equations essentially describe the behaviour of those particles about a point in a small-volume element, the particle velocities lying within a small range about a given value. The interactions with all other velocity groups, volume elements, and any externally applied electric and magnetic fields are taken into account. In many cases, equations of a fluid type may be derived from the kinetic equations; they express the conservation of mass, momentum, and energy per unit volume, with one such set of equations for each particle type.

DETERMINATION OF PLASMA VARIABLES

The basic variables useful in the study of plasma are number densities, temperatures, electric and magnetic field strengths, and particle velocities. In the laboratory and in space, both electrostatic (charged) and magnetic types of sensory devices called probes help determine the magnitudes of such variables. With the electrostatic probe, ion densities, electron and ion temperatures, and electrostatic potential differences can be determined. Small search coils and other types of magnetic probes yield values for the magnetic field; and from Maxwell's electromagnetic equations the current and charge densities and the induced component of the electric field may be found. Interplanetary spacecraft have carried such probes to nearly every planet in the solar system, revealing to scientists such plasma phenomena as lightning on Jupiter and the sounds of Saturn's rings and radiation belts. In the early 1990s, signals were being relayed to the Earth from several spacecraft approaching the edge of the plasma boundary to the solar system, the heliopause.

In the laboratory the absorption, scattering, and excitation of neutral and high-energy ion beams are helpful in determining electron temperatures and densities; in general, the refraction, reflection, absorption, scattering, and interference of electromagnetic waves also provide ways to determine these same variables. This technique has also been employed to remotely measure the properties of the plasmas in the near-space regions of Earth using the incoherent scatter radar method. The largest single antenna is at the National Astronomy and Ionosphere Center at Arecibo in Puerto Rico. It has a circumference of 305 metres and was completed in 1963. It is still used to probe space plasmas to distances of 3,000 km (2,000 miles). The method works by bouncing radio waves from small irregularities in the electron gas that occur owing to random thermal motions of the particles. The returning signal is shifted slightly from the transmitted one—because of the Doppler-shift effect—and the velocity of the plasma can be determined in a manner similar to the way in which the police detect a speeding car. Using this method, the wind speed in space can be found, along with the temperature, density, electric field, and even the types of ions present. In geospace the appropriate radar frequencies are in the range of 50 to 1,000 megahertz (MHz), while in the laboratory, where the plasma densities and plasma frequencies are higher, microwaves and lasers must be used.

Aside from the above methods, much can be learned from the radiation generated and emitted by the plasma itself; in fact, this is the only means of studying cosmic plasma beyond the solar system. The various spectroscopic techniques covering the entire continuous radiation spectrum determine temperatures and identify such non-thermal sources as those pulses producing synchrotron radiations.

WAVES IN PLASMAS

The waves most familiar to people are the buoyancy waves that propagate on the surfaces of lakes and oceans and break onto the world's beaches. Equally familiar, although not necessarily recognized as waves, are the disturbances in the atmosphere that create what is referred to as the weather. Wave phenomena are particularly important in the behaviour of plasmas. In fact, one of the three criteria for the existence of a plasma is that the particle-particle collision rate be less than the plasma-oscillation frequency. This in turn implies that the collective interactions that control the plasma gas depend on the electric and magnetic field effects as much as, or more so than, simple collisions. Since waves are able to propagate, the possibility exists for force fields to act at large distances from the point where they originated.

Ordinary fluids can support the propagation of sound (acoustic) waves, which involve pressure, temperature, and velocity variations. Electromagnetic waves can propagate even in a vacuum but are slowed down in most cases by the interaction of the electric fields in the waves with the charged particles bound in the atoms or molecules of the gas. Although it is important for a complete description of electromagnetic waves, such an interaction is not very strong. In a plasma, however, the particles react in concert with any electromagnetic field (e.g., as in an electromagnetic wave) as well as with any pressure or velocity field (e.g., as in a sound wave). In fact, in a plasma sound wave the electrons and ions become slightly separated owing to their difference in mass, and an electric field builds up to bring them back together. The result is called an ion acoustic wave. This is just one of the many types of waves that can exist in a plasma. The brief discussion that follows touches on the main types in order of increasing wave-oscillation frequency.

LOW-FREQUENCY WAVES

At the lowest frequency are Alfvén waves, which require the presence of a magnetic field to exist. In fact, except for ion acoustic waves, the existence of a background magnetic field is required for any wave with a frequency less than the plasma frequency to occur in a plasma. Most natural plasmas are threaded by a magnetic field, and laboratory plasmas often use a magnetic field for confinement, so this requirement is usually met, and all types of waves can occur.

Alfvén waves are analogous to the waves that occur on the stretched string of a guitar. In this case, the string represents a magnetic field line. When a small magnetic field disturbance takes place, the field is bent slightly, and the disturbance propagates in the direction of the magnetic field. Since any changing magnetic field creates an electric field, an electromagnetic wave results. Such waves are the slowest and have the lowest frequencies of any known electromagnetic waves. For example, the solar wind streams out from the Sun with a speed greater than either electromagnetic (Alfvén) or sound waves. This means that, when the solar wind hits Earth's outermost magnetic field lines, a shock wave results to "inform" the incoming plasma that an obstacle exists, much like the shock wave associated with a supersonic airplane. The shock wave travels toward the Sun at the same speed but in the opposite direction as the solar wind, so it appears to stand still with respect to Earth. Because there are almost no particle-particle collisions, this type of collisionless shock wave is of great interest to space plasma physicists who postulate that similar shocks occur around supernovas and in other astrophysical plasmas. On Earth's side of the shock wave, the heated and slowed solar wind interacts with Earth's atmosphere via Alfvén waves propagating along the magnetic field lines.

The turbulent surface of the Sun radiates large-amplitude Alfvén waves, which are thought to be responsible for heating the corona to 1,000,000 K. Such waves can also produce fluctuations in the solar wind, and, as they propagate through it to Earth, they seem to control the occurrence of magnetic storms and auroras that are capable of disrupting communication systems and power grids on the planet.

Two fundamental types of wave motion can occur: longitudinal, like a sound or ion acoustic wave, in which particle oscillation is in a direction parallel to the direction of wave propagation; and transverse, like a surface water wave, in which particle oscillation is in a plane perpendicular to the direction of wave propagation. In all cases, a wave may be characterized by a speed of propagation (u), a wavelength (λ), and a frequency (ν) related by an expression in which the velocity is equal to the product of the wavelength and frequency, namely, $u = \lambda\nu$. The Alfvén wave is a transverse wave and propagates with a velocity that depends on the particle density and the magnetic field strength. The velocity is equal to the magnetic flux density (B) divided by the square root of the mass density

(ρ) times the permeability of free space (μ_o) — that is to say, $B/\sqrt{\mu_o\rho}$. The ion acoustic wave is a longitudinal wave and also propagates parallel to the magnetic field at a speed roughly equal to the average thermal velocity of the ions. Perpendicular to the magnetic field a different type of longitudinal wave called a magnetosonic wave can occur.

HIGHER FREQUENCY WAVES

In these waves the plasma behaves as a whole, and the velocity is independent of wave frequency. At higher frequencies, however, the separate behaviour of ions and electrons causes the wave velocities to vary with direction and frequency. The Alfvén wave splits into two components, referred to as the fast and slow Alfvén waves, which propagate at different frequency-dependent speeds. At still higher frequencies these two waves (called the electron cyclotron and ion cyclotron waves, respectively) cause electron and cyclotron resonances (synchronization) at the appropriate resonance frequencies. Beyond these resonances, transverse wave propagation does not occur at all until frequencies comparable to and above the plasma frequency are reached.

At frequencies between the ion and electron gyrofrequencies lies a wave mode called a whistler. This name comes from the study of plasma waves generated by lightning. When early researchers listened to natural radio waves by attaching an antenna to an audio amplifier, they heard a strange whistling sound. The whistle occurs when the electrical signal from lightning in one hemisphere travels along the Earth's magnetic field lines to the other hemisphere. The trip is so long that some waves (those at higher frequencies) arrive first, resulting in the generation of a whistlelike sound. These natural waves were used to probe the region of space around Earth before spacecraft became available. Such a frequency-dependent wave velocity is called wave dispersion because the various frequencies disperse with distance.

The speed of an ion acoustic wave also becomes dispersive at high frequencies, and a resonance similar to electron plasma oscillations occurs at a frequency determined by electrostatic oscillations of the ions. Beyond this frequency no sonic wave propagates parallel to a magnetic field until the frequency reaches the plasma frequency, above which electroacoustic waves occur. The wavelength of these waves at the critical frequency (ω_p) is infinite, the electron behaviour at this frequency taking the form of the plasma oscillations of Langmuir and Tonks. Even without particle collisions, waves shorter than the Debye length are heavily damped—i.e., their amplitude decreases rapidly with time. This phenomenon, called Landau damping, arises because some electrons have the same velocity as the wave. As they move with the wave, they are accelerated much like a surfer on a water wave and thus extract energy from the wave, damping it in the process.

Containment

Magnetic fields are used to contain high-density, high-temperature plasmas because such fields exert pressures and tensile forces on the plasma. An equilibrium configuration is reached only when at all points in the plasma these pressures and tensions exactly balance the pressure from the motion of the particles. A well-known example of this is the pinch effect observed in specially designed equipment. If an external electric current is imposed on a cylindrically shaped plasma and flows parallel to the plasma axis, the magnetic forces act inward and cause the plasma to constrict, or pinch. An equilibrium condition is reached in which the temperature is proportional to the square of the electric current. This result suggests that any temperature may be achieved by making the electric current sufficiently large, the heating resulting from currents and compression. In practice, however, since no plasma can be infinitely long, serious energy losses occur at the ends of the cylinder; also, major instabilities develop in such a simple configuration. Suppression of such instabilities has been one of the major efforts in laboratory plasma physics and in the quest to control the nuclear fusion reaction.

A useful way of describing the confinement of a plasma by a magnetic field is by measuring containment time (τ_c), or the average time for a charged particle to diffuse out of the plasma; this time is different for each type of configuration. Various types of instabilities can occur in plasma. These lead to a loss of plasma and a catastrophic decrease in containment time. The most important of these is called magnetohydrodynamic instability. Although an equilibrium state may exist, it may not correspond to the lowest possible energy. The plasma, therefore, seeks a state of lower potential energy, just as a ball at rest on top of a hill (representing an equilibrium state) rolls down to the bottom if perturbed; the lower energy state of the plasma corresponds to a ball at the bottom of a valley. In seeking the lower energy state, turbulence develops, leading to enhanced diffusion, increased electrical resistivity, and large heat losses. In toroidal geometry, circular plasma currents must be kept below a critical value called the Kruskal-Shafranov limit, otherwise a particularly violent instability consisting of a series of kinks may occur. Although a completely stable system appears to be virtually impossible, considerable progress has been made in devising systems that eliminate the major instabilities. Temperatures on the order of 10,000,000 K at densities of 10^{19} particles per cubic metre and containment times as high as $\frac{1}{50}$ of a second have been achieved.

APPLICATIONS OF PLASMAS

The most important practical applications of plasmas lie in the future, largely in the field of power production. The major method of generating electric power has been to use heat sources to convert water to steam, which drives turbogenerators. Such heat sources depend on the combustion of fossil fuels, such as coal, oil, and natural gas, and fission processes in nuclear reactors. A potential source of heat might be supplied by a fusion reactor, with a basic element of deuterium-tritium plasma; nuclear fusion collisions between those isotopes of hydrogen would release large amounts of energy to the kinetic energy of the reaction products (the neutrons and the nuclei of hydrogen and helium atoms). By absorbing those products in a surrounding medium, a powerful heat source could be created. To realize a net power output from such a generating station—allowing for plasma radiation and particle losses and for the somewhat inefficient conversion of heat to electricity—plasma temperatures of about 100,000,000 K and a product of particle density times containment time of about 10^{20} seconds per cubic metre are necessary. For example, at a density of 10^{20} particles per metre cubed, the containment time must be one second. Such figures are yet to be reached, although there has been much progress.

In general, there are two basic methods of eliminating or minimizing end losses from an artificially created plasma: the production of toroidal plasmas and the use of magnetic mirrors. A toroidal plasma is essentially one in which a plasma of cylindrical cross section is bent in a circle so as to close on itself. For such plasmas to be in equilibrium and stable, however, special magnetic fields are required, the largest component of which is a circular field parallel to the axis of the plasma. In addition, a number of turbulent plasma processes must be controlled to keep the system stable. In 1991 a machine called the JET (Joint European Torus) was able to generate 1.7 million watts of fusion power for almost 2 seconds after researchers injected titrium into the JET's magnetically confined plasma. It was the first successful controlled production of fusion power in such a confined medium.

Besides generating power, a fusion reactor might desalinate seawater. Approximately two-thirds of the world's land surface is uninhabited, with one-half of this area being arid. The use of both giant fission and fusion reactors in the large-scale evaporation of seawater could make irrigation of such areas economically feasible. Another possibility in power production is the elimination of the heat–steam–mechanical energy chain. One suggestion depends on the dynamo effect. If a plasma moves perpendicular to a magnetic field, an electromotive force, according to Faraday's law, is generated in a direction perpendicular to both the direction of flow of the plasma and the magnetic field. This dynamo effect can drive a current in an external circuit connected to electrodes in the plasma, and thus electric power may be produced without the need for steam-driven rotating machinery. This process is referred to as magnetohydrodynamic (MHD) power generation and has been proposed as a method of extracting power from certain types of fission reactors. Such a generator powers the auroras as the Earth's magnetic field lines tap electrical current from the MHD generator in the solar wind.

The inverse of the dynamo effect, called the motor effect, may be used to accelerate plasma. By pulsing cusp-shaped magnetic fields in a plasma, for example, it is possible to achieve thrusts proportional to the square of the magnetic field. Motors based on such a technique have been proposed for the propulsion of craft in deep space. They have the advantage of being capable of achieving large exhaust velocities, thus minimizing the amount of fuel carried.

A practical application of plasma involves the glow discharge that occurs between two electrodes at pressures of one-thousandth of an atmosphere or thereabouts. Such glow discharges are responsible for the light given off by neon tubes and such other light sources as fluorescent lamps, which operate by virtue of the plasmas they produce in electric discharge. The degree of ionization in such plasmas is usually low, but electron densities of 10^{16} to 10^{18} electrons per cubic metre can be achieved with an electron temperature of 100,000 K. The electrons responsible for current flow are produced by ionization in a region near the cathode, with most of the potential difference between the two electrodes occurring there. This region does not contain a plasma, but the region between it and the anode (i.e., the positive electrode) does.

Other applications of the glow discharge include electronic switching devices; it and similar plasmas produced by radio-frequency techniques can be used to provide ions for particle accelerators and act as generators of laser beams. As the current is increased through a glow discharge, a stage is reached when the energy generated at the cathode is sufficient to provide all the conduction electrons directly from the cathode surface, rather than from gas between the electrodes. Under this condition the large cathode potential difference disappears, and the plasma column contracts. This new state of electric discharge is called an arc. Compared with the glow discharge, it is a high-density plasma and will operate over a large range of pressures. Arcs are used as light sources for welding, in electronic switching, for rectification of alternating currents, and in high-temperature chemistry. Running an arc between concentric electrodes and injecting gas into such a region causes a hot, high-density plasma mixture called a plasma jet to be ejected. It has many chemical and metallurgical applications.

NATURAL PLASMAS

It has been suggested that the universe originated as a violent explosion about 10 billion years ago and initially consisted of a fireball of completely ionized hydrogen plasma. Irrespective of the truth of this, there is little matter in the universe now that does not exist in the plasma state. The observed stars are composed of plasmas, as are interstellar and interplanetary media and the outer atmospheres of planets. Scientific knowledge of the universe has come primarily from studies of electromagnetic radiation emitted by plasmas and transmitted through them and, since the 1960s, from space probes within the solar system.

EXTRATERRESTRIAL FORMS

In a star the plasma is bound together by gravitational forces, and the enormous energy it emits originates in thermonuclear fusion reactions within the interior. Heat is transferred from the interior to the exterior by radiation in the outer layers, where convection is of greater importance. In the vicinity of a hot star, the interstellar medium consists almost entirely of completely ionized hydrogen, ionized by the star's ultraviolet radiation. Such regions are referred to as H II regions. The greater proportion by far of interstellar medium, however, exists in the form of neutral hydrogen clouds referred to as H I regions. Because the heavy atoms in such clouds are ionized by ultraviolet radiation (or photoionized), they also are considered to be plasmas, although the degree of ionization is probably only one part in 10,000. Other components of the interstellar medium are grains of dust and cosmic rays, the latter consisting of very high-energy atomic nuclei completely stripped of electrons. The almost isotropic velocity distribution of the cosmic rays may stem from interactions with waves of the background plasma.

Throughout this universe of plasma there are magnetic fields. In interstellar space magnetic fields are about 5×10^{-6} gauss (a unit of magnetic field strength) and in interplanetary space 5×10^{-5} gauss, whereas in intergalactic space they could be as low as 10^{-9} gauss. These values are exceedingly small compared with Earth's surface field of about 5×10^{-1} gauss. Although small in an absolute sense, these fields are nevertheless gigantic, considering the scales involved. For example, to simulate interstellar phenomena in the laboratory, fields of about 10^{15} gauss would be necessary. Thus, these fields play a major role in nearly all astrophysical phenomena. On the Sun the average surface field is in the vicinity of 1 to 2 gauss, but magnetic disturbances arise, such as sunspots, in which fields of between 10 and 1,000 gauss occur. Many other stars are also known to have magnetic fields. Field strengths of 10^{-3} gauss are associated with various extragalactic nebulae from which synchrotron radiation has been observed.

SOLAR-TERRESTRIAL FORMS

The most notable natural plasmas are those that occur in the space environment around Earth. Some of these plasmas create currents that have caused power outages on Earth's surface.

REGIONS OF THE SUN

The visible region of the Sun is the photosphere, with its radiation being about the same as the continuum radiation from a 5,800 K blackbody. Lying above the photosphere is the chromosphere, which is observed by the emission of line radiation from various atoms and ions. Outside the chromosphere, the corona expands into the ever-blowing solar wind), which on passing through the planetary system eventually encounters the interstellar medium. The corona can be seen in spectacular fashion when the Moon eclipses the bright photosphere. During the times in which sunspots are greatest in number (called the sunspot maximum), the corona is very extended and the solar wind is fierce. Sunspot activity waxes and wanes with roughly an 11-year cycle. During the mid-1600s and early 1700s, sunspots virtually disappeared for a period known as the Maunder minimum. This time coincided with the Little Ice Age in Europe, and much conjecture has arisen about the possible effect of sunspots on climate. Periodic variations similar to that of sunspots have been observed in tree rings and lake-bed sedimentation. If real, such an effect is important because it implies that the Earth's climate is fragile.

In 1958 the American astrophysicist Eugene Parker showed that the equations describing the flow of plasma in the Sun's gravitational field had one solution that allowed the gas to become supersonic and to escape the Sun's pull. The solution was much like the description of a rocket nozzle in which the constriction in the flow is analogous to the effect of gravity. Parker predicted the Sun's atmosphere would behave just as this particular solar-wind solution predicts rather than according to the solar-breeze solutions suggested by others. The interplanetary satellite probes of the 1960s proved his solution to be correct.

INTERACTION OF THE SOLAR WIND AND THE MAGNETOSPHERE

The solar wind is a collisionless plasma made up primarily of electrons and protons and carries an outflow of matter moving at supersonic and super-Alfvénic speed. The wind takes with it an extension of the Sun's magnetic field, which is frozen into the highly conducting fluid. In the region of Earth, the wind has an average speed of 400 km (250 miles) per second; and, when it encounters the planet's magnetic field, a shock front develops, the pressures acting to compress the field on the side toward the Sun and elongate it on the nightside (in Earth's lee away from the Sun). Earth's magnetic field is therefore confined to a cavity called the magnetosphere, into which the direct entry of the solar wind is prohibited. This cavity extends for about 10 Earth radii on the Sun's side and about 1,000 Earth radii on the nightside.

Inside this vast magnetic field a region of circulating plasma is driven by the transfer of momentum from the solar wind. Plasma flows parallel to the solar wind on the edges of this region and back toward Earth in its interior. The resulting system acts as a secondary magnetohydrodynamic generator (the primary one being the solar wind itself). Both generators produce potential on the order of 100,000 volts. The solar-wind potential appears across the polar caps of Earth, while the magnetospheric potential appears across the auroral oval. The latter is the region of the Earth where energetic electrons and ions precipitate into the planet's atmosphere, creating a spectacular light show. This particle flux is energetic enough to act as a new source of plasmas even when the Sun is no longer shining. The auroral oval becomes a good conductor; and large electric currents flow along it, driven by the potential difference across the system. These currents commonly are on the order of 1,000,000 amperes.

The plasma inside the magnetosphere is extremely hot (1–10 million K) and very tenuous (1–10 particles per cubic cm). The particles are heated by a number of interesting plasma effects, the most curious of which is the auroral acceleration process itself. A particle accelerator that may be the prototype for cosmic accelerators throughout the universe is located roughly 1 Earth radius above the auroral oval and linked to it by all-important magnetic field lines. In this region the auroral electrons are boosted by a potential difference on the order of 3–6 kilovolts, most likely created by an electric field parallel to the magnetic field lines and directed away from Earth. Such a field is difficult to explain because magnetic field lines usually act like nearly perfect conductors. The auroras occur on magnetic field lines that—if it were not for the distortion of Earth's dipole field—would cross the equatorial plane at a distance of 6–10 Earth radii.

Closer to Earth, within about 4 Earth radii, the planet wrests control of the system away from the solar wind. Inside this region the plasma rotates with Earth, just as its atmosphere rotates with it. This system can also be thought of as a magnetohydrodynamic generator in which the rotation of the atmosphere and the ionospheric plasma in it create an electric field that puts the inner magnetosphere in rotation about Earth's axis. Since this inner region is in contact with the dayside of Earth where the Sun creates copious amounts of plasma in the ionosphere, the inner zone fills up with dense, cool plasma to form the plasmasphere. On a planet such as Jupiter, which has both a larger magnetic field and a higher rotation rate than Earth, planetary control extends much farther from the surface.

THE IONOSPHERE AND UPPER ATMOSPHERE

At altitudes below about 2,000 km (1,200 miles), the plasma is referred to as the ionosphere. Thousands of rocket probes have helped chart the vertical structure of this region of the atmosphere, and numerous satellites have provided latitudinal and longitudinal information. The ionosphere was discovered in the early 1900s when radio waves were found to propagate "over the horizon." If radio waves have frequencies near or below the plasma frequency, they cannot propagate throughout the plasma of the ionosphere and thus do not escape into space; they are instead either reflected or absorbed. At night the absorption is low since little plasma exists at the height of roughly 100 km (60 miles) where absorption is greatest. Thus, the ionosphere acts as an effective mirror, as does the Earth's surface, and waves can be reflected around the entire planet much as in a waveguide. A great communications revolution was initiated by the wireless, which relied on radio waves to transmit audio signals. Development continues to this day with satellite systems that must propagate through the ionospheric plasma. In this case, the wave frequency must be higher than the highest plasma frequency in the ionosphere so that the waves will not be reflected away from the Earth.

The dominant ion in the upper atmosphere is atomic oxygen, while below about 200 km (120 miles) molecular oxygen and nitric oxide are most prevalent. Meteor showers also provide large numbers of metallic atoms of elements such as iron, silicon, and magnesium, which become ionized in sunlight and last for long periods of time. These form vast ion clouds, which are responsible for much of the fading in and out of radio stations at night.

THE LOWER ATMOSPHERE AND SURFACE OF EARTH

A more normal type of cloud forms at the base of Earth's plasma blanket in the summer polar mesosphere regions. Located at an altitude of 85 km (50 miles), such a cloud is the highest on Earth and can be seen only when darkness has just set in on the planet. Hence, clouds of this kind have been called noctilucent clouds. They are thought to be composed of charged and possibly dusty ice crystals that form in the coldest portion of the atmosphere at a temperature of 120 K (-150 °C, or -240 °F). This unusual medium has much in common with dusty plasmas in planetary rings and other cosmic systems. Noctilucent clouds have been increasing in frequency throughout the 20th century and may be a forerunner of global change.

High-energy particles also exist in the magnetosphere. At about 1.5 and 3.5 Earth radii from the centre of the planet, two regions contain high-energy particles. These regions are the Van Allen radiation belts, named after the American scientist James Van Allen, who discovered them using radiation detectors aboard early spacecraft. The charged particles in the belts are trapped in the mirror system formed by Earth's magnetic dipole field.

Plasma can exist briefly in the lowest regions of the Earth's atmosphere. In a lightning stroke an oxygen-nitrogen plasma is heated at approximately 20,000 K with an ionization of about 20 percent, similar to that of a laboratory arc. Although the stroke is only a few centimetres thick and lasts only a fraction of a second, tremendous energies are dissipated. A lightning flash between the ground and a cloud, on the average, consists of four such strokes in rapid succession. At all times, lightning is occurring somewhere on Earth, charging the surface negatively with respect to the ionosphere by roughly 200,000 volts, even far from the nearest thunderstorm. If lightning ceased everywhere for even one hour, Earth would discharge. An associated phenomenon is ball lightning. There are authenticated reports of glowing, floating, stable balls of light several tens of centimetres in diameter occurring at times of intense electrical activity in the atmosphere. On contact with an object, these balls release large amounts of energy. Although lightning balls are probably plasmas, so far no adequate explanation of them has been given.

Considering the origins of plasma physics and the fact that the universe is little more than a vast sea of plasma, it is ironic that the only naturally occurring plasmas at the surface of Earth besides lightning are those to be found in ordinary matter. The free electrons responsible for electrical conduction in a metal constitute a plasma. Ions are fixed in position at lattice points, and so plasma behaviour in metals is limited to such phenomena as plasma oscillations and electron cyclotron waves (called helicon waves) in which the electron component behaves separately from the ion component. In semiconductors, on the other hand, the current carriers are electrons and positive holes, the latter behaving in the material as free positive charges of finite mass. By proper preparation, the number of electrons and holes can be made approximately equal so that the full range of plasma behaviour can be observed.

MAGNETIC FIELDS

The importance of magnetic fields in astrophysical phenomena has already been noted. It is believed that these fields are produced by self-generating dynamos, although the exact details are still not fully understood. In the case of Earth, differential rotation in its liquid conducting core causes the external magnetic dipole field (manifest as the North and South poles). Cyclonic turbulence in the liquid, generated by heat conduction and Coriolis forces (apparent forces accompanying all rotating systems, including the heavenly bodies), generates the dipole field from these loops. Over geologic time, Earth's field occasionally becomes small and then changes direction, the North Pole becoming the South Pole and vice versa. During the times in which the magnetic field is small, cosmic rays can more easily reach Earth's surface and may affect life forms by increasing the rate at which genetic mutations occur.

Similar magnetic-field generation processes are believed to occur in both the Sun and the Milky Way Galaxy. In the Sun the circular internal magnetic field is made observable by lines of force apparently breaking the solar surface to form exposed loops; entry and departure points are what are observed as sunspots. Although the exterior magnetic field of Earth is that of a dipole, this is further modified by currents in both the ionosphere and magnetosphere. Lunar and solar tides in the ionosphere lead to motions across Earth's field that produce currents, like a dynamo, that modify the initial field. The auroral oval current systems discussed earlier create even larger magnetic-field fluctuations. The intensity of these currents is modulated by the intensity of the solar wind, which also induces or produces other currents in the magnetosphere. Such currents taken together constitute the essence of a magnetic storm.

CHAPTER 9
CLUSTERS

A toms and molecules are the smallest forms of matter typically encountered under normal conditions and are in that sense the basic building blocks of the material world. There are phenomena, such as lightning and electric discharges of other kinds, that allow free electrons to be observed, but these are exceptional occurrences. It is of course in its gaseous state that matter is encountered at its atomic or molecular level; in gases each molecule is an independent entity, only occasionally and briefly colliding with another molecule or with a confining wall.

In contrast to the free-molecule character of gases, the condensed phases of matter—as liquids, crystalline solids, and glasses are called—depend for their properties on the constant proximity of all their constituent atoms. The extent to which the identities of the molecular constituents are maintained varies widely in these condensed forms of matter. Weakly bound solids, such as solid carbon dioxide (dry ice), or their liquid counterparts, such as liquid air or liquid nitrogen, are made up of molecules whose properties differ only slightly from the properties of the same molecules in gaseous form; such solids or liquids are simply molecules packed tightly enough to be in constant contact. These are called van der Waals solids or liquids, after Johannes D. van der Waals, the Dutch physicist who described the weak forces that just manage to hold these materials together if they are cold enough. In other solids, like diamond, graphite, silicon, or quartz, the individual atoms retain their identity, but there are no identifiable molecules in their structures. The forces between the constituent atoms are roughly as strong as the forces that hold atoms together in the strongly bound covalent molecules that make up most common substances. Negatively charged electrons act as a "glue" to hold the positively charged nuclei together and are more or less confined to the vicinity of the so-called home-base nuclei with which they are associated; they are not free to roam through the entire solid or liquid. These materials are said to be covalently bound and are electrical insulators. They are best described as neutral atoms held together by covalent bonds and are essentially one giant molecule.

Another kind of bonding found in condensed matter is exhibited by sodium chloride, ordinary table salt, which is composed of positive sodium ions (Na^+) and negative chloride ions (Cl^-). Such ionic compounds are held together by the mutual attraction of the oppositely charged ions; because of their locations, these attractions are stronger than the repulsions of the ions with like charges. Each ion in an ionic crystal is surrounded by nearest neighbours of opposite charge. The consequence is that the binding energies of ionic compounds are large, comparable to those of strongly bound covalent substances.

Metallic bonding is another type of binding found in condensed matter. Electrons moving between the positive atomic cores (i.e., the nuclei plus inner-shell, tightly bound electrons) form an electron cloud; the attractions between the positive cores and the negative charges that make up the cloud hold metals together. Metals differ from covalently bound insulators in that those electrons responsible for the cohesion of the metals move freely throughout the metal when given the slightest extra energy. For example, under the influence of the electric field produced in a copper wire when its ends are connected to the terminals of a battery, electrons move through the wire from the end connected to the battery's negative pole toward the end connected to its positive pole. An electric field applied to a metal generates an electric current, but the same electric field applied to a covalent insulator does not. The net binding forces between electrons and atomic cores of a metal are comparable in strength to those that hold ionic compounds together.

As mentioned previously, liquids constitute a condensed or dense phase of matter, but their atomic arrangement differs from that of solids. In a liquid the constituent atoms are only slightly farther apart than they are in a solid, but that small difference is significant enough to allow the atoms or molecules that constitute a liquid to move around and to assume a full range of geometric configurations. Atoms of the same kind can trade places and can wander through the liquid by the random-walk process called diffusion. In general, materials that can form solids can also form liquids, but some, such as carbon dioxide, can only enter the liquid state under excess pressure. At least one substance, helium, can form a liquid while having no known solid form.

Materials that form solids and liquids can exhibit another form, one that may be solidlike or liquidlike but that has properties somewhat different from those of the bulk. This is the form of matter consisting of exceedingly small particles that are called clusters. Clusters are aggregates of atoms, molecules, or ions that adhere together under forces like those that bind the atoms, ions, or molecules of bulk matter; because of the manner in which they are prepared, clusters remain as tiny particles at least during the course of an experiment. There are clusters held together by van der Waals forces, by ionic forces, by covalent bonds, and by metallic bonds. Despite the similarity of the forces that bind both clusters and bulk matter, one of the fascinating aspects of clusters is that their properties differ from those of the corresponding bulk material; that characteristic affords the opportunity to learn about the properties of bulk matter by studying how, as the number of constituent particles increases, the properties of clusters evolve into those of bulk matter. For example, a cluster of 20 or 30 atoms typically has a melting point far lower than that of the corresponding bulk. The electrical properties of clusters also differ in some instances from those of the bulk matter: clusters of only a few atoms of mercury are insulators, held together by weak van der Waals forces, but clusters of hundreds of mercury atoms are metallic. One of the puzzles posed by clusters is the question of how properties of small clusters evolve with size into properties of bulk matter.

COMPARISON WITH BULK MATTER

Several characteristics differentiate clusters from molecules and bulk matter. They differ from bulk matter, first and foremost, in size; whether three particles bound together constitute a cluster is a matter of choice and convention, but an aggregate of four or more atoms or molecules certainly comprises a cluster. Such a small cluster would differ markedly from bulk matter in almost all its properties. A second difference between clusters and bulk matter is the variability of the properties of clusters with the number of their constituent particles. The properties of a lump of bulk matter remain unchanged by the addition or subtraction of a few atoms or molecules, whereas the properties of a small cluster vary significantly and, in general, neither uniformly nor even in the same direction with a change in the number of constituent particles. Medium-size clusters have properties that vary smoothly with the number of constituent particles (denoted N), but their properties, such as the melting point, differ significantly from those of the corresponding bulk. Large clusters have properties that vary smoothly with N and clearly merge into those of their bulk counterparts. This distinction, while not extremely precise, is quite useful. For example, the average binding energies—that is, the average energy per constituent atom or molecule required to separate the particles from each other—vary widely with N for small clusters. The reason for this wide range is that clusters of certain values of N, known as magic numbers, can take on unusually stable geometric structures that yield large binding energies, while others with different small values of N have no especially stable forms and therefore only relatively low binding energies. The binding energies of medium-size clusters vary rather smoothly with N, but they are in general considerably lower than the binding energies of bulk matter. The most important reason for this trend is that in a body of bulk matter almost all the particles are in the interior, while in a cluster most of the particles are on the surface. In a cluster of 13 atoms of copper or argon, for example, 12 of the atoms are on the surface. In a cluster of 55 argon atoms, 42 atoms are on the surface, and, in a cluster of 137 argon atoms, 82 are on the surface. Surface atoms are bonded only to atoms in their own layer and to those directly beneath them, so they have fewer atoms holding them to the main body of matter, whether cluster or bulk, than do atoms in the interior. Hence, the average binding energies of atoms in clusters are normally considerably less than those of bulk matter.

An important difference between clusters, in particular small- and medium-size clusters, and bulk solids is the structure that is assumed by their most stable form. Most bulk solids are crystalline. This means that their atomic structures consist of periodic lattices—i.e., structures that repeat over and over so that every unit composed of a few neighbouring atoms is indistinguishable from other groups of atoms that have exactly the same arrangement. In a simple cubic crystal, for example, all the atoms lie at the corners of cubes (in fact at a point common to eight equivalent cubes), and all these lattice points are identical. Such structures are called periodic. Most clusters, by contrast, have structures that are not periodic; many have the form of icosahedrons, incomplete icosahedrons, or other polyhedral structures that cannot grow into periodic lattices. One of the challenging puzzles of cluster science is to explain how, as an aggregate grows, it transforms from a polyhedral cluster-type structure into a crystalline lattice-type structure.

Furthermore, some properties of clusters reflect their small size in more subtle ways that depend on quantum mechanical phenomena. These are generally much more pronounced in exceedingly small systems than in bulk or macroscopic samples. One such property is the nature of the energy levels occupied by the electrons. In a macroscopic sample the energies of the states available to an electron are, in principle, discrete but are merged into bands consisting of many energy levels. Within each band the intervals of energy between those discrete levels are too tiny to be discerned; only the gaps between the bands are large enough to be important because they correspond to ranges of energy that are forbidden to the electrons. In fact, it is the contrast in the mobility of electrons that differentiates insulators from electrical conductors. In even a very cold metal, only an infinitesimal amount of excess energy is required to promote a few electrons into the previously empty energy levels in which they can move freely throughout the material. If an electric field is applied to the metal, the negatively charged electrons move toward the positive pole of the field so that a net current flows in the metal. It is the motion of these electrons, driven by an applied field, that makes metals conductors of electricity. In an insulator the electrons fill all the energy levels up to the top of the highest-energy occupied band. This means that at least the full energy of the forbidden interval, called the band gap, must be imparted to any electron to promote it to an allowed state where it may travel readily through the material. In an insulator this is far more energy than is normally available, and so no electrons are in states that allow them to move freely; such materials cannot conduct electric currents.

Clusters containing only a small number of metal atoms have so few available quantum states for their electrons that these states must be considered discrete, not as components of a dense band of available states. In this sense, small clusters of metal atoms are like conventional molecules rather than like bulk metals. Medium-size clusters of metal atoms have electronic energy states that are close enough together to be treated like the bands of bulk metals, but the conducting properties of these clusters are different from those of the bulk. Electrons driven by a constant electric field in a bulk metal can travel distances that are extremely long compared with atomic dimensions before they encounter any boundaries at the edges of the metal. Electrons in metal clusters encounter the boundaries of their cluster in a much shorter distance. Hence, metal clusters do not conduct electricity like bulk metals; if they are subjected to rapidly oscillating electric fields, such as those of visible, infrared, or microwave radiation, their "free" electrons are driven first one way and then back in the opposite direction over distances smaller than the dimensions of the cluster. If they are subjected to constant or low-frequency electric fields, such as the common 60-hertz fields that drive ordinary household currents, the electrons reach the boundaries of their clusters and can go no farther. Thus, the equivalent of conduction is not seen at low frequencies.

COMPARISON WITH MOLECULES

The manner in which clusters differ from molecules is more of a categorical nature than one of physical properties. Molecules have a definite composition and geometry; with few exceptions clusters can be made of any number of particles and may have any of several geometries. For example, the 13-atom cluster has the form of a regular icosahedron of 12 argon atoms around a central atom and is particularly stable.

Despite their multiplicity of structures, small clusters of fixed size, undergoing vibrations of small amplitude around a single geometry, are in most respects indistinguishable from molecules. If such clusters are given energy that is not great enough in magnitude to break them into separate parts, they may assume other geometries, alternating among these structural forms. This phenomenon is rarely seen with conventional molecules, but it is not unknown for energized molecules to exhibit more than one structure and to pass among them.

All in all, small clusters are much like molecules and are often considered to be molecules, while very large clusters are quite similar to bulk matter. The properties of clusters whose size is between these extremes may be like either or like neither.

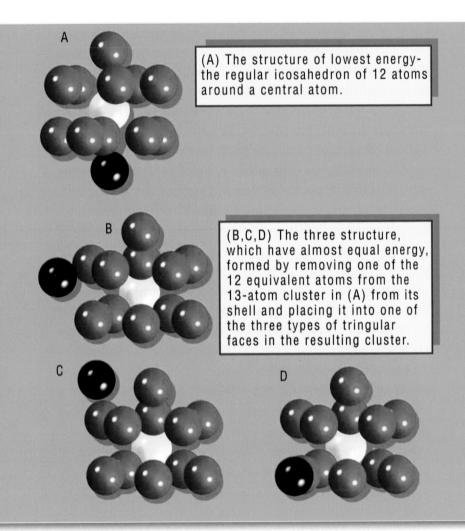

A

(A) The structure of lowest energy-
the regular icosahedron of 12 atoms
around a central atom.

B

(B,C,D) The three structure,
which have almost equal energy,
formed by removing one of the
12 equivalent atoms from the
13-atom cluster in (A) from its
shell and placing it into one of
the three types of tringular
faces in the resulting cluster.

C

D

The four lowest-energy structures of the 13-atom cluster of argon. Copyright Encyclopædia Britannica; rendering for this edition by Rosen Educational Services

METHODS OF STUDY

Clusters can be studied by experiment, by theoretical analysis, and by simulation with computer-generated models. For several reasons they cannot be studied in the same manner as bulk matter. First, if individual clusters are allowed to coalesce into a mass, they will actually turn into bulk matter, so they must be kept separated. Second, it is desirable (but not always possible) to conduct experiments that distinguish the size and structure of each kind of cluster under observation. Because of these two considerations, experiments with clusters are usually more difficult than those with either specific molecules or bulk matter. Most of the difficulties arise from the same properties that make clusters interesting: the ease with which their sizes and compositions are varied and the variety of structures available for clusters of almost any given size.

PREPARATION OF CLUSTERS

Because of these difficulties, most experiments on clusters have been carried out with the clusters isolated in the gas phase; a few studies have been done with them in solution or in frozen matrices. Clusters can be prepared in the gas phase and then either studied in that form or captured into solvents or matrices or onto surfaces. They may be made by condensation of atoms or molecules or by direct blasting of matter from solids. In the most generally used method, a gas containing the gaseous cluster material is cooled by passing it under high pressure through a fine hole or slot. The expansion cools the gas rapidly from its initial temperature—usually room temperature but much higher if the cluster material is solid at room temperature—to a temperature not far above absolute zero. If, for example, argon gas is expanded in this way, it condenses into clusters if the pressure is not too high and the aperture is not too small; if the conditions are too extreme, the argon instead turns to snow and condenses.

Inert gases are often used as the medium by which other materials, in a gaseous or vaporous state, are transported from the ovens or other sources where they have been gasified and through the jets that cool them and turn them into clusters. One especially popular and interesting method in which solids are vaporized is by the action of intense laser beams on solid surfaces. Often called ablation, this process is an effective means of vaporizing even highly refractory materials like solid carbon. The ablated material is then carried through the cooling jet by an inert gas such as helium or argon.

IONIZATION AND SORTING OF CLUSTERS

Once the clusters have been formed, they can be studied in a variety of ways. One of the first techniques was simply to ionize the clusters, either with ultraviolet radiation (usually from a laser) or by electron impact. The gaseous ionized clusters are accelerated by an electric field and then analyzed according to their masses; these results immediately reveal the number of atoms or molecules in the cluster. The analysis yields the distribution of the relative abundances of clusters of different sizes in the beam. If the experiment is done with considerable care, the abundance distribution corresponds to the true relative stabilities of the clusters of different sizes. However, like many experiments with clusters, these can either provide results consistent with the equilibrium conditions that reflect those relative stabilities, or they can give results that reflect the rates of the cluster-forming processes rather than the equilibrium characteristics, as the latter may take far longer to reach than the time required to form clusters.

Because of the conditions under which clusters are formed, their distributions contain many different sizes and, in some instances, different shapes. Because chemists seek to characterize clusters of a single size and geometry, the clusters must first be sorted on that basis. If the clusters carry charge, they can be separated according to size with a mass spectrometer that sorts charged particles with approximately the same energy according to their masses. This is usually done by deflecting the charged clusters or ions with an electric or magnetic field; the smaller the mass, the greater is the deflection. This is one of the most effective ways of preparing a beam of clusters of only a single selected mass. It does not eliminate the problem of multiple structures, however.

A technique that can sometimes be used to sort clusters according to their size and structure is a two-step process in which one cluster species at a time is excited with the light from a laser and is then ionized with light from a second laser. This process, called resonant two-photon ionization, is highly selective if the clusters being separated have moderately different absorption spectra. Since this is frequently the case, the method is quite powerful. As the experimenter varies the wavelength of the first exciting laser, a spectrum is produced that includes those wavelengths of light that excite the cluster. If the wavelength of the second ionizing laser is varied, the method also yields the ionization potential, which is the minimum energy that the photon in the ionizing beam must possess in order to knock an electron out of the cluster. Such data help to reveal the forces that bind the cluster together and give some indication of how the cluster will react with atoms, molecules, or other clusters.

COMPUTER SIMULATION OF CLUSTER BEHAVIOUR

A powerful tool for studying clusters is computer simulation of their behaviour. If the nature of the forces between the individual atoms or molecules in a cluster is known, then one can construct a computer model that represents the behaviour of those atoms or molecules by solving the equations of motion of the cluster. To describe the cluster in terms of classical mechanics, the Newtonian equations of motion are solved repeatedly—namely, force equals mass times acceleration, in which the forces depend on the instantaneous positions of all the particles. Hence, these equations are simultaneous, interlinked equations; there is one set of three (for the three instantaneous coordinates of each particle) for each atom or molecule. The results can take one of three forms: (1) the positions and coordinates of the atoms, given in tables, (2) the average properties of the entire cluster, or (3) animations. Tables are too cumbersome for most purposes, and specific average properties are frequently what the investigator seeks. Animated sequences show the same content as the tables but far more efficiently than extensive tables do. In fact, animations sometimes reveal considerably more than is expected by scientists.

It is also possible to construct computer models of clusters based on quantum mechanics instead of Newton's classical mechanics. This is especially appropriate for clusters of hydrogen and helium, because the small masses of their constituent atoms make them very quantumlike in the sense that they reveal the wavelike character that all matter exhibits according to quantum mechanics. The same kinds of data and inferences can be extracted from quantum mechanical calculations as from classical ones, but the preparation and visualization of animations for such clusters are much more demanding than their classical mechanical counterparts.

STRUCTURE

The abundance distributions for several kinds of clusters show that there are certain sizes of clusters with exceptional stability, analogous to the exceptional stability of the atoms of the inert gases helium, neon, argon, krypton, and xenon and of the so-called magic number nuclei—i.e., the sequence of unusually stable atomic nuclei beginning with the a-particle, or helium nucleus. Such unusual stability suggests that its interpretation should be associated with the closing of some kind of shell, or energy level. The overall structure that determines the cluster's stability is generally called its shell structure.

CLUSTERS WITH ICOSAHEDRAL STRUCTURES

Clusters of atoms bound by van der Waals forces or by other simple forces that depend only on the distance between each pair of atoms have unusual stability when the cluster has exactly the number of atoms needed to form a regular icosahedron. The first three clusters in this series have, respectively, 13, 55, and 147 atoms. In the 13-atom cluster, all but one of the atoms occupy equivalent sites. The 55-atom cluster in this series consists of a core—which is just the 13-atom icosahedron—plus 12 more atoms atop

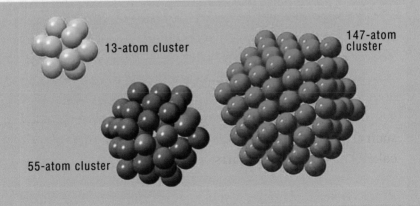

13-atom cluster

147-atom cluster

55-atom cluster

The first three complete icosahedral structures of 13, 55, and 147 particles. These are the structures taken on by clusters of 13, 55, and 147 atoms of neon, argon, krypton, and xenon, for example. Copyright Encyclopædia Britannica; rendering for this edition by Rosen Educational Services

the 12 vertices of the icosahedron and 30 more atoms, one in the centre of each of the 30 edges of the icosahedron. The 147-atom cluster consists of a 55-atom icosahedral core, 12 more atoms at the vertices of the outermost shell, one atom in the centre of each of the 20 faces, and two atoms along each of the 30 edges between the vertices. The shell structure that provides special stabilities in this class of clusters is determined by the individual stabilities of the shells of the atoms themselves.

CLUSTERS OF SIMPLE METAL ATOMS

A different kind of extraordinary stability manifests itself in clusters of simple metal atoms. The shell structure for this class of clusters is determined by the electrons and the filling of those shells that have energy states available to the electrons. The numbers of electrons corresponding to closed electron shells in metal clusters are 8, 20, 40, 58, ... The electron structure can be modeled by supposing that the positively charged cores consisting of the protons and inner-shell electrons of all the cluster's atoms are smeared out into a continuous, attractive background, while the valence, or outer-shell, electrons are delocalized (i.e., shared among all atoms in the cluster). The electron environment is much like a well or pit with a flat bottom and a moderately steep wall. The determination of the energy states available for electrons in such a simplified model system is relatively easy and gives a good description of clusters of more than about eight or nine alkali atoms— i.e., lithium, sodium, potassium, rubidium, or cesium. The single valence, or outer-shell, electron of each alkali atom is treated explicitly, while all the others are considered part of the smeared-out core. Since each alkali atom has only one valence electron, the unusually stable clusters of alkalis consist of 8, 20, 40, . . . atoms, corresponding to major shell closings. This model is not as successful in treating metals such as aluminum, which have more than one valence electron.

NETWORK STRUCTURES

Still another kind of particularly stable closed shell occurs in clusters sometimes called network structures. The best-known of these is C_{60}, the 60-atom cluster of carbon atoms. In this cluster the atoms occupy the sites of the 60 equivalent vertices of the soccer ball structure, which can be constructed by cutting off the 12 vertices of the icosahedron to make 12 regular 5-sided (regular pentagonal) faces. The icosahedron itself has 20 triangular faces; when its vertices are sliced off, the triangles become hexagons. The 12 pentagons share their edges with these 20 hexagonal faces. No two pentagons have any common edge in this molecule or cluster (C_{60} may be considered either). The resulting high-symmetry structure has been named buckminsterfullerene, after R. Buckminster Fuller, who advocated using such geometric structures in architectural design.

Other network compounds of carbon are also known. To form a closed-shell structure, a network compound of carbon must have exactly 12 rings of 5 carbon atoms, but the number of rings of 6 carbon atoms is variable. Shells smaller than C_{60} have been discovered, but some of their constituent pentagons must share edges; this makes the smaller network compounds less stable than C_{60}. Shells larger than C_{60}, such as C_{70}, C_{76}, and C_{84}, are known and are relatively stable. Even tubes and "onions" of concentric layers of carbon shells have been reported in observations made with modern electron microscopes

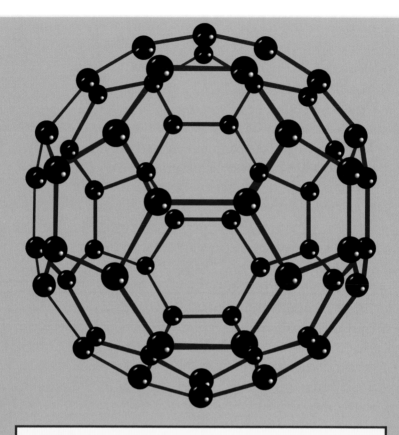

The geometry is that of a soccer ball with a carbon atom at each vertex.

The structure of C$_{60}$, buckminsterfullerene. Copyright Encyclopædia Britannica; rendering for this edition by Rosen Educational Services

known as scanning tunneling microscopes. These devices are powerful enough to reveal images of extremely small clusters and even individual foreign atoms deposited on clean surfaces.

The network compounds of carbon, which make up the class called fullerenes, form compounds with alkali and other metals. Some of these compounds of fullerenes combined with metals, such as K_3C_{60}, become superconductors at low temperatures; that is to say, they lose all resistance to electric current flow when they are cooled sufficiently. The class of network compounds as a group had been imagined from time to time, but only in the late 1980s were they realized in the laboratory and shown to have closed-shell network structures.

PHYSICAL PROPERTIES

Clusters share some of the physical properties of bulk matter, a few of which are rather surprising. Clusters of all substances except helium and possibly hydrogen are solidlike at low temperatures as expected. The atoms or molecules of a cluster remain close to their equilibrium positions, vibrating around these positions in moderately regular motions of small amplitude. This is characteristic of all solids; their atoms are constrained to stay roughly in the same position at all times. In a liquid or a gas, the atoms or molecules are free to wander through the space accessible to the substance. A gas or vapour has so much empty space relative to the volume occupied by the particles that the particles move almost unhindered, colliding only occasionally with other particles or with the walls of the container. A liquid is typically almost as dense as a solid but has some empty spaces into which the atoms or molecules can easily move. Hence, the particles of a liquid can diffuse with moderate ease. (Water is an exception; its density as a liquid is higher than its density as ice, because ice has an unusually open structure in comparison with most solids, and this open structure collapses when ice turns to water.) Clusters can be liquidlike if they are warm enough, but typically the temperatures at which clusters can become liquid are much lower than the melting points of the corresponding bulk solids. If temperatures are measured on the Kelvin scale, small clusters become liquidlike at temperatures of roughly half the bulk melting temperatures. For example, solid argon melts at approximately 80 K (-190 °C, or -320 °F), while small clusters of argon become liquid at about 40 K (-230 °C, or -390 °F).

LIQUID AND SOLID PHASES

Some clusters are expected to show a gradual transition from solidlike to liquidlike, appearing slushy in the temperature range between their solidlike and liquidlike zones. Other clusters are expected to show, as seen in computer simulations, distinct solidlike and liquidlike forms that qualitatively resemble bulk solids and liquids in virtually every aspect, even though they may exhibit quantitative differences from the bulk. Solid clusters, for example, show virtually no diffusion, but the particles of a liquid cluster can and do diffuse. The forces that hold a particle in place in a solid cluster are strong, comparable to those of a bulk solid; but those in a liquid cluster include, in addition to forces comparable in strength to those in solids, some forces weak enough to allow a particle to wander far from its home base and find new equilibrium positions. Those same weak forces are responsible for making a liquid cluster compliant; that is, weak forces allow the liquid to accommodate any new force, say, a finger inserted into water. Ice will not yield to such an intruding force, but when a finger is placed into liquid water, the water molecules move aside under the force of the finger. This is much like the behaviour of a bulk liquid. The greatest differences between bulk solids and liquids and solid and liquid clusters arise from the fact that a large fraction of the particles of a cluster are on its surface. As a result, the particle mobility that characterizes liquids and enables them to exhibit diffusion and physical compliance is enhanced in a cluster, for the cluster can easily expand by enlarging the spaces between particles and can also transfer particles from its interior to its surface, leaving vacancies that enhance the mobility of the interior particles. The large surface area, together with the curved shape of the cluster's surface, make it easier for particles to leave a cluster than to leave the flat surface of a bulk liquid or solid. An important consequence is that the vapour pressure of a cluster is higher than the vapour pressure of the corresponding bulk, and accordingly the boiling point of a liquid cluster—i.e., the temperature at which the vapour pressure of a liquid is equal to the pressure of the surrounding atmosphere—is lower than that of the corresponding bulk liquid. The vapour pressure of clusters decreases with increasing cluster size, while the boiling point increases.

Perhaps the greatest difference between clusters and bulk matter with regard to their transformation between solid and liquid is the nature of the equilibrium between two phases. Bulk solids can be in equilibrium with their liquid forms at only a single temperature for any given pressure or at only a single pressure for any given temperature. A graph of the temperatures and pressures along which the solid and liquid forms of any given substance are in equilibrium is called a coexistence curve. One point on the coexistence curve for ice and liquid water is 0 °C (32 °F) and one atmosphere of pressure. A similar curve can be drawn for the coexistence of any two bulk phases, such as liquid and vapour; a point on the coexistence curve for liquid water and steam is 100 °C (212 °F) and one atmosphere of pressure. Clusters differ sharply from bulk matter in that solid and liquid clusters of the same composition are capable of coexisting within a band of temperatures and pressures. At any chosen pressure, the proportion of liquid clusters to solid clusters increases with temperature. At low temperatures the clusters are solid, as described above. As the temperature is increased, some clusters transform from solid to liquid. If the temperature is raised further, the proportion of liquid clusters increases, passing through 50 percent, so that the mixture becomes predominantly liquid clusters. At sufficiently high temperatures all the clusters are liquid.

No cluster remains solid or liquid all the time; liquid-like clusters occasionally transform spontaneously into solidlike clusters and vice versa. The fraction of time that a particular cluster spends as a liquid is precisely the same as the fraction of clusters of that same type within a large collection that are liquid at a given instant. That is to say, the time average behaviour gives the same result as the ensemble average, which is the average over a large collection of identical objects. This equivalence is not limited to clusters; it is the well-known ergodic property that is expected of all but the simplest real systems.

ELECTRIC, MAGNETIC, AND OPTICAL PROPERTIES

Other significant physical properties of clusters are their electric, magnetic, and optical properties. The electric properties of clusters, such as their conductivity and metallic or insulating character, depend on the substance and the size of the cluster. Quantum theory attributes wavelike character to matter, a behaviour that is detectable only when matter is examined on the scale of atoms and electrons. At a scale of millimetres or even millionths of millimetres, the wavelengths of matter are too short to be observed. Clusters are often much smaller than that, with the important consequence that many are so small that when examined their electrons and electronic states can exhibit the wavelike properties of matter. In fact, quantum properties may play an important role in determining the electrical character of the cluster. In particular, as described previously, if a cluster is extremely small, the energy levels or quantum states of its electrons are not close enough together to permit the cluster to conduct electricity.

Moreover, an alternative way to view this situation is to recognize that a constant electric force (i.e., the kind that drives a direct current) and an alternating force (the kind that generates alternating current) can behave quite differently in a cluster. Direct current cannot flow in an isolated cluster and probably cannot occur in a small cluster even if it is sandwiched between slabs of metal. The current flow is prohibited both because the electrons that carry the current encounter the boundaries of the cluster and because there are no quantum states readily available at energies just above those of the occupied states, which are the states that must be achieved to allow the electrons to move. However, if a field of alternating electric force is applied with a frequency of alternation so high that the electrons are made to reverse their paths before they encounter the boundaries of the cluster, then the equivalent of conduction will take place. Ordinary 60-cycle (60-hertz) alternating voltage and even alternations at radio-wave frequencies switch direction far too slowly to produce this behaviour in clusters; microwave frequencies are required.

Magnetic properties of clusters, in contrast, appear to be rather similar to those of bulk matter. They are not identical, because clusters contain only small numbers of electrons, which are the particles whose magnetic character makes clusters and bulk matter magnetic. As a result, the differences between magnetic properties of clusters and of bulk matter are more a matter of degree than of kind. Clusters of substances magnetic in the bulk also tend to be magnetic. The larger the cluster, the more nearly will the magnetic character per atom approach that of the bulk. The degree of this magnetic character depends on how strongly the individual electron magnets couple to each other to become aligned in the same direction; the larger the cluster, the stronger is this coupling.

The optical properties of weakly bound clusters are much like those of their component atoms or molecules; the small differences are frequently useful diagnostics of how the cluster is bound and what its structure may be. Optical properties of metal clusters are more like those of the corresponding bulk metals than like those of the constituent atoms. These properties reveal which cluster sizes are unusually stable and therefore correspond to "magic-number" sizes. Optical properties of covalently bound clusters are in most cases—e.g., fullerenes—unlike those of either the component atoms or the bulk but are important clues to the structure and bonding of the cluster.

CHEMICAL PROPERTIES

The chemical properties of clusters are a combination of the properties of bulk and molecular matter. Several kinds of clusters, particularly those of the metallic variety, induce certain molecules to dissociate. For example, hydrogen molecules, H_2, spontaneously break into two hydrogen atoms when they attach themselves to a cluster of iron atoms. Ammonia likewise dissociates when attaching itself to an iron cluster. Similar reactions occur with bulk matter, but the rate at which such gases react with bulk metals depends only on how much gaseous reactant is present and how much surface area the bulk metal presents to the gas. Metal powders react much faster than dense solids with the same total mass because they have much more surface area. Small and medium-size clusters, on the other hand, show different reactivities for every size, although these reactivities do not vary smoothly with size. Furthermore, there are instances, such as reactions of hydrogen with iron, in which two different geometric forms of clusters of a single size have different reaction rates, just as two different molecules with the same elemental composition, called chemical isomers, may have different reaction rates with the same reactant partner. In the case of molecules, this is not surprising, because different isomers typically have quite different structures, physical properties, and reactivities and do not normally transform readily into one another. Isomers of clusters of a specific chemical composition, however, may well transform into one another with moderate ease and with no excessive increase in energy above the amount present when they formed. If the reaction releases energy (i.e., it is exothermic) in sufficient quantity to transform the cluster from solid to liquid, a cluster may melt as it reacts.

Some of the interesting chemistry of clusters is set in motion by light. For example, light of sufficiently short wavelength can dissociate molecules that are captured in the middle of a cluster of nonreactive atoms or molecules. A common question is whether the surrounding molecules or atoms form a cage strong enough to prevent the fragment atoms from flying apart and from leaving the cluster. The answer is that, if there are only a few surrounding atoms or molecules, the fragments escape their initial cage, and, if the energy of the light is high enough, at least one of the fragments escapes. On the other hand, if there are enough nonreacting cage atoms or molecules in the cluster to form at least one complete shell around the molecule that breaks up, the cage usually holds the fragments close together until they eventually recombine.

A related sort of reaction, another example of competition between a particle's attempt to escape from a cluster and some other process, occurs if light is used to detach an excess electron from a negative ion in the middle of an inert cluster. If, for example, light knocks the extra electron off a free, negatively charged bromine molecule, Br_2^-, the electron of course escapes. If the charged molecule is surrounded by a few inert molecules of carbon dioxide (CO_2), the electron escapes almost as readily. If 10 or 15 CO_2 molecules encase the Br_2^-, the electron does not escape; instead, it loses its energy to the surrounding molecules of CO_2, some of which boil off, and then eventually recombines with the now neutral bromine molecule to re-form the original Br_2^-.

The chemical properties of fullerenes and other network compounds have become a subject of their own, bridging molecular and cluster chemistry. These compounds typically react with a specific number of other atoms or molecules to form new species with definite compositions and structures. Compounds such as K_3C_{60} mentioned previously have the three potassium atoms outside the C_{60} cage, all as singly charged ions, K^+, and the ball of 60 carbon atoms carries three negative charges to make the entire compound electrically neutral. Other compounds of C_{60}, such as that made with the metal lanthanum, contain the metal inside the carbon cage, forming a new kind of substance. It is possible to add or take away hydrogen atoms from C_{60} and its larger relatives, much as hydrogen atoms can be added or removed from some kinds of hydrocarbons; in this way some of the chemistry of this class of clusters is similar to classical organic chemistry.

One of the goals of cluster science is the creation of new kinds of materials. The possible preparation of diamond films is one such application; another example is the proposal to make so-called superatoms that consist of an electron donor atom in the centre of a cluster of electron acceptors; the fullerene clusters containing a metal ion inside the cage seem to be just such a species but with much more open structures than had been previously envisioned. Molecular electronics is another goal; in this technology clusters would be constructed with electrical properties much like those of transistors and could be packed together to make microcircuits far smaller than any now produced. These applications are still theoretical, however, and have not yet been realized.

Clusters do indeed form a bridge between bulk and molecular matter. Their physical and chemical properties are in many instances unique to their finely divided state. Some examples of clusters, such as the network clusters of carbon, are new forms of matter. Nevertheless, such clusters, particularly the small and middle-size ones, not only exhibit behaviours of their own but also provide new insights into the molecular origins of the properties of bulk matter. They may yield other new materials—e.g., possibly far more disordered, amorphous glasslike substances than the glasses now in common use—and at the same time give rise to deeper understanding of why and how glasses form at all.

CONCLUSION

Although basic ideas about matter trace back to Newton and even earlier to Aristotle's natural philosophy, further understanding of matter, along with new puzzles, began emerging in the early 20th century. Einstein's theory of special relativity (1905) shows that matter (as mass) and energy can be converted into each other according to the famous equation $E = mc^2$, where E is energy, m is mass, and c is the speed of light. This transformation occurs, for instance, during nuclear fission, in which the nucleus of a heavy element such as uranium splits into two fragments of smaller total mass, with the mass difference released as energy. Einstein's theory of gravitation, also known as his theory of general relativity (1916), takes as a central postulate the experimentally observed equivalence of inertial mass and gravitational mass and shows how gravity arises from the distortions that matter introduces into the surrounding space-time continuum.

The concept of matter is further complicated by quantum mechanics, whose roots go back to Max Planck's explanation in 1900 of the properties of electromagnetic radiation emitted by a hot body. In the quantum view, elementary particles behave both like tiny balls and like waves that spread out in space—a seeming paradox that has yet to be fully resolved. Additional complexity in the meaning of matter comes from astronomical observations that began in the 1930s and that show that a large fraction of the universe consists of "dark matter." This invisible material does not affect light and can be detected only through its gravitational effects. Its detailed nature has yet to be determined, but it may be an as yet undiscovered elementary particle.

On the other hand, through the contemporary search for a unified field theory, which would place three of the four types of interactions between elementary particles (the strong force, the weak force, and the electromagnetic force, excluding only gravity) within a single conceptual framework, physicists may be on the verge of explaining the origin of mass. Although a fully satisfactory grand unified theory (GUT) of physics has yet to be derived, one component— the electroweak theory of Sheldon Glashow, Abdus Salam, and Steven Weinberg (who shared the 1979 Nobel Prize for Physics for this work)—predicts that an elementary subatomic particle known as the Higgs boson imparts mass to all known elementary particles. There is as yet no experimental evidence that the Higgs boson exists, however, and physicists are eager to search for it, using the Large Hadron Collider, which is the most powerful particle accelerator available.

amorphous solid Any noncrystalline solid in which the atoms and molecules are not organized in a definite lattice pattern.

aqueous Made from, with, or by water.

coefficient Any of the factors of a product considered in relation to a specific factor; specifically, a constant factor of a term as distinguished from a variable.

colligative Depending on the number of particles (as molecules) and not on the nature of the particles.

colloid A substance that consists of particles dispersed throughout another substance but whose particles are incapable of passing through a semipermeable membrane.

covalent bond The interatomic linkage that results from the sharing of an electron pair between two atoms, arising from the electrostatic attraction of their nuclei for the same electrons.

critical point The set of conditions under which a liquid and its vapour become identical.

diffusion coefficient The constant of proportionality between the flow of a material and the gradient of its concentration.

diffusion thermoeffect The physics effect in which an imposed concentration difference causes a temperature difference to develop.

dipole A pair of equal and opposite electric charges or magnetic poles of opposite sign separated by a distance.

eutectic The one mixture of a set of substances able to dissolve in one another as liquids that, of all such mixtures, liquefies at the lowest temperature.

fugacity A measure of the tendency of a component of a liquid mixture to escape, or vaporize, from the mixture.

immiscible Incapable of mixing or attaining homogeneity.

lepton Any member of a class of subatomic particles that respond only to electromagnetic, weak, and gravitational forces, but not by strong force.

manometer An instrument for measuring the pressure of gases and vapors.

mole A standard scientific unit for measuring large quantities of very small entities such as atoms, molecules, or other specified particles.

osmosis The diffusion of a solvent through a semipermeable membrane.

polymer A chemical compound or mixture of compounds formed by polymerization and consisting essentially of repeating structural units.

radiometer A four-vaned mill that spins when light is absorbed by the vanes.

thermal transpiration The situation in which, given equal initial pressure, gas will flow from the low-temperature side to the high-temperature side, causing the high-temperature pressure to increase.

thermodynamics The science of the relationship between heat, work, temperature, and energy.

viscosity A matter transport property characterized by the resistance to flow.

BIBLIOGRAPHY

PHASES

Gerhard L. Salinger and Francis Weston Sears, *Thermodynamics, Kinetic Theory, and Statistical Thermodynamics* (1975), is a classic introduction. A detailed application of thermodynamic principles to phases, phase changes, and phase diagrams is given in Mats Hillert, *Phase Equilibria, Phase Diagrams, and Phase Transformations: Their Thermodynamic Basis* (1998).

Works focusing on phase equilibria in geology and petrology include W.G. Ernst, *Petrologic Phase Equilibria* (1976), a concise introduction to phase equilibria that assumes some knowledge of thermodynamics; Ernest G. Ehlers and Harvey Blatt, *Petrology: Igneous, Sedimentary, and Metamorphic* (1982), an introduction to phase equilibria of petrologic systems; and Ernest G. Ehlers, *The Interpretation of Geological Phase Diagrams* (1972, reprinted 1987), which provides step-by-step nonmathematical procedures for understanding phase diagrams. A more recent work is Thomas M. Will, *Phase Equilibria in Metamorphic Rocks: Thermodynamic Background and Petrological Applications* (1998).

GASES

Three excellent introductions to the kinetic theory of gases at an elementary level are Joel H. Hildebrand, *An Introduction to Molecular Kinetic Theory* (1963, reissued 1966); Sidney Golden, *Elements of the Theory of*

Gases (1964); and Gerhard L. Salinger and Francis W. Sears, *Thermodynamics, Kinetic Theory, and Statistical Thermodynamics* (1975). An accessible popular work that touches some of these issues is Hans Christian von Baeyer, *Warmth Disperses and Time Passes: A History of Heat* (1999; originally published as *Maxwell's Demon: Why Warmth Disperses and Time Passes*, 1998).

Books that focus on historical development include Stephen Brush (ed.), *Kinetic Theory*, 3 vol. (1965–72), a set of famous historical papers along with introductory commentaries and summaries by the editor; Stephen Brush, *The Kind of Motion We Call Heat: A History of the Kinetic Theory of Gases in the 19th Century*, 2 vol. (1976, reissued 1986), a thorough historical account without much mathematics, and *Statistical Physics and the Atomic Theory of Matter: From Boyle and Newton to Landau and Onsager* (1983), which requires a thorough scientific background; Elizabeth Garber, Stephen Brush, and C.W.F. Everitt (eds.), *Maxwell on Molecules and Gases* (1986), a compilation of early writings on the kinetic theory of gases by the English physicist James Clerk Maxwell; and J.S. Rowlinson (ed.), *J.D. van der Waals: On the Continuity of the Gaseous and Liquid States* (1988), a translation of the seminal 1873 thesis by the Dutch physicist J.D. van der Waals, with an excellent introduction by the editor that surveys modern developments in the theory of liquids and solutions.

LIQUIDS

A classic survey of the liquid state by a pioneer in the field is given in J.S. Rowlinson (ed.), *J.D. van der Waals: On the Continuity of the Gaseous and Liquid States* (1988), with an extensive bibliography. J.N. Murrell and E.A. Boucher, *Properties of Liquids and Solutions*, 2nd ed. (1994), is a short introduction to the physics and chemistry of the liquid state. A general approach to the chemical thermodynamics of pure substances and solutions is given in the classic text Gilbert Newton Lewis and Merle Randall, *Thermodynamics*, 2nd ed., rev. by Kenneth S. Pitzer and Leo Brewer (1961). J.S. Rowlinson and F.L. Swinton, *Liquids and Liquid Mixtures*, 3rd ed. (1982), gives a thorough treatment of the physics of fluids and of the statistical mechanics of the equilibrium properties of simple pure liquids and liquid mixtures; the work also contains a data bibliography and is primarily for research-oriented readers.

More specialized books include John P. O'Connell, John M. Prausnitz, and Bruce E. Poling, *The Properties of Gases and Liquids*, 5th ed. (2001), which focuses on the vapour-liquid transition and evaluates techniques for estimating and correlating properties of gases and liquids, as well as tabulating the properties of 600 compounds; and John M. Prausnitz, Ruediger N. Lichtenthaler, and Edmundo Gomes de Azevedo, *Molecular Thermodynamics of Fluid-Phase Equilibria*, 3rd ed. (1998), which is written from a chemical-engineering point of view.

Those interested in the properties of water from the physical and chemical standpoint, and in terms of biological function, will find accessible introductory descriptions in Sidney Perkowitz, "The Rarest Element," *The Sciences*, 39:(1): 34–38 (Jan./Feb. 1999); and Mark W. Denny, *Air and Water: The Biology and Physics of Life's Media* (1993).

CRYSTALS

Works on solids in general include Lawrence H. Van Vlack, *Elements of Materials Science and Engineering*, 6th ed. (1989), an elementary textbook; Charles Kittel,

Introduction to Solid State Physics, 8th ed. (2005), a standard college textbook; and Linus Pauling, *The Nature of the Chemical Bond and the Structure of Molecules and Crystals*, 3rd ed. (1960, reissued 1989), a classic work on chemical bonding.

For crystalline solids in particular, Alan Holden and Phylis Morrison, *Crystals and Crystal Growing* (1960, reissued 1982), is a readable illustrated treatment; Richard P. Feynman, *The Feynman Lectures on Physics: From Crystal Structure to Magnetism*, vol. 3 (1999), is also highly accessible as a sound recording.

Richard Dalven, *Introduction to Applied Solid State Physics*, 2nd ed. (1990), is an intermediate-level textbook on semiconductors and semiconducting devices.

Books on magnetism include David Jiles, *Introduction to Magnetism and Magnetic Materials*, 2nd. ed. (1998); and Robert C. O'Handley, *Modern Magnetic Materials: Principles and Applications* (2000).

Fullerenes are reviewed in Wanda Andreoni, *The Physics of Fullerene-Based and Fullerene-Related Materials* (2000); and Mildred S. Dresselhaus, Gene Dresselhaus, and Phaedon Avouris (eds.), *Carbon Nanotubes: Synthesis, Structure, Properties, and Applications* (2001)

LIQUID CRYSTALS

Works on solids in general include Lawrence H. Van Vlack, *Elements of Materials Science and Engineering*, 6th ed. (1989), an elementary textbook; Charles A. Wert and Robb M. Thomson, *Physics of Solids*, 2nd ed. (1970), an intermediate-level text; Charles Kittel, *Introduction to Solid State Physics*, 6th ed. (1986), the standard college textbook; Neil W. Ashcroft and N. David Mermin, *Solid State Physics* (1976), an advanced textbook; George E. Bacon, *The Architecture of Solids* (1981), an introduction to bonding and structure; and Linus Pauling, *The Nature of the Chemical Bond and the Structure of Molecules and Crystals*, 3rd ed. (1960, reissued 1989), the classic reference work on chemical bonding.

The history of liquid crystals in particular is surveyed by H. Kelker, "History of Liquid Crystals," *Molecular Crystals and Liquid Crystals*, 21(1 and 2):1–48 (May 1973). The Nobel Prize acceptance lecture by P.G. de Gennes, "Soft Matter," *Reviews of Modern Physics*, 64(3):645–648 (July 1992), sets liquid crystals in a broader scientific context. Discussions of special topics in liquid crystals, frequently at a level close to this book, may be found in the periodical *Condensed Matter News* (bimonthly). More technical presentations are given in P.G. de Gennes, *The Physics of Liquid Crystals* (1974); S. Chandrasekhar, *Liquid Crystals*, 2nd ed. (1992); and P.S. Pershan, *Structure of Liquid Crystal Phases* (1988). Applications of liquid crystals are described in E. Kaneko, *Liquid Crystal TV Displays* (1987); and J. Funfschilling, "Liquid Crystals and Liquid Crystal Displays," *Condensed Matter News*, 1:12–16 (1991).

AMORPHOUS SOLIDS

Works on solids in general include Lawrence H. Van Vlack, *Elements of Materials Science and Engineering*, 6th ed. (1989), an elementary textbook; Charles A. Wert and Robb M. Thomson, *Physics of Solids*, 2nd ed. (1970), an intermediate-level text; Charles Kittel, *Introduction to Solid State Physics*, 6th ed. (1986), the standard college textbook; Neil W. Ashcroft and N. David Mermin, *Solid State Physics* (1976), an advanced textbook; George E. Bacon, *The Architecture of Solids* (1981), an introduction to bonding and structure; and Linus Pauling, *The Nature of the Chemical Bond and the Structure of Molecules and Crystals*,

3rd ed. (1960, reissued 1989), the classic reference work on chemical bonding.

On amorphous solids in particular, a lucid introductory text accessible to a nontechnical reader is Richard Zallen, *The Physics of Amorphous Solids* (1983), with coverage of structural models for the various classes of amorphous solids as well as percolation theory, a modern paradigm for disordered systems. A classic advanced work is N.F. Mott and E.A. Davis, *Electronic Processes in Non-crystalline Materials*, 2nd ed. (1979), which features many of the theoretical contributions of Nobel Laureate coauthor Mott. A text providing a thorough treatment of oxide glasses is J. Zarzycki, *Glasses and the Vitreous State* (1991; originally published in French, 1982). A reference work with wide coverage of recent research topics, including detailed treatment of chalcogenide glasses, is S.R. Elliott, *Physics of Amorphous Materials*, 2nd ed. (1990). A comprehensive collection of detailed reviews is contained in R.W. Cahn, P. Haassen, and E.J. Kramer (eds.), *Materials Science and Technology*, vol. 6, *Glasses and Amorphous Materials*, ed. by J. Zarzycki (1991), including coverage of glass technology, formation, and structure, oxide glasses, chalcogenide glasses, metallic glasses, polymeric glasses, and the optical, electric, and mechanical properties of glasses. Amorphous silicon is treated in detail in another work, R.A. Street, *Hydrogenated Amorphous Silicon* (1991).

QUASICRYSTALS

Works on solids in general include Lawrence H. Van Vlack, *Elements of Materials Science and Engineering*, 6th ed. (1989), an elementary textbook; Charles A. Wert and Robb M. Thomson, *Physics of Solids*, 2nd ed. (1970), an intermediate-level text; Charles Kittel, *Introduction to*

Solid State Physics, 6th ed. (1986), the standard college textbook; Neil W. Ashcroft and N. David Mermin, *Solid State Physics* (1976), an advanced textbook; George E. Bacon, *The Architecture of Solids* (1981), an introduction to bonding and structure; and Linus Pauling, *The Nature of the Chemical Bond and the Structure of Molecules and Crystals*, 3rd ed. (1960, reissued 1989), the classic reference work on chemical bonding.

Introductions to quasicrystals in particular are available in David R. Nelson, "Quasicrystals," *Scientific American*, 255(2):43–51 (August 1986); Peter W. Stephens and Alan I. Goldman, "The Structure of Quasicrystals," *Scientific American*, 264(4): 44–47, 50–53 (April 1991); and P.J. Steinhardt, "Icosahedral Solids: A New Phase of Matter?," *Science*, 238(4831): 1242–47 (Nov. 27, 1987). Martin Gardner, "Mathematical Games," *Scientific American*, 236(1):110–112, 115–121 (January 1977), discusses Penrose tilings and their remarkable properties. More technically detailed works are D.P. DiVencenzo and P.J. Steinhardt (eds.), *Quasicrystals: The State of the Art* (1991); and the series *Aperiodicity and Order*, ed. by Marko V. Jarić (1988–).

PLASMA

Yaffa Eliezer and Shalom Eliezer, *The Fourth State of Matter: An Introduction to the Physics of Plasma*, 2nd ed. (2001), is a useful starting point for general readers. More advanced texts, some with applications in nuclear fusion and in terrestrial plasmas, include Francis F. Chen, *Introduction to Plasma Physics and Controlled Fusion* (1984); Michael C. Kelley and Rodney A. Heelis, *The Earth's Ionosphere: Plasma Physics and Electrodynamics* (1989); R.J. Goldston and P.H. Rutherford, *Introduction to Plasma*

Physics (1995, reissued 2000); and Masahiro Wakatani and Kyoji Nishikawa, *Plasma Physics: Basic Theory with Fusion Applications*, 3rd rev. ed. (2000), which begins at an introductory level.

Overviews of nuclear fusion efforts involving plasmas include Ruth Howes and Anthony Fainberg (eds.), *The Energy Sourcebook: A Guide to Technology, Resources, and Policy* (1991); and National Research Council (U.S.), Fusion Science Assessment Committee, *An Assessment of the Department of Energy's Office of Fusion Energy Sciences Program* (2001). An accessible description of one approach to fusion energy production is Gerald Yonas, "Fusion and the Z Pinch," *Scientific American*, 279(2): 40–45 (August 1998).

Robert H. Eather, *Majestic Lights: The Aurora in Science, History, and the Arts* (1980), is a broad treatment of the aurora, with numerous illustrations. An accessible account of research on the solar plasma is given in Robert Irion, "Our Tortured Star," *New Scientist*, 162(2184): 44–48 (May 1, 1999).

CLUSTERS

Michael A. Duncan and Dennis H. Roubray, "Microclusters," *Scientific American*, 261(6):110–115 (December 1989), provides a general introduction and survey for nonscientists. Works presenting the results of recent research include R. Stephen Berry, "When the Melting and Freezing Points Are Not the Same," *Scientific American*, 263(2): 68–72, 74 (August 1990), written for nonscientists, a description of the melting and freezing of clusters and their relation to bulk melting and freezing; and several collections of conference proceedings: P. Jena, B.K. Rao, and S.N. Khanna (eds.),

Physics and Chemistry of Small Clusters (1987), covering a wide variety of topics within cluster science; S. Sugano, Y. Nishina, and S. Ohnishi (eds.), *Microclusters* (1987); G. Scoles (ed.), *The Chemical Physics of Atomic and Molecular Clusters* (1990), at the graduate-student level; S. Sugano, *Microcluster Physics* (1991), accessible to scientifically literate readers; and *Zeitschrift für Physik*, part D, vol. 19 and 20 (1991) and vol. 26 (1993), the proceedings of the international conferences on small particles and inorganic clusters held in 1990 and 1992, respectively.

INDEX